The Hillary Trap

The
Hillary
Trap

LOOKING FOR
POWER IN ALL THE
WRONG PLACES

Laura Ingraham

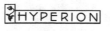

New York

Book design by Jennifer Daddio

Library of Congress Cataloging-in-Publication Data

Ingraham, Laura.
    The Hillary trap : looking for power in all the
wrong places / by Laura Ingraham.— 1st ed.
        p. cm.
    ISBN: 0-7868-6333-1
    1. Feminism—United States. 2. Women—
United States—Social conditions. 3. Clinton,
Hillary Rodham. 4. Presidents' spouses—United
States—Biography. I. Title.

HQ1426 .I59 2000
305.42'0973—dc21
                                    00-024781

FIRST EDITION

1   3   5   7   9   10   8   6   4   2

For my mother
Anne Caroline
(1920–1999)

Acknowledgments

Before I began this project, my writer friends told me about the hell and elation I would discover when I wrote my first book. They warned me not to take it on unless I believed in my thesis, and was willing to dig deep—even if that meant challenging some old assumptions. They were right. Without a doubt, if it weren't for the encouragement and support of friends and family, I would have never been able to write this book. In the early days of writing and researching, my mother was a constant source of inspiration. During her nine-month battle against lung cancer, she somehow found the energy to prop me up when I was doubting myself. She passed away in May of last year, but her memory still inspires me, and her spirit helped me finish what I started. Thank you, Mom.

My three brothers have been a perpetual force for good in my life, helping me make the transition from tomboy to athlete to lawyer to talk show host to writer. Curtis is my touchstone with the past and taught me how to cope with death and dying through the loving care he gave to his partner Richard in his last days. Jim and his wife Stephanie provided a living example of the patience and selflessness that a happy marriage requires. Brooks, even from far-away Korea, was in my mind during much of the time I wrote this book. His own love of music, literature, and art always reminding me that politics is just a small slice of life. My father has steadfastly supported my career and all its turns, showing me that it's never too late to pick yourself up. Lorraine and Joe Martynowicz, my "second parents" during my years in Connecticut, continue to be inspirations of love and generosity. As for their daughter Pam Cooke, now a mother of two—what can I say? Let's just hope your daughter doesn't cause half the trouble we did.

There are so many friends whose patience, guidance, good cheer, and assistance prevented me from falling into the Book Trap. Each has added something uniquely wonderful to my life—the enduring kindness of Bob Brauneis, who has been there with me through the stormiest of seas; the wise advice and shared dog fanaticism of Katie Sexton, who was with me in the last days of my mother's life; the loyalty and laughter of Lia Macko, who at the ripe old age of twenty-eight teaches me about female strength and perseverance every day; the kindhearted gestures of her mother, Karen Macko, who is living proof that there are angels in this world; the love of my "Washington parents" Chuck and Ina Carlsen, who were a constant help in managing my life (and Troy) when there didn't seem to be enough hours in the day; the satirical observations of Melinda Sidak (the original Straight-Talk Express), who has the three most beautiful sons I've ever known; the contagious optimism of Lee Habeeb, who is always there when I need him most; the much-missed effervescence of Amy Downing, whose risotto is better than her running; my old Georgetown pals Ethan and Karen Leder, who are living proof that marrying your high school sweetheart can be magic; and the sunny demeanors, assistance, and loyalty of my former television staff—Matthew Hosford, Jennifer Weems, and Jeff Macedo.

I am the lucky beneficiary of the careful analysis and endless encouragement of David Ignatius, who one day will play tennis as well as he writes; the historical and political insights of Stephen Vaughn, who is one of the smartest people on the planet; the sage advice and constant humor of Kate and Cliff Brokaw, who have one of the most comfortable sofa beds in Manhattan; the compassion and counsel of Arianna Huffington and her mother, who provided a luxurious and fun West Coast base of operations; the constant encouragement and teasing of Joe and Jill Robert, who gave me lessons in the art of the vacation; the dry humor and manuscript review of Jim Warren, who was the best permanent guest a talk show host could hope for; the powerful friendship of Maryann O'Donnell, who has taught me about the real meaning of "sister-hood"; the constant pep talks of Jon Ledecky, who saw me through the transition from one reviled profession to another (law to media); the support of Alex Azar, who shared greasy breakfasts with me at the Supreme Court and continues to be a mainstay of political insights; the caring ways of Jonathan Schiller, who gives lawyers a good name; the wit and wisdom of Paul Cappuccio, who showed me how to take a leap and land well; and the empathy and political smarts of Will Feltus, who serves up the best gumbo and top-spin forehand in town.

Other friends and mentors to whom I owe a great deal: Justice Clarence Thomas, Dinesh D'Souza, George Will, Tom Brokaw, Erik Sorenson, Henry Kissinger, Don Imus, Bob Bennett, Brian Williams, Bruce Cummings, Sue and Frank Reichel, Gary Bauer, Jeff Hart, Ricki and Larry Silberman, Deborah Colloton, Michael Bloomberg, Rod Satterwhite, Wendy Long, Emmett Flood, Valerie Ross, Jon L. Thornton, and all the teachers at Glastonbury High School. Sheryl Henderson Blunt and Mark Stricherz provided wonderful, well-organized research. I found the work of Clinton biographers Roger Morris, David Brock, and Joyce Milton thought-provoking and excellent resources in my early days of writing. The writings and research of John Lott, and the help of Don Kates, was of immense help. The suggestions and encouragement of author

Cathy Young also proved invaluable, as did much of the research gathered over the years by the Independent Women's Forum.

Finally, I owe a deep gratitude to my agent Lynn Chu, who believed in this project from day one, and kept me centered by telling me to be true to myself. And I will always remember the initial help of Michael Ovitz, who first brought my work to Hyperion's attention. Thanks also to Jennifer Barth, my original editor, who kept my feet to the fire and was interested enough to follow my progress even after she moved on to another publishing house. And lastly, my thanks to my editor Peternelle van Arsdale, who pushed me to test my thesis page after page, and produce a book I could be proud of. We did it.

Laura Ingraham

Contents

Introduction

It was her 52nd birthday, and finally Hillary Rodham Clinton seemed to be stepping out of her husband's long shadow. Surrounded by fifteen hundred of her political friends and supporters, she stood on the stage of the Ford Center for the Performing Arts on Broadway. For three decades the good political wife, at last it would be Hillary's chance to stand front and center. New York's liberal elite had gathered to cheer her on and open their wallets. Rosie O'Donnell, Alec Baldwin, and Mia Farrow were there, along with a long list of investment bankers and $500-an-hour lawyers. This evening was to be a celebration of Hillary's liberation and rebirth. Tonight, she would begin speaking in her own voice—not as the First Lady, not as a wronged wife, not even as a woman—as a prospective candidate for the U.S. Senate.

Yet amidst all the hoopla, Hillary Rodham Clinton, even in her new pursuit of elected office, was walking straight into a trap—one of her own making. On this night, Hillary's dependence on her husband—on his political organization and his friends and contributors—to define her and deliver to her the power she has always craved, was complete.

Bill Clinton mounted the dais. His demeanor captured the conflicts and contradictions of the couple's twenty-four-year marriage. Biting his lip, voice choked with emotion, he described Hillary as an independent and self-reliant woman, an ideal candidate. That night he was the one who exuded dependence. A scent of legacy filled the air. President Clinton seemed to think that by passing the baton to his wife, he could script a last—this time happy—chapter to his messy political life. He seemed almost desperate to tell the crowd that their marriage had in fact been good for her.

They had just celebrated their wedding anniversary and Bill took the opportunity to reminisce. His only hesitation in marrying Hillary, he admitted, had been his fear of preventing her from "sharing her gifts" in the public arena. He extolled his wife's lifelong commitment to health care, child welfare, education, and women's rights. As he spoke, Hillary watched and smiled, the perfect echo of the adoring wife that Nancy Reagan had symbolized before her.

"The best gift that I can give the American people now is to do my best to make sure that they know the person I love most in the world is without any doubt the most able, the most passionate, the most committed, the most visionary public servant I have ever known," he said, beaming. The First Couple tenderly embraced, then, and the audience roared.

It was a touching display—but one requiring a near total willing suspension of disbelief. To compartmentalize with this crowd, you had to be able to pretend that the events of the past several years never happened. Consider how, for their whole marriage, this man had publicly humiliated his wife with his rampant philandering. Anyone rooting for Hillary might have wished that her husband would just get off the stage so that she might take the microphone and finally tell us who she really was and what she believed in—not as his political wife but as a candidate. But of course that was precisely what she couldn't do. She owes everything to Bill. For all her feminism, Hillary has never learned to stand on her own.

Hillary's political or cultural influence, and her celebrity, is still a function of Bill's position, just as it has always been. Without the backdrop of her husband's sordid tale and her consequent victimization, Hillary's luster would fade. This is a trap for her. She has been granted power by her spouse in the form of sheer celebrity. Yet as her husband's power dwindles in his final months as president, Hillary's dilemma is about to be exposed.

I wondered how a woman so impeccably educated and credentialed and prepared for independence could have made such a devil's bargain. Is the applause of the Broadway crowd really for her left-wing politics? Or sympathy for her martyrdom? What a story of irony and of tragedy—a woman, once so promising, now finally trying to collect her just reward, one she clearly expects to be as grand as the humiliation she has been forced to endure. Was this the promise of feminism? Were women now to submit to any indignity, even a sham marriage, for access to power and fame? Thirty-five years after Betty Friedan's groundbreaking book, *The Feminine Mystique*, women are still in thrall to a remarkably traditional image of wifely subordination—emblemized by none other than Hillary Rodham Clinton, the one woman, we are told, who is supposed to stand for the very opposite.

Her birthday bash marked the official kickoff of Hillary's payback, the pundits all said. Once the Lewinsky story broke, politically Bill needed her more than she needed him. If Hillary had walked out in January 1998 instead of taking to the airwaves to denounce the "vast right-wing conspiracy," what little there was of the Clinton legacy would have been obliterated. She would have forced him and the country to reckon with reality. Instead, during the thirteen-month investigation and impeachment, she defended him and attacked his political enemies, allowing him to regroup. There were stories, carefully leaked to the press, of her distress after the president's August 1998 admission of an "inappropriate relationship" with the young intern. Television footage displayed the two walking at a chilly distance in Martha's Vineyard. Sympathy for her plight grew. Keenly aware of the perception by some that she tolerated her husband's adolescent sexcapades as a raw power-grab or a twisted codependent compulsion, she now carefully crafted her counterimage. She was her own person—a person who stood against threats to her family. Ken Starr was the real threat, not her cheating husband.

The spin worked. Disgust for her husband's potential criminality soon subsided into distaste for his caddishness. Only fourteen months later, Hillary was a Senate candidate, basking in the adoring glow of an A-list crowd.

Was this the life that bright, ambitious Hillary Rodham imagined for herself as she worked her way through college and law school? Is Hillary's brand of calculated opportunism the life we want for our own daughters?

Hillary came of age at the beginning of the modern women's movement, when feminist thinkers demanded and largely achieved equal rights and opportunities for women. She received the best education available to women of her generation. At her elite seven sisters school, Wellesley, Hillary was transformed—in the manner of the time—from a "Goldwater Girl" from Park Ridge, Illinois, to a member of the anti-Vietnam youth movement. In 1968, her junior year, she was elected student government president. Like her future husband, who was then attending Georgetown University, Hillary relished campus meetings and discussion groups on political and social issues. She had begun to organize campus antiwar teach-ins to chants of "We Want the World and We Want It Now!" Her classmates later described Hillary as more of a conciliator than a radical, but the conformist who in 1964 had been a Young Republican now marched, along with the rest of her peers, to the tune of a different drummer.

In 1967–68, she worked for Democrat Eugene McCarthy and liberal Republican Nelson Rockefeller. She got an A on her thesis on Lyndon Johnson's ill-fated community-action programs in his War on Poverty (which she has never allowed Wellesley to unseal); her adviser, Alan Schecter, describes her innocuously as a "pragmatic liberal." Her 1969 Wellesley commencement speech, neither particularly bold nor particularly inspirational, reflects a starry-eyed left-liberalism fairly standard for the time. Campus demonstrations were noble, Hillary said: "unabashedly an attempt to forge an identity . . . [a] coming to terms with our own humanness." They were expressions of student concern about "[t]he issues of sharing and responsibility, and of assuming power and responsibility." Hillary expresses similar sentiments to this day. She went on to say that "our prevailing acquisitive, and competitive corporate life, including, tragically, the universities, is not the way of life for us." What *was* this new way of life the new generation longed for? "We're searching for more immediate, ecstatic, and penetrating modes of living." Interestingly, she concluded somewhat disparagingly that "New Left collegiate protests" possessed a "very strange conservative strain," finally waving her hands to say airily that it all was "a very unique American experience. It's such a great adventure."

Neither openly defiant nor angry, she nevertheless embraced radical ideals and the speech conveys her sense of membership in an elite group entitled to lead. Ever the conformist, Hillary signed on to the trendy leftism of her generation, including its expectation that government could and should boldly remake society. Her notions of how she and her group would do that, exactly, remained fuzzy and ill-defined.

As a Yale law student, Hillary began to develop a significant network among liberal Democrats. She won a Yale grant to work on migrant worker rights for Senator Walter Mondale, chipped in at the founding of the upstart progressive *Yale Review of Law and Social Order*, and moderated a few angry campus protests. At Yale, she met Peter Edelman and his wife, Marian Wright Edelman, who later founded the Children's Defense Fund. The Edelmans were to break angrily with the Clintons after the president signed the GOP's welfare reform bill in 1995 and his politics suddenly veered right; but in the early seventies, Marian helped inspire Hillary's view that big government and rights advocacy could solve all of society's ills. In a June 1970 speech before the League of Women Voters, Hillary called for revolutionary social and economic change, far beyond mere civil rights advocacy: "Our social indictment has broadened . . . Where we once advocated civil rights, we now advocate a realignment of political and economic power . . . How much longer can we let the corporations run us?"

By the age of twenty-three, Hillary was parroting every hip left-wing theme espoused by the in-crowd of the time and forging links to what would soon be the new liberal establishment. To Hillary and her friends, the world was less about personal achievement and fulfillment through individual initiative and hard work than about what government could do to give people the lives to which they are *entitled*. It wasn't enough that government ensure equal opportunity—in Hillary's world government needed to redistribute wealth and engineer far-reaching social change. Corporations (free enterprise) were bad. Only government, led by the good, could ensure the good. By edict, society could be remade.

In November 1970, she met William Jefferson Clinton in the stacks of the Yale law library. Already the consummate politician, Hillary was captivated by his mind and his charm. By the fall of 1972, she took on a postgraduate research job instead of a high-powered career to stay with him at Yale in his last year of law school. It would also form the basis of her lifelong specialization in children and women's rights.

Finishing up at Yale, Hillary set out for Washington and Marian Wright Edelman's Children's Defense Fund to litigate on behalf of children and the poor. The group advocated for protections against child abuse but was also a breeding ground for the most radical views about civil rights, generally arguing that children's rights should supersede almost any competing concerns of parents. In January 1974, Hillary was chosen for a prized staff position at the House Judiciary Committee during the Nixon Watergate impeachment inquiry. When Nixon resigned, Hillary made a decision that would forever change her life—to move to Fayetteville, Arkansas, bucking the feminist admonition that women shouldn't "sell out" their own careers for a man and the antiwar admonition not to "sell out" to the establishment. Hillary intended to join the establishment and re-create it, "to bore from within," as the saying goes.

Bill and Hillary wed in 1975. An indispensable political asset to her husband, she worked tirelessly to help him win a congressional seat. He lost that first race but their partnership paid off when he was elected Arkansas attorney general in 1976 and then governor in 1978. He lost the governorship in 1980, but Hillary helped him take it back in 1984, where he would serve until his election as president in 1992. Even as she confided in friends that he had been seeing other women along the campaign trail, Hillary remained the toughest, most committed campaigner for Bill Clinton. Gone was her talk of evil corporations and the need for economic and political realignment. Now Hillary was the establishment—the governor's wife. When she took a job teaching at the University of Arkansas Law School in 1975, or when she joined the Rose Law Firm in 1977, it was always her husband who greased the wheels for her.

Correspondingly, she was the good wife to make Bill more electable. She discovered the virtues of marital compromise, as her marriage brought her political influence. (Elizabeth Dole, by contrast, held two different cabinet posts before she ever married Bob.) Hillary pulled it all off, successfully playing both the traditional wife who puts her husband's career before her own and the liberated, independent feminist.

No First Lady in American history, except perhaps Hillary's idol Eleanor Roosevelt, has been as controversial—as admired, as reviled, as talked about—as Hillary. She seems to symbolize how much things have changed for American women. She seems to keep three balls in the air at once—marriage, motherhood, and career—just like us all. She seems to be a First Lady with a mind and an agenda of her own. She's the "First Partner," as *Glamour* magazine put it and, chimed the *Boston Globe*, as a couple the Clintons were "the first First Family of the feminist generation." From the moment Hillary debuted on the national stage, her sisters in the Woodstock generation identified. "To many women, and especially to professional women, Hillary Clinton is the first First Lady who is one of them," wrote *Detroit News* columnist Laura Berman. Lavish media profiles of Hillary painted a strong, discerning, sharp-thinker who was also compassionate, caring, and devoted to social issues. She has been made over into our role model in chief.

Her husband, however, in retrospect, is less like the enlightened, egalitarian New Man perfectly paired with his feminist mate than the old-fashioned pig to whom philandering is a male prerogative so long as you continue to serve up your wife's meal ticket. His behavior isn't just something Hillary tolerated. She encouraged it by doing public damage control. To deflect the threat Gennifer Flowers's revelation of her extramarital affair with Bill Clinton posed to his presidential campaign, Hillary faced a national audience to both "stand by her man" and fervently deny just that—ironically managing to appeal to both sides of the liberal-conservative divide. Six years later, she took to the airwaves again to blame the "vast right-wing conspiracy" for all those tales of an affair with an intern. After the smoking blue dress made further lies and denials impossible, Hillary still played the loyal, wronged wife, rationalizing to *Talk* magazine that the blame for Bill's bad behavior lay with two dead women: his mother and grandmother, who caused his problems by competing for his affection.

The First Feminist had morphed into the First Victim.

By then it was a well-worn masquerade. Serious scandals engulfed her husband's administration—including several implicating Hillary herself. Yet she was always the victim. It was never Hillary's fault. Hillary was never wrong. She was wronged. She was unfairly targeted, by independent counsel Ken Starr, by former business partner Jim McDougal—by anyone who disagreed with her. But not everyone was buying the modern damsel-in-distress line. Hillary's cattle futures bonanza was revealed as a payoff and her evasions under oath about her legal work for Madison Guaranty after the belated "discovery" of her billing records (helpfully annotated by Vince Foster) in the White House had stung. The joke now was that the description "First Partners" was short for "First Partners in Crime."

Both partners have responded to allegations of wrongdoing by stonewalling, shifting responsibility, and spinning one convoluted explanation after another. Through it all we are supposed to believe that Hillary is at once an uncannily smart lawyer with a discerning mind and a total naif in business and legal affairs. The "little woman defense" was first introduced by Bill during the 1992 Democratic primary debates, when his rival Jerry Brown raised questions about Whitewater and Hillary's work at the

Rose Law Firm. Clinton, the man who had been banging more women than a revolving door, kicked into a chivalrous how-dare-you-pick-on-my-wife mode. "I think now they know I've got some old-fashioned values," he crowed to the press afterward. "If somebody jumps on my wife, I'm gonna jump 'em back."

Meanwhile, the little woman herself shuttles back and forth between feminist outrage and feminine helplessness: "This is the sort of thing that happens to women who have their own careers and own lives," she sniffs in response to serious questions of conflicts of interest in her legal practice. She attributes her windfall from cattle futures to dumb luck and reading the *Wall Street Journal*, not the Arkansas commodities trader who actually did the deal for the Governor's wife. She dismisses her work on Jim McDougal's shady business ventures as nothing more than low-level legal assistance (despite being a senior partner in the Rose firm).

Hillary is the ultimate "feminist of convenience"—demanding equal treatment or special treatment, whichever suits her at the moment. This hypocrisy is well illustrated by the Clinton Administration's ill-fated attempt in 1993 to keep the work of Hillary's health care reform task force shrouded in secrecy. After introducing the concept of the First Couple as a "copresidency," in the next breath the Clintons argued that the First Lady could be deemed, legally, as nothing more than a private citizen, so that the health care sessions would not be a matter of public record. Once again, the theme emerges of a woman who wanted it all, by any means necessary, but who wouldn't put herself on the line, or on the record, to get there.

All this would seem to make Hillary Rodham Clinton a dubious candidate for First Feminist. Yet prominent women of the left continue to cheerlead for her. Criticism is quickly declared to be thinly disguised sexism. When scrutiny of Hillary's role in Whitewater intensified in 1994, Democratic consultant Ann Lewis told *USA Today* that the male Washington establishment was taking out its "repressed resentment" of women in politics on Hillary. Her colleague Lynn Cutler saw the investigation of Hillary as one more link in the patriarchal chain: "This is what happens to women who stand up, step forward, and speak out." "First Lady's Fight Symbolizes the War against Strong Women," shrieked a headline in the *Kansas City Star*. Even *Glamour* magazine took time out from "Makeup Dos and Don'ts" to bemoan attacks on Hillary Clinton as part of an "agenda to move us all backwards."

For many moms who are carpooling, mothering, and working their way through life, on the surface Hillary is a strong, self-reliant woman who kept a family together and still found time to fight for women and children's betterment. Yet if women really modeled their lives after Hillary's, they'd think that the path to personal strength and security is through their husbands, or government. Somehow the inspiring message of early feminists—that women can do anything—has a big caveat attached to it. Women can do anything IF a powerful husband or institution makes it possible. Long ago, Hillary fell into a trap of dependence on a husband who repeatedly violated their marital trust. This was winked at as a private deal for political power. Now Hillary wants us to follow her into the same trap—scramble for the scraps of power and authority to be found in your husband's wake. With Hillary as the reigning role model, you can count on groupies like Monica to be found not far behind.

Politically, the policies Hillary advocates would also keep women as dependent—on lawmakers, unions, the police, even the United Nations— as she is on Bill. Though she uses conservative rhetoric as camouflage, since that is what is popular this fifteen minutes, Hillary's actual policy prescriptions depend on liberal big government solutions that have a thirty-year record of failure. We need to be very suspicious of a world that penalizes marriage and stay-at-home moms; a world where economic outcomes must be mandated by new laws and bureaucracies; a world where balancing work and child-rearing is to be a federal concern, not an individual choice; a world that deals with violence against women in workshops and vigils instead of by giving women the means and the confidence to defend themselves; a world of instant New Age spirituality, that often treats Judeo-Christian and other mainstream religious convictions based on millennia of accumulated wisdom with mockery and contempt.

So if we are admiring Hillary, what are we admiring her for? Her independence—or for bringing back a Neanderthal tolerance for the extramarital shenanigans of married men? A dedicated champion of education or a cheerleader for many of the trends that have ruined our public schools? A woman to lead us across that fabled bridge to the twenty-first century or one trapped in the hackneyed thinking and rhetoric of 1969? Finally, what does her example teach us about ourselves and our lives?

The ultimate Hillary trap is believing that we can have it all, and that someone or something else can help us get there. Her personal and political choices are a series of shortcuts to nowhere. When Hillary finally had a chance to strike out on her own by running for the New York Senate, she was still stuck in the trap that she unwittingly built decades before, because she still depended upon her husband for her success. Her only chance of winning would be if Bill Clinton pulled out all the stops and campaigned hard for her as he did the night of her birthday.

A lot of people say they feel sorry for Hillary. After all, she has gone through so much, lived under the bright lights, endured endless inquiries into every aspect of her life.

But I say nonsense.

My mother, who passed away as I was writing this book, was someone for whom empathy was truly in order. She grew up dirt poor in the Depression, lost her mother at fourteen, had no money to go to college and so took a job in the local thread factory. She married for love. She raised four children on little money through ingenuity, thrift, and twenty-five years of waitressing. Like Hillary, she stayed in an unhappy marriage. In those days there were few alternatives. She could have played the victim and blamed the world but instead she persevered with the talents and skills that she had. Ordinary women like this taught me and many other women in America how to stand on our own, how to fight for ourselves and our principles. My mother never used the word "gender" in her lifetime, yet from her I learned that inner strength and independence are only possible if we take responsibility for our mistakes and learn from them. In that sense, my mother was more of a modern woman than Hillary could ever hope to be.

This book is not a biography of Hillary Rodham Clinton or another rehash of the Clinton scandals. It is an attempt to show a new generation of women that the promise of the future is found in our individual liberty, not in a cycle of dependence that Hillary, I think, represents—dependence on special "women's" or other group privileges, on government, or on the men that we marry. While Hillary's supporters say she represents the future, I see her mired hopelessly in the stale, outmoded thinking of her youth. Young women, in many ways, have already moved beyond Hillary's old-fashioned politics and retrograde values, and jumped over her traps. Where she is dependent, we are self-reliant; where she is still pushing the Nanny State, we are succeeding in the Opportunity Society; where she is sanctimonious, we are purposefully outrageous; where she is bureaucratic, we are entrepreneurial.

Sometimes, however, the traps are hard to see. They are hidden in policies that promise female advancement and protection, or rationalizations that condone a man's adulterous behavior for the sake of keeping the relationship together. But we cannot take the bait. For no woman wants to end up as Hillary did on that stage—listening to a liar and cheat define who she is.

1.

The
Sisterhood
Trap

A tour of Hillary's world begins with what she has often made out to be the most important fact about her: She's a woman. For Hillary, that's not a statement of biology or even culture, but a political creed. And that's the point at which Hillary Clinton starts to veer off the road of good sense and toward folly.

Hillary's commitment to "women's issues" reminds me of the old story about the man who loved humanity—it was just people he couldn't stand. To Hillary, women are political "sisters" first and people second. She has crisscrossed the globe talking about empowering this sisterhood and setting women free, but at every stop she advances a liberal agenda that reduces women to yet another interest group seeking yet another government handout. By reducing womanhood to a political platform, Hillary creates the ultimate trap for those who choose to follow her: the trap of groupthink and identity politics. For being a truly liberated woman means being your own person—not a victim whining for special privileges or a mindless soldier of anyone's political agenda, liberal or conservative. When the Hillarys of the world talk about sisterhood, women who want real equality and power should Just Say No.

Predictably, Hillary has tried to turn her reputation as a champion of women's rights to political advantage in her race for the U.S. Senate. In May 1999 she announced her Senate exploratory committee. The Albany *Times-Union* said she was hoping "to court . . . women voters" and "to highlight her commitment to issues of concern to women voters, including public education, child care for working women, and the role of women in society." New York *Daily News* columnist Lars-Erik Nelson enthused about her "claim to the women's vote." Well, yes, Hillary is a woman, and she speaks for some women. But does she speak for all, or even for a majority?

A feminist credo from the 1960s was that "the personal is political." But in Hillary's world, sisterhood is anything but personal: It's a purely political concept of women as a group united by common interests and goals—goals that Hillary and her left-liberal sisterhood define. Hmmm. Where was sisterhood when Kathleen Willey, Paula Jones, and Juanita Broadrick came forward to say they were groped—and in one case, even raped—by Hillary's husband? To the sisterhood, I guess they don't count as "women."

What *is* sisterhood, anyway? The way I see it, it's about laughing and crying with your girlfriends, about cheering on their successes and commiserating in their failures. It's about being able to rely on them as individuals, not a collective mass defined by faceless organizations or vague notions of community. Sisterhood is about trust, which is only meaningful on a personal level. Yes, "female bonding" often includes joking about male foibles and sharing horror stories of men behaving badly; mostly, such "girl talk" really is personal and not political. It certainly doesn't mean—sorry, Hillary!—that we're ready to embrace some sort of common political agenda.

Women are not the unified bloc that recent rhetoric about the "gender gap" implies. While polls show that women are more likely to be interested in issues like health and education, the obvious truth is that men, too, go to hospitals and care about their children's schooling. And on the other hand, we care about jobs and taxes just like the guys do. The same policies that benefit our brothers, fathers, and husbands—policies that boost the economy, protect citizens from crime, and strengthen families—benefit us as well. There is, as we'll see later in this chapter, no gulf between the political values of men and women. For the most part, despite what the pundits may say, we don't even vote all that differently. Hillary's brand of gender politics—the idea that women are naturally drawn to a particular social agenda—is no better than the old notion that women are naturally drawn to nursing, or teaching, or cooking.

Once, slogans like "Sisterhood = Power" were legitimate rallying cries—back in the early days of "women's lib," when fifty thousand women joined Betty Friedan and Gloria Steinem marching down Fifth Avenue in New York, and young collegiate Hillary Rodham devoured the writings of Germaine Greer and Simone de Beauvoir. Back then, women were bound together in one important sense—they still confronted gross stereotyping and discrimination. They banded together to demand equal treatment and opportunity and beat back the image of the helpless, delicate female dependent on men to protect and care for them.

I'm glad those battles were fought and won, but let's face it, those days are gone. Today women and girls are virtually everywhere they want to be, and it didn't happen during the Clinton Administration. When I attended Dartmouth College in the 1980s, nearly half of the student body was female. Women made up half of my 1991 graduating class at the University of Virginia Law School. Somehow, I managed to make it to Dartmouth and to law school without being drilled about "gender sensitivity" and without being trained to think of every win or loss as saying something about gender. The women's movement helped give me opportunities that women of earlier generations didn't have, but from then on it was up to me to succeed through my own hard work. My outlook wasn't predetermined by my sex, it was informed by my family, friends, and experiences. In fact, the only time I remember the word "gender" coming up was in biology class (I think it had something to do with fruit flies). As for the word "sisterhood," it was akin to phrases like "groovy, man" or "far out!"—an amusing rhetorical relic from a bygone age.

Of course, there is lingering discrimination—there always will be.

People treat other people unjustly on the basis of all kinds of things that have nothing to do with our true selves and intrinsic merits—on our looks, our tone of voice, on the social set we belong to, on misleading or ridiculous first impressions. Life is unfair to practically everybody. But that's no reason women should see themselves as a lifetime member of the P.O.C. (Perpetually Oppressed Club). Unfortunately, in spite of everything that common sense should tell us, gender identity politics of the kind Hillary espouses have gradually worked their way into the laws, the schools, and the universities.

These days, even a women's soccer team's triumphs get politicized. Remember all those GIRLS RULE and GIRL POWER signs in the stands at the Women's World Cup Soccer games in the summer of 1999? Harmless and cute on the surface, but almost defensively hyped in the media as some glorious chapter in women's unending political struggle. Sure, the triumph of Team USA was exciting and it was great to cheer on Mia Hamm—because it was a superb athletic performance. So why the gender mania? One commentator on CNN's *Inside Politics* got so carried away she gushed that if a woman runs for president thirty years from now "and you interview her and say what was the defining moment of your childhood, I think she will answer, 'the 1999 Women's World Cup.'"

During the World Cup tournament, the media endlessly brought up Title IX, the federal law banning sex discrimination in schools. We were supposed to think that the players wouldn't have been there without Title IX. First of all, that's not so obvious. The history of civil rights legislation, from race to gender and beyond, is that civil rights laws have been enacted in response to social changes. They don't initiate social change. In the case of Title IX, there was a growing popular interest in and concern for women's athletics and the politicians ratified what was already going on in the culture. (To some extent, the same can be said of the Civil Rights Act: By 1964, when it was passed, women were already making significant inroads in business and the professions.) Mixing sports and politics in the World Cup detracted from the simple fact that these women were among the best athletes in the country. Those women athletes made it to the top through practice, grit, and sheer determination—not because gender-conscious politicians handed their victory to them.

Hillary was in the stands, watching the final soccer game, just as she has been at nearly every high-visibility women's event during her years as First Lady. One of her most famous moments was her speech at the United Nations Fourth World Conference on Women in Beijing in 1995. Hillary proclaimed that it was "time to act on behalf of women every-where . . . women will never gain full dignity until their human rights are respected and protected . . . However different we may appear, there is far more that unites us than divides us." But this sunny, vacuous vision was belied by what was really going on in Beijing. In a witty, incisive report in *National Review*, British journalist Anne Applebaum detailed the rift that was developing between Western feminists and their sisters in the less developed world:

> *Most of the Third World women were interested in very basic issues: the horrors of female circumcision, legal systems which prevent women from owning property, hunger and illiteracy. . . . The Western agenda was somewhat different: it ranged from lesbian rights to the need for women's studies at universities to "Gender Stereotyping and Sexism in Advertising" . . .*

Third World delegates in Beijing were bewildered and annoyed by the Western feminist dominance of the conference agenda. "Our issues are much more basic: We need education, we need a health system that works," said one Kenyan woman. She found it strange that most of her developed world "sisters" were so much more concerned with the availability of birth control and abortion than with the availability of lifesaving gender-neutral medicines like penicillin.

Certainly there are abuses of women that need to be exposed and stopped. Genital mutilation in Africa, wife burning in India, forced abortions in China. These are outrages. But how do these horrific actions connect with any "women's agenda" in American politics? When feminism tries to link these bloody crimes against women with workplace issues in our advanced society, they're just piggybacking on the suffering of the truly oppressed. The complaints of Western feminists look like petty self-absorption when you line them up against human rights abuses in Third World military dictatorships. Clitoridectomy and denial of maternity leave are simply *not* equivalent offenses against womankind. To patch together the gross injustices done to women in places like Nigeria with the relatively minor difficulties women face in their everyday lives in the United States into one giant collage of women's oppression, so as to rally women as one monolithic political voting block, is political opportunism of the most odious sort.

Let's get our priorities straight: Volunteer for a couple of weeks at Freedom House or Human Rights Watch if you want to see what human oppression is all about. In this diverse multicultural world of ours, oppression comes mainly from brutal repressive governments—not from your husband or the mythical patriarchy.

Republicans can be just as guilty of using gender for political gain. Before she pulled out of the 2000 presidential race, Republican Elizabeth Dole played the gender card, too, glowing about how her candidacy sent a positive message to young women. In response to a tough question about traditional GOP support for a constitutional ban on abortion, Dole lamented that because of the "inordinate focus" on that topic, "urgent issues such as domestic violence, child care, sexual harassment, women's health, and the financial security of women" were being neglected. It was a carefully scripted response to show Dole's sensitivity to "women's issues." But it plays to the same demagoguery that Hillary and her acolytes specialize in—the notion that violence, health care, and Social Security are somehow "female" special interests, rather than human issues that concern men, too.

Hillary didn't invent gender politics. But she was the first First Lady to use her position as a bully pulpit for the sisterhood and to do "consciousness raising" among lawmakers. As we will see, she and her feminist allies have had a major impact on what is happening in politics, in the class-room, in courts, and in the workplace, big-time. Politicians are often ridiculed for making a lot of promises and doing nothing, but what they actually *do*—with money taken out of your paycheck—is often worse. Even conservative politicians like Senators Orrin Hatch and John McCain are so cowed by the feminist lobby that they go out of their way to assure us that theirs is a "pro-women" agenda. Look, Ma, I'm sensitive! Today's female-friendly politicians stir a stew of vaguely defined issues such as violence against women, women's medical needs, or girls' education. They ladle it out to the public whenever it seems politically advantageous, however expensive, and however ridiculous. When these policies become law, the real beneficiaries are mainly bureaucrats, lobbyists and activists, not individual women or their daughters.

Women's Crusades: Fighting for Justice or Promoting Myth-Information?

Convincing a new generation of women that they ought to pledge allegiance to their gender is one clever way to keep us politically dependent, while giving us a false sense of security that the sisterhood is always looking out for our interests. This is the False Sisterhood Trap in a nutshell. With all the advances and choices women enjoy today, how do Hillary and her sisters keep the gender fixation alive? By creating the impression that rampant discrimination is still prevalent but in covert and disguised form.

Perhaps the most frightening of these claims is that the male-dominated American medical establishment has been willfully neglecting women's health. It's a charge that Hillary Rodham Clinton made in a July 1993 appearance at a fundraiser for a breast cancer screening center at UCLA. She brought a mostly female crowd nearly to tears, and to deafening applause, when she described the "unfair emotional burden inflicted on women because of the inequities of the system." But the real kicker was her claim that women have been discriminated against in the all-important world of medical research. "We have been on the medical and scientific sidelines," she complained.

Hillary wasn't breaking any new ground. In 1991, a bipartisan group of women in Congress charged that women were victims of systematic discrimination in medicine. "One of the reasons our hormones rage is that we're so often written off and trivialized," proclaimed liberal Senator Barbara Mikulski (D-MD). Senator Olympia Snowe (R-ME) seconded her Democratic sister: "There is a bias in federal research," she stated. "Medical research is largely done and conducted on men." As evidence, the congresswomen cited the fact that only thirteen percent of the total research budget of the National Institutes of Health (NIH) was devoted to diseases affecting women and that major federally funded heart disease studies had used exclusively men as participants. Representative Patricia Schroeder (D-CO) painted an ominous picture of the "boys' club" ignoring female health problems. "People tend to fund what they fear first," she opined in a television interview. "A majority of the House and Senate and other people never feared breast cancer, ovarian cancer, osteoporosis, so we feel they've been underfunded." The accusation sent shivers through the spine of many a male legislator. How would they respond when a female constituent asked, "Are you one of those politicians who don't care about women's health?"

No one wanted to be so "insensitive" as to point out that if thirteen percent of all federal medical research dollars went to specifically female health problems, a mere seven percent was earmarked for men's diseases such as prostate and testicular cancer. Eighty percent of the money was going to the study of diseases that affect both sexes—including heart disease, which kills ten times as many women annually as does breast cancer, and lung cancer, which has killed more women than breast cancer in every year since 1989. That didn't stop Hillary Clinton from declaring at the 1993 fundraiser at UCLA, "If we have technology sophisticated enough to direct missiles to targets thousands of miles away, then we [ought to] have technology sophisticated enough to detect every fatal lump in a woman's breast." (Leave it to Hillary to turn health care into a struggle between the Pentagon and women's breasts!) Never mind that we also don't have technology sophisticated enough to distinguish a lethal fast-growing prostate tumor from a slow-growing one that does not require surgery.

In fact, it's interesting to note that between 1981 and 1985, long before women's health was turned into a political issue, five federal dollars were spent on breast cancer for every dollar spent on prostate cancer. By 1997, when prostate cancer claimed almost as many victims as breast cancer (41,800 versus 43,900), NIH spent more than $410 million on breast cancer research compared to a paltry $105 million for prostate cancer. So is it time for a Men's Health Equity Act?

As for major heart disease studies that included only male patients, there were actually good reasons for such policies. Judith LaRosa and Vivian Pinn, who used to work in the NIH Office of Research on Women's Health, acknowledged in a 1993 article in the *Journal of the American Medical Women's Association* that until the age of sixty-five, women are at very low risk for severe cardiac disease—so to test, for example, the benefits of a daily dose of aspirin in preventing heart attacks, researchers would have to recruit at least three times as many women as men to get equally valid results. Sometimes male-only studies are just good science: First you study the group most at risk or the group least medically complicated. Once you obtain the results, then you figure out whether further testing in other groups is warranted. In light of this, the exclusion of women seems to have been based on valid and gender-neutral concerns, not male chauvinism. It is worth noting that in the same period when male-only heart disease research was done, trials of treatments for hypertension, which affects both sexes at similar rates, included both women and men.

In the 1999 book *Ceasefire!: Why Women and Men Must Join Forces to Achieve True Equality*, journalist Cathy Young reports that over two-thirds of all studies and clinical trials reported in medical literature from 1966 to 1990 were two-sex studies—while of the remaining third, more than half were female-only. Diseases for which women are at higher risk than men, such as arthritis or osteoporosis, have been studied primarily in women;

there have been more all-female than all-male studies of diabetes, kidney disease, and chemotherapy. Dr. Sally Satel, a lecturer at the Yale University School of Medicine, also finds no evidence of anti-female bias in medical research. She points out that as early as 1979, over ninety percent of active clinical trials being conducted under the auspices of the NIH involved both men and women; the rest were evenly divided between all-male and all-female participants.

Women's health advocates have complained that from 1977 to 1993 the Food and Drug Administration barred women of childbearing potential from the early stages of drug trials. These rules were adopted to protect the fetuses of pregnant mothers and allowed an exception for women with life-threatening illnesses to take part in the early testing of promising new drugs. In all other cases, once the basic safety of a drug was established, women were fully involved in the later stages of trials monitoring its use and effects. According to Dr. Ruth Merkatz, special assistant to the FDA commissioner for women's health, FDA surveys in 1983 and 1988 found that "both sexes had substantial representation in clinical trials conducted before FDA approval of drugs."

Bluntly put, the notion that modern medicine has benefitted men while ignoring women is one of the nuttiest ideas ever put forth by feminists. In fact, it's more plausible to argue that women have gained more from medical progress than men. Until this century, women on average died younger than men; today, we're living seven years longer. Thanks to medical progress, we no longer have hundreds of thousands of young women dying in childbirth, and we've all but gotten rid of infectious diseases like smallpox, cholera, and tuberculosis, which used to kill off a lot of women *and* men at a young age. So far, science hasn't done anywhere near as good a job against the afflictions that kill men at a younger age than women (mainly heart disease). So if you're grateful for being alive and having a good chance to live to be eighty or more as a woman, don't thank Hillary, Pat Schroeder, or the Capitol Hill sisterhood. Thank "patriarchal medicine," however maligned it is by the women's studies mavens for taking over health care from the female healers and midwives.

Nevertheless, a lot of people bought the "male bias in medicine" myth. By the time Hillary and Bill moved into 1600 Pennsylvania Avenue, the sisterhood had organized thousands of American women to fight against this alleged bias. The activists, many of them breast cancer survivors, gathered millions of signatures to demand more money for research on breast cancer. They marched on Washington, where their leaders met with President Clinton and the First Lady. It was an occasion for the First Partners to score political points with a voting bloc essential to Bill's re-election, and they did. Bill and Hillary assured the advocates that more money would go to breast cancer research and that women would never again be treated as "second-class citizens" in health care.

Members of Congress knew that the political fallout among women voters could be disastrous if they didn't act like they "cared" about women's health soon. So in 1993 Congress passed the Women's Health Equity Act, allocating $805 million to women's health and mandating that women be included in every federally funded clinical study. Republicans and Democrats all heaved a heavy sigh of relief. They'd covered their butts. Now they could point to their vote as proof that are indeed "sensitive to women's health concerns."

Most Congressmen and Senators were so panicked about losing their female constituency they didn't bother to question the facts underlying the allegations of bias against women by the medical establishment. During the congressional deliberations, anyone who voiced reservations over the Women's Health Equity Act was immediately savaged by women's health lobbyists. Scientists who warned that it was unwise to allow politicians to dictate the makeup of medical research studies were branded as heartless tools of the male establishment.

The women's health crusade shows what can happen when women become a special interest group. Due to the cries about "shortchanged women," special funds are now set aside for women's health, supposedly to correct the imbalance. A network of six National Centers of Excellence in Women's Health—a public-private partnership partly funded by the U.S. Public Health Service—was created in 1996, and expanded to eighteen by

1999. Meanwhile, there are no centers for men's health, and doctors still don't know enough about prostate cancer to be able to decide whether surgery for a newly diagnosed tumor will be beneficial or harmful. Should women be concerned about this? After all, it's the lives of our fathers, brothers, husbands, and sons that we're talking about.

Besides, not everything that's done in the name of women's health actually benefits women. The tendency to hype the perils to women's health, such as the activists' sloganeering about the "breast cancer epidemic"—"One in eight, we can't wait!"—has frightened a lot of women into needless paranoia. The actual numbers don't paint such a grim picture. The one-in-eight statistic is the cumulative lifetime risk of breast cancer for an eighty-five-year-old woman; however, average life expectancy for white women is seventy-nine and for black women, seventy-four. As you age beyond fifty, people's risk of cancers of all kinds increases; cancer predominantly strikes the elderly. But because of politically fomented breast-cancer hysteria, women of all ages are more scared than informed. A 1999 Harris poll found that forty percent of women believe they will get breast cancer. In fact, even among women who live to eighty-five, just over twelve percent will get it. And only 1.3 percent of all women in their forties will be stricken by breast cancer in the next ten years.

Screechy interest-group-generated rhetoric about "male medicine" can also pressure many women into making bad health care choices. Feminist health counseling groups, for instance, often take the view that hysterectomy—unless absolutely essential to save a woman's life—is an evil act of female mutilation. Certainly, there are instances when doctors have been too eager to recommend this radical surgery. But there are also instances when feminist groups have been too eager to discourage it. One woman who fell into the clutches of such a sisterhood, Ellen Bertone of Pennington, New Jersey, described her experience in a 1997 letter to the *New York Times*: "I postponed [a hysterectomy] for several years because I had been made to fear it and . . . to feel that I was submitting to manipulation by the patriarchal medical profession, and that I was somehow failing if I gave in and had the surgery." She added that when she finally had the surgery, her health improved dramatically and she bitterly regretted the delay: "I had suffered needlessly for several years."

On the political level, too, sound medical judgment often goes out the window when politics take over. A good example is the Women's Health Initiative, a massive, $625 million study launched by the NIH with great fanfare in 1991, under the leadership of women's health advocate Berna-dine Healy. Two years after the study was begun, a review panel of the Institute of Medicine of the National Academy of Sciences (IOM) appointed by Congress issued a devastating report. It concluded that the study was so poorly designed it was of little scientific use. Furthermore, the women enrolled in the trials weren't properly advised of the possible health risks. According to the journal *Nature*, the IOM committee said that "politics, not science, [had] dissuaded it from outright cancellation of the study . . . committee members were besieged by women's health groups who said that canceling the study would be a sign that the NIH does not care about women."

Prominent political women seemed offended at the very idea that the project should be subjected to critical review. "Billions of dollars have been spent to do research on men," wailed Dr. Bernadine Healy, former head of the NIH. "Now a relatively modest study comes along to do studies on women, and it is subject to this kind of scrutiny." Pat Schroeder charged that the IOM report was yet another vicious patriarchal attempt to short-change women. (The review panel was made up of seven women and four men and chaired by a woman.) Schroeder promised to "make sure that nobody cuts the corners on us one more time." Of course, nobody was planning to cut corners on women, but facts have never stopped politi-cians from making hay with gender demagoguery.

Women's health remains a favorite arena for posturing by politicos of both parties and sexes. Complaints about "drive-through mastectomies" by stingy HMOs refusing to pay for more than twenty-four hours of post-sur-gery hospitalization have prompted calls for action in Washington, with

Hillary Clinton joining the chorus. While this may sound like a worthy cause, the problem has been massively exaggerated: A survey reported in *The Atlanta Journal* found that only six percent of mastectomy patients in HMOs went home quickly, usually because they wanted to. (Where's the concern for patients who have undergone surgery for equally devastating but gender-neutral diseases like colon cancer?) And in 1997, when a National Cancer Institute panel of doctors and consumer advocates concluded that scientific evidence did not warrant routine annual mammograms for women in their forties, Congress quickly intervened and pressured the NCI to reverse this recommendation.

Two years later, women's health was again the buzzword in the debate over the "patients' bill of rights" intended to protect patients from abuses by insurance companies and HMOs. While Republicans and Democrats disagreed over the scope of these protections, both versions of the bill focused on women's needs: namely allowing women to stay in the hospital at least forty-eight hours after breast surgery and to choose their gynecologist as their primary doctor.

Women may feel gratified by all the attention lavished on their health. But this special status makes me cringe. It's politics by chromosome, based on pandering and opportunism. Essentially, we're being patted on the head and told, "Now, now, little ladies, we'll look out for you, and you just honor and obey your protectors." Ironically, even some women's advocates are starting to express misgivings about the women's health vogue. National Women's Health Network executive director Cindy Pearson has said that it's a "double-edged sword," since politicians may feel compelled to "choose to make medical decisions through legislation that they think are helpful to women, which are often arguable." Some also detect a whiff of paternalism in the legislators' eagerness to "intervene in the way doctors and private health insurance companies conduct themselves when the patients are women." That's exactly right. But when you turn women into a special interest group, that's what you get.

Another pet project of the gender police is the equally mythical problem of "shortchanged girls." In 1994, Congress passed the Women's
Educational Equity Act (WEEA), authorizing millions of dollars to fight
alleged anti-girl bias in education. A better name might be the Gender
Equity Experts' Employment Act. Supporters of the bill invoked dubious
studies by the American Association of University Women (a group for
which, as we will see, politically correct zealotry has long displaced educational goals). "Where nine-year-old girls were once confident that they
could conquer the world, girls at age eleven suddenly begin doubting their
worth," declared the ubiquitous Pat Schroeder. The AAUW research
"refutes the common assumption that boys and girls are treated equally in
our educational system," chimed in Senator Ted Kennedy, never one to
stand by when females are in peril.

That time, at least, two Republican senators, Nancy Kassebaum of
Kansas and Kay Bailey Hutchison of Texas, tried to slow down the steam-
roller. They made the modest proposal that the WEEA be held up for a
year pending a more rigorous review of the sexism-in-schools research.
The feminist-educrat lobby quickly sprang to action. At a House-Senate
conference, an AAUW representative warned Kassebaum and Hutchison
about the female retaliation that awaited them if they did anything to
weaken or stall the gender-equity legislation. No one else came to their
support and the rebellion was quashed.

This drama replayed itself in 1999, when some Republicans—including "moderates" like New Jersey Congresswoman Marge Roukema—
wanted to cut off the funding for WEEA, pointing out that the goals of
gender equity in education had been achieved and the program had out-
lived its usefulness. The AAUW and other "progressive" groups mobilized
yet again, and Democrats like Patsy Mink of Hawaii earnestly argued that
there was still a need to "balance the scales." As we'll see in the next chapter, the educational "scales" have in many ways tipped in favor of girls, and
if they are "shortchanged" it's not by gender bias but by the overall dumb-
ing-down of education to which Hillary's friends have contributed quite a
bit. But as usual, the gendercrats were not about to let the facts get in the

way. Funding for WEEA was triumphantly restored by a 311 to 111 vote in the House. Not only did the Democrats overwhelmingly support it, but so did half of the Republicans.

The Clinton Administration has gotten into the act as well. In 1996, under the stewardship of Friend of Hillary and Health and Human Services (HHS) secretary Donna Shalala, the HHS Department launched a public education campaign called "Girl Power!"—intended, according to the HHS press release, to "encourage and empower nine- to fourteen-year-old girls to make the most of their lives." That sounds like a worthy goal, and "Girl Power!" includes many initiatives no one could quarrel with: promoting sports; fitness and healthy nutrition; preventing drug use, smoking, and teenage sex. But since when are drug use, poor health habits, and teen sex problems for girls only? Here's one example of how dishonest this "girl power" propaganda can be: The HHS press release cites a study showing that ninth-grade girls are twice as likely as boys to "have thought seriously about attempting suicide" and to have attempted it in the past year. It conveniently forgets to mention that boys actually *commit suicide five times more often*. This isn't sisterhood—it's female chauvinism. As women, don't we care about our sons as much as we do about our daughters?

Or take another noble cause-turned-feminist pork: violence against women. The Violence Against Women Act (VAWA) passed in 1994 as part of the omnibus crime bill, is one of the most cherished accomplishments of the Capitol Sisters. Hillary Clinton has touted it as one of her husband's greatest gifts to women. While campaigning for Chuck Schumer for the U.S. Senate in New York in 1998, she declared that women should boot out Republican Alfonse D'Amato because, among other things, he had voted against VAWA. Actually, the irony is that D'Amato had cosponsored VAWA in the Senate (along with several other Republicans, including Orrin Hatch, Arlen Specter, and the great defender of women Bob Packwood), and voted against the anticrime bill because it contained too many feel-good programs like "midnight basketball." Like many other exercises in legislative chivalry, VAWA was, alas, largely a bipartisan effort.

Who could possibly be against a bill that protects women from violence? Unfortunately, what we have here is stealth radical feminism. Sure, VAWA has some bits no one could quarrel with. For instance, it requires the states to pay for medical exams for rape victims and to enforce orders of protection against abusive spouses issued in another state. It also provides grants to improve security in parking lots and bus, train, and subway stations—though one may ask why such matters should be handled by the federal government rather than by state and local authorities, who are in a much better position to address specific safety issues, which may differ from one community to the next.

But VAWA also ensures a steady stream of federal grants to groups like the National Coalition Against Domestic Violence, whose mission statement reads like an over-the-top parody of political correctness: The abuse of women, we are told, is related to "sexism, racism, classism, anti-Semitism, able-bodyism, ageism, and other oppressions." VAWA reclassifies sexual assault and domestic violence as gender bias crimes for which women can file federal civil rights suits against their attackers. Does this do much for women who are raped or battered? Actually, no. There is little chance of collecting monetary damages from the typical perp (federal statistics and many other studies show that men who attack women are likely to be uneducated, unemployed, alcoholics, or drug abusers), and it doesn't make sense to go through the arduous and lengthy litigation unless there's big money involved. Only a handful of VAWA suits have been filed since 1994, mostly involving wealthy husbands in divorce cases or deep-pocket entities like a college that allegedly mishandled a student's complaint of date rape.

Provisions that make such litigation possible may be more pointless than harmful, but the real shame is that the VAWA lobby seemed more interested in scoring political points and winning federal dollars for feminist projects than in protecting women. Activists talk about the symbolic importance of court rulings that treat battering and rape as part of a male "war against women," but victims of such crimes presumably would like to see more focus on putting their attackers behind bars for longer terms. Yet in 1993, when Senator Joseph Biden (D-DE) tried to include stiffer jail sentences for rapists in VAWA, women's groups nixed the idea, denouncing such provisions as "aimed at black males."

You might think that VAWA supporters would be passionately concerned for the underprivileged. In fact, instead of funding services in poor urban areas where women are most likely to be victims of rape and other violence, VAWA shells out millions to "date rape education" on college campuses—programs where young women are told, falsely, that one in four female students gets raped in college. If that statistic were accurate, parents would be insane to let their daughters go off to college. But, however self-evidently ridiculous, this statistic has taken root in the public imagination. It is obtained by defining rape down. One leading date rape educator, Dr. Andrea Parrot of Cornell University, asserts that a woman who is "psychologically pressured" into sex is "as much a victim of rape as the person who is attacked on the streets." A woman who lives in a neighborhood where she has to worry about being attacked on the street probably won't find this argument convincing.

This sort of misguided "education" about rape is only one instance of how VAWA puts ideology over women's real-life needs. It also promotes ignorance about the relationship between drugs and alcohol and crimes against women. When I checked out the Department of Justice website with information on how to apply for VAWA grants (no, I wasn't thinking of getting one for myself), one thing I learned was that no grants are given to programs that focus on substance abuse. Was that a typo? After all, the website also tells us that alcohol is involved in three out of four sexual assaults on college campuses and all the data show that the majority of batterers abuse alcohol or illicit drugs. But according to the new orthodoxy at the Justice Department, the abuse of women is caused by "beliefs and attitudes that women are subordinate to men and that men have the right to exercise power and control over women"—so, even if most sexual aggressors and woman-beaters are junkies or alcoholics, drinking and drugs must be treated as entirely separate problems from the violence.

Clearly, VAWA is not the dream legislation for women that it's been made out to be. Has it been good for women at all? Bonnie Campbell, the first director of the federal Violence Against Women Office, points to a drop in murders of spouses and intimate partners. But that's not very convincing, since the decline is part of a twenty-year trend. Visiting a battered women's shelter in 1998, Hillary Clinton crowed about a Justice Department report showing that from 1993 to 1996, incidents of domestic violence had dropped by twenty-three percent. There is no evidence that VAWA was the reason for the decline. Domestic violence numbers go up and down from year to year; in 1993, for example, they rose by twelve percent from 1992. According to the same Justice Department report, VAWA has been a total failure on at least one count—the percentage of battered women who seek police assistance has barely budged, despite millions spent on police sensitivity training.

Women benefitted most from the overall drop in crime, not from any specially targeted violence-against-women measures. For all the feminist complaints that the biggest threat women face comes from the men in their lives, government statistics show that only about twenty percent of violent crimes against women are committed by husbands and boyfriends; attacks by strangers account for more than a third (the rest are by non-intimate acquaintances). That means women have benefitted even more from the drop in stranger crime than they have from the drop in domestic violence (in the mid-1990s both types of crime have declined at the same rate). Whether it's medicine, education, or crime, women and girls gain far more from across-the-board improvements than from anything the politicos set out to do "for women." Still, women are always expected to be wowed by legislation that treats them as a special interest group—the political equivalent of a cheap pickup line.

Sisterhood Isn't for Everyone

What's depressing is that the cheap pickup line so often works. Hillary and her feminist supporters have successfully played the gender card whenever there's a risk that conservatives might win and liberals might lose. A striking example of this gender opportunism came in July 1999, when Hillary, appearing by her husband's side at the White House, assailed the Republicans' plan for a $792 billion tax cut as "antiwoman." Actually, the Republican proposal had a welcome bonus for working women—an end to the "marriage penalty" that pushes the joint income of two employed spouses into a higher tax bracket. The proposed tax cut (minuscule, and phased-in over several years) would have at least given working women some modest tax relief, allowing them to keep a bit more of their income. Hillary and others, again using gender-scare tactics, warned that the Republican plan would have harmed Medicare (which serves more women than men because women live longer). Feminist groups should have been the first to call the marriage penalty sexist, since it sometimes makes it more advantageous for a woman to quit her job. But the only women's group to champion the elimination of the marriage penalty was the Independent Women's Forum, an organization of which I am a proud member and one that feminists routinely savage as a puppet of the patriarchy.

It's not just tax cuts that are derided as "antiwoman." You're antiwoman when you think single moms on welfare should be required to work, or when you think America's U.N. dues shouldn't fund abortions in other countries. So what about those women who support tax cuts, limited government, and a strong defense? Or who think female-specific legislation like the Violence Against Women Act is more about making male politicians feel good than helping women? In Hillary's world they—we—are "unwomen."

If you're wondering whether you fall in the woman or unwoman category, here's a handy reference list. Copy it. Stick it on the refrigerator:

Women	Unwomen
Women who live on government checks	Women who start private businesses
Activists who fight for the rights of spotted owls	Activists who fight for the rights of private landowners

Women	Unwomen
Supporters of the right to choose abortion	Supporters of the right to choose their children's schools
Goddess worshipers	Evangelical Christians
Our Bodies, Ourselves owners	Gun owners
Opponents of sex discrimination	Opponents of race or gender preferences
Protesters against the male establishment	Protesters against high taxes
Accuse Republicans of sexual harassment	Accuse Democrats of sexual harassment
Democrats	Republicans

Some feminists take that last party-label category literally. Back in 1984, I remember seeing a sign at a feminist rally: ARE YOU A WOMAN OR ARE YOU FOR REAGAN? YOU CAN'T BE BOTH. Gulp! There I was, classified as a member of a third sex. Luckily I didn't suffer too much of an identity crisis, since Ronald Reagan actually captured the majority of the female vote that year, and I ended up working in his White House two years later. But this kind of demonization is sadly typical. In 1993, Gloria Steinem campaigned against pro-choice Republican Kay Bailey Hutchison in the Senate race and jeered her as a "female impersonator."

The so-called "gender gap" that emerged in the 1980s seemed to offer proof of the feminist contention that women voted as a bloc. Their claim isn't entirely unfounded. In the 1994 midterm congressional elections, men voted Republican fifty-seven percent to forty-three percent while women voted Democratic fifty-four percent to forty-six percent; and women did get Bill Clinton re-elected in 1996, which led me to question the wisdom of women's suffrage (relax, I'm kidding!).

However, while more women vote Democratic than Republican, describing this phenomenon as a "gender gap" is simplistic and misleading. Break down how women vote by other demographic categories and the pattern suggests more of a "married/single gap" or a "racial gap" than a straight gender gap. Single women are more likely to vote Democratic, while married women gravitate toward Republican candidates. Black women vote overwhelmingly Democratic, even more than black men. Meanwhile, white women tend to be Republican—with fifty-five percent voting Republican in 1994, compared to sixty-two percent of white men. Professional women split their vote evenly between both parties. Although that group tends to be more liberal on social issues, they like the conservative message of lower taxes, self-reliance, and personal responsibility.

Despite the real political divide among women, the Left clings to the idea of the gender gap as an important weapon in its arsenal. Democratic pollsters Stan Greenberg and Celinda Lake tell *The Washington Post*, "Men and women absolutely disagree about which party would be better on the economy, taxes, crime." But on underlying ideological issues, many women embrace what feminists regard as "male" attitudes. Several polls in the mid-1990s showed that similar numbers of women and men (about two out of three) agreed that "government is almost always wasteful and inefficient" and that "the federal government has become so large and powerful that it poses an immediate threat to the rights and freedoms of ordinary citizens."

Women do seem to favor, by a margin of about ten percent, a government that's actively involved in solving people's problems and providing services, polls show. This is partly because women are more likely to benefit from government largesse—for example, two-thirds of food stamp recipients and residents in federally subsidized housing are single mothers and their kids. Maybe not many food stamp recipients vote. But women are also vastly overrepresented in public-sector jobs, and so when the GOP talks about cutting the pork out of government, they complain. The reason women tend to trust government more than men could thus be more related to self-interest than any innate "female" sense of compassion.

The peddlers of the false sisterhood have a vested interest in convincing women that it is right to demand that there always be a "government safety net." Once again, the trap is set. Through a slick combination of pandering and fear-mongering, the Hillarys send a steady stream of messages to women that "we know what's good for you," and conservatives just don't "care." Of course in the "politics of caring," as columnist George Will has dubbed it, being "pro-women" means being pro-government, or rather, being for a government that "feels." (Wasn't it our president's predilection for government feeling—or rather, feeling up—that ended up getting him impeached?) For all their scoffing at old notions of male chivalry, feminists like Hillary are calling for Uncle Sam to the rescue!

Clearly, many women have fallen into the Hillary Trap of political sisterhood, substituting a left-liberal slate of political beliefs in place of their own independent thinking. Polls show that a lot of women buy the idea that conservatives are heartless numbers-crunchers and just don't get it. Well, you have to admit that most of them haven't a clue about how to appeal to women voters. Republicans have a weird, nerdy passion for battles over "continuing resolutions" and "CBO surplus estimates" that would bore most men, let alone women. But even if you feel your eyes glazing over, you would do well to trust the guy wearing green eye shades mumbling boringly about cost-benefit equations over the rotund sloganeer with the great makeover.

Unfortunately, we can't expect conservative Republicans to stand up to feminist follies anymore. Cowed by the vast power of the sisterhood, a lot of them gave up years ago: To win women's allegiance, they are voting reflexively for any program with gender rhetoric attached. Lots of so-called conservatives voted for VAWA and the Family Medical Leave Act, while holding their noses in private.

Politicians of both parties, reading polls and press reports like tea leaves, often assume along with essayist Barbara Ehrenreich that women are born socialists, eager to share and care—naturally drawn, as it were, to the party of the Nanny State. Men, on the other hand, are said to be more self-reliant and to see government as more of an obstacle than a help. In a 1996 column in *Time*, Ehrenreich elaborated on her theories of the caring Woman versus the detached Man, contending that women's continuing role as primary caregiver to children and the elderly makes them, well, more evolved:

*Cut off from daily contact with the weak and the needy, and hypnotized
by the zero-sum ethic of televised sports, men were bound to be seduced
by the social Darwinism of the political right, with its vision of the world
as a vast playing field for superstar linebackers and heroic entrepreneurs
on leave from* The Fountainhead. *Women, on the other hand, are more
likely to have a vested interest in the notion of human interdependence.*

That phrase "human interdependence" has Hillary's "village" written all
over it, a world where a government welfare office is more connected to
human needs than an entrepreneur who creates jobs.

By promoting such stereotypes, feminists are sacrificing their own
hard-won achievements. After all, one of the best things to come out of the
women's movement was the message of self-reliance and self-sufficiency.
The demeaning stereotype of the fragile woman, ever-dependent upon a
man to put food on the table and a roof over her head has been banished
forever. Yet Hillary's brand of feminism forces upon women new stereotypes—like the liberal soccer mom who wants an activist government to
protect her and her family. Women demanding that government serve
them might seem, on the surface, to empower women. But true empowerment means making it without demanding special privileges based on who
you are and without relying on the government to bail you out if things go
wrong. Women now own nearly forty percent of the nation's small businesses and start new ventures at twice the rate of men. And guess what?
These women are far more concerned about exorbitant taxes and absurd
regulations, just like their male counterparts, than they are about what the
sisterhood has designated as "women's issues." Elinor Burkett, a liberal
journalist who wrote a book called *The Right Women* has this to say about
the comfortable stereotype of women as perpetually pro-government:

*While the explosion in woman-owned businesses has caused a revolution
in the American economy, it has provoked an even greater revolution in
the lives and perspectives of these female entrepreneurs. Women who
have always believed that big government is essential to providing a social*

safety net wind up furious at the government for interfering in the econ-
omy. Women who once trusted that the government would help them
pursue the American Dream have come to believe that the American
Dream would be accessible if not for the feds.

I have had a chance to observe firsthand the pattern that Burkett
describes.

A few years ago, I was doing a piece for *CBS News* on the regulation of
the wine industry. I talked to a few winery owners in Sonoma and Napa
Valley. Julie Williams was a co-owner of Frog's Leap Winery. (Try their '95
zinfandel, by the way.) Now in her forties, she and her husband started
their winery years before, and began turning out some terrific, modestly
priced wines that were soon marketed by retailers across the country.
When I first started chatting with Julie, she seemed like the classic liberal
feminist—no makeup, earth mom, speaking in hushed tones.

But then Julie started talking about the "overwhelming federal, state,
and local regulations" of the wine industry and suddenly she started to
sound like a dyed-in-the-wool Reagan conservative. She wasn't "the super-
rich," but the government treated her as if she had unlimited money
to hire accountants and lawyers. By the time I left Frog's Leap, I wasn't
thinking that I had just met a cool *woman* business owner, but that I had just
met a cool business owner. Julie loves wine-making and wishes the government wasn't so often an impediment to her life and her business. She defied
gender stereotypes and in that sense she is the true woman of our age.

The gendercrats who thrive in Hillary's world don't seem to know what
to do with "unwomen" like Julie. When Hillary was touting the glories of
her health care reform plan before a rapt Congress, Representative Jim
Ramstad (R-MN) asked her about the burden the plan would impose on
small businesses. "I can't be responsible for saving every undercapitalized
entrepreneur in America," Hillary imperiously replied. (Can you imagine
her saying, "I can't be responsible for saving every child in America" or "I
can't be responsible for saving every federal program that claims to help
inner-city women"? Never.)

But the American entrepreneurs to whom she referred with such sneering contempt are increasingly women—like Kathy Posner, the head of a marketing firm in Chicago who fired off an angry letter to the editor of the *Chicago Sun-Times* blasting Hillary's "arrogance and disregard" for people like herself: "I am a small business owner. I was not undercapitalized as of September 30, but I will be undercapitalized if the Clinton plan comes to fruition because the government will be burdening me with a tax bill that I never had before." There are nearly nine million Kathy Posners out there, and they make their living by avoiding traps in the business world. Will they fall for the Hillary Trap of gender politics?

Forever caught in the time warp of 1969, Hillary and today's feminists with few exceptions haven't yet come to terms with the fact that, as a group, women are politically diverse. Seeing women through the gender prism makes them seem one-dimensional, products of groupthink and lockstep liberal politics. For women who lean heavily on their membership in this "oppressed class," gender becomes self-limiting. During Hillary's "listening tour" as she contemplated a bid for the U.S. Senate, she assured audiences that she would fight for issues "that women care about." But not all women, thanks. The only "women's issues" in Hillary's world are social services—anything vaguely family related that creates bigger government programs. How great would it be if the next time Hillary boasts about her advocacy on behalf of women, a female voter asked, "Glad you're so concerned about the struggles of women, Mrs. Clinton. My concern is about high taxes, so what are you going to do to cut federal spending?"

Uh, next question.

Because Hillary and her followers define sisterhood in political terms, inclusivity is out. Membership in the sisterhood is enforced by an ideological apartheid dividing liberal Democrats from the unwomen of the GOP. Conservative women are total pariahs. Even liberal Republican women, who pass all left-liberal litmus tests on abortion, women's health legislation, and the Equal Rights Amendment (time warp alert), are deemed well-intentioned but enlightened dupes of the white male GOP establishment.

Senator Olympia Snowe, the liberal Republican from Maine, can tell you how gender apartheid works. In 1984, then-Congresswoman Snowe cochaired with Democratic Congresswoman Pat Schroeder the Congressional Caucus for Women's Issues. Gender-pressured by the sisterhood, Snowe used her position to support just about every left-wing "pro-women" piece of legislation to come out of Congress—the Family and Medical Leave Act, the Women's Health Equity Act, the Sexual Harassment Free Schools Act, the Act for Better Child Care, the Child Support Enforcement Improvements Act. I myself disagree with all of them and would vote against Madame Snowe if I ever got the chance. Nevertheless, the feminists from NOW still didn't consider Snowe one of them. When Snowe decided to run for a vacant Senate seat in Maine in 1994, NOW supported her Democratic challenger Tom Andrews. It didn't matter that the policies Snowe supported were just the sort of big-government social spending that feminists love. NOW tried to spin its endorsement of Snowe's male Democratic opponent as a sign of its gender neutrality—look, we support men, too! NOW spokeswoman Lois Reckitt proclaimed, "Sometimes, we have to look beyond gender—to the issues." What more could NOW have wanted to extract from Snowe on the "issues"? The explanation is obvious: Right gender, wrong party. A similar party-line move was the New Jersey NOW chapter's support in the 1990 Senate race for Democrat Bill Bradley over moderate pro-choice, pro-feminist Republican Christine Todd Whitman.

The more threatened the feminists in Hillary's world feel, the nastier they get. When the 1996 GOP convention featured a lineup of female speakers—Elizabeth Dole, Representative Susan Molinari, Senator Kay Bailey Hutchison, Govenor Christine Todd Whitman—NOW vice president Rosemary Dempsey scoffed, "I'm not surprised at all. Republicans know how to use women."

This is not to say that women shouldn't criticize other women—of course they should, when it's about substance. During Kay Bailey Hutchison's Senate race, Molly Ivins, the tart-tongued Texas newspaper columnist, dismissed her as a vapid "Breck girl," for her blonde, well-groomed hair. Feminists have also ridiculed members of the conservative Independent Women's Forum such as Wendy Lee Gramm and Lynne Cheney, as nothing more than puppets of their famous Republican husbands—never mind that Gramm is a distinguished economist and Cheney a former chair of the National Endowment for the Humanities. Girl power means never having to say you're Republican.

Belittling women's achievement with cracks about their looks is precisely the kind of thinking a hundred years of feminism has been fighting against. I cite as authority none other than Hillary Clinton, who once told a group of eighth-graders during a discussion of sexism, "Sometimes our contributions are blocked or made fun of or ignored because of how we look." Yes, it happens. And sometimes, Hillary, the culprits are your own sisters.

Here's how weird the gender mavens get: In their zeal to protect their political agenda, Hillary's henchwomen end up blasting women who dared to criticize the egregious sexual improprieties of Hillary's husband. I know, because I've often been on the receiving end of these personal attacks. In late 1998, as the House was moving to impeach the president for lying about his affair with Monica Lewinsky, West Coast leftist law professor Susan Estrich published a piece in *Legal Times* titled: "Sex Scandal Spawns Clinton-Bashing Peroxide Pundettes." She was denouncing me and other conservative women for dissing her man Bill. Incredible! Here was a progressive female legal mind resorting to the old male chauvinist line—blondes are just airheads. Estrich charged that we were not on TV for our "wit, insight, knowledge, and experience," but solely because of our looks.

This was what Clinton feminists had resorted to—reverse "wolf whistling." She described us as "modern-day bunnies," members of a club where "long legs, short skirts, low necklines" are preferred. It didn't matter that three of us were attorneys (Ann Coulter, Barbara Olson and I), or that the other two were also working professionals (Kellyanne Fitzpatrick runs and solely owns her own polling firm and Danielle Crittenden is a widely published journalist).

To be fair, Hillary Clinton herself has not engaged in this feminist neo-misogyny. What she has done is help create the atmosphere in which this intolerant view of womanhood is acceptable. After all, key to the First Couple's survival strategy for the past seven years has been the demonization of the opposition as fascists and racists at every turn. Loyal operatives like James Carville and Ann Lewis do the dirty work so that politicians like Hillary can keep their hands clean. Needless to say, Hillary does not object when her political sisters blast away at other women who won't sign on the dotted line.

I'm not the kind of person who goes ballistic over every "dumb blonde" joke. But where are feminist watchdogs like Laura Flanders when conservative women get tarred and feathered? Writing in the left-wing magazine *In These Times*, Flanders jeered that "With all that conservative bombast and blonde hair blowing, it's hard to tell those perky pundits apart." My favorite insult came from writer Katha Pollitt, who in *The Nation* imagined a nightmare television network that was "an endless right-wing TV talk show." The show would include a feature where conservative women would "give dating tips to restlessly single Laura Ingraham ('Leopard-print miniskirts? Scary! No wonder guys don't call back')." She devoted the rest of this column to denouncing misogyny around the world.

About that miniskirt. I wore it for a cover photo of *The New York Times Magazine* in February 1995. The article was about the new conservative "opinion elite" invading Washington. The theme: This is not your father's brand of conservatism. After the miniskirt picture, nearly every article written about me seized on it as evidence that I was a gadfly. Hey, it was just a skirt! And it was borrowed, too! Surely, the sisterhood would be there to support my right to choose . . . clothing, right? Not quite. Feminist Susan Faludi, who devoted pages of her book *Backlash* to the evils of stereotyping, dubbed me "a leopard-skin miniskirted socialite." *The Washington Post*'s Megan Rosenfeld informed readers that I am "fond of leopard prints and short skirts." And when media big sister Marjorie Williams, a prolific and talented writer for *Vanity Fair*, profiled me for the magazine's January 1997 issue, she, too, highlighted the stupid miniskirt: "Meet Laura Ingraham, the brand-new pundit with a provocative arsenal of miniskirts [and] party invitations."

There I was, trying to make it in what I thought was the boys' club of the media, and my biggest detractors weren't the suits in the boardroom, they were the women who had already made it. Sure, I expected to get slammed by the president's supporters when I devoted so much of my on-air time to criticizing his policies and his ethics. What was surprising was that—with the exception of some wonderfully supportive women at *NBC News*—feminists were so vicious. By the time the First Couple called for an end to the "politics of personal destruction," Hillary's feminist supporters had already turned it into an art form.

Women, Don't Unite—Just Be Honest

So is there such a thing as sisterhood? On some level, I think there is. We do have a common interest in the dignity and equality of women, which has been denied for most of human history. And we do embrace our sisters in less developed countries who still live with daily abuse and oppression. Beyond these core human rights issues, however, women will often disagree about what dignity and equality means: to some, it's more parity in the workplace; to others, more respect for the traditional female sphere of home and family. What do we want for ourselves, here and now, at the beginning of a new century? A new set of limiting stereotypes based on gender politics? Or what our grandmothers only dreamed of—the chance to think freely and be judged according to our merits and character?

Hillary Clinton wants to turn womanhood into a liberal pledge of allegiance. To be a real woman, she and her allies imply, you have to buy into a list of policy prescriptions that range from federal health care to federal child care. That's the Hillary Trap of false sisterhood. By campaigning as a woman first, Hillary is using gender in a way that ultimately undermines the ideas real feminism ought to be about. She should sell her liberal policies on their merits—not try to shame us into supporting them. In rejecting those ideas, we're not antiwoman. We're thinking for ourselves.

Indeed, there is encouraging evidence that growing numbers of women are not seduced by the pretty but empty slogans of sisterhood. In late 1999 and early 2000, as Hillary was inching closer to a formal announcement of her Senate candidacy, polls showed that only 47 percent of women in New York State, down from 58 percent a year earlier, planned to give her their votes. Among white women, support for Hillary was down to 35 percent. According to a January 16, 2000, story in the *Washington Post*, interviews with individual voters showed that while many women wanted to support the candidacy of a strong and accomplished woman, they also had reservations about Hillary—either because they believed that she had not accomplished much, or because they didn't like the baggage she came with (including the baggage currently occupying the Oval Office.)

Hillary is such an unlikely role model for a self-respecting woman, if you think about it. I don't care how many inspirational speeches she gives while she's globe-trotting at taxpayer expense about bringing "new dignity and respect to women and girls all over the world." A prominent woman in the public eye who puts up with chronic marital infidelities and acts as an unpaid defense attorney for a husband who humiliates her and her daughter is not standing up for women's dignity. It's even worse when she colludes in trashing women victimized by her husband's egregious sexual misconduct and attempts to excuse his behavior by blaming his dead mother and grandmother.

The only kind of sisterhood that can work is one in which we treat each other with decency and respect as people, even as we respectfully disagree about issues. Instead of this simple prescription, Hillary Clinton invites us into an artificial community defined by our anatomy. She wants us to share an ideology based on gender. That kind of sisterhood denies our individuality and our true diversity as women. It lures us into a new dependency—on the sisterhood, spouting its half-truths and pleas for special treatment—and that's every bit as limiting as our old dependency on men.

In subsequent chapters, we will see how the Hillary Trap sabotages women from cradle to grave, in every sphere of their lives from the workplace to marriage and family to personal safety. It starts early in life with the miseducation of America's daughters.

2

The

Education

Trap

When Hillary Clinton finally decided in late November 1999 to end the guessing game about whether she would run for retiring Senator Daniel Patrick Moynihan's newly vacated New York Senate seat, she chose a friendly forum. It was classic Hillary. The blue-and-white United Federation of Teachers banner forming a striking TV backdrop, Mrs. Clinton stood on the podium next to UFT president Randi Weingarten. Reporters later described the scene as a scripted question-and-answer session. "We need someone to push this [education] agenda," Weingarten told Hillary. "And we need someone to be the successor to Pat Moynihan, who really cares about education. So is it yes or no?"

Hillary answered, "Yes." Throngs of reporters had flown in for the event, after being tipped off by the First Lady's staff. Weingarten embraced Hillary to applause and cheers from the union rank and file. Like the Clintons' January 1998 "impromptu" waltz on the beach or Hillary's solitary walks in Martha's Vineyard post-Monica, the event had been carefully staged to seem spontaneous. Standing arm in arm with teachers, Hillary's explicit message to the public was "I'm the candidate who cares about our children's future."

But what was the *real* message of that even? After all, it was not against the scrubbed walls and scuffed linoleum of a struggling urban public school that Hillary posed for the cameras, but at the well-appointed quarters of a teachers' union. What it showed was that the "education" candidate was in the pocket of a powerful special interest group. It showed how dependent the outwardly confident Hillary was upon her organized labor friends and their campaign contributions.

Hillary's choice of the teacher's union conference to announce her candidacy also spoke volumes about the educational agenda that she champions. While the UFT does support some education innovations such as charter schools, it virulently opposes school vouchers, which would give a portion of the money that the government currently pumps into the public schools directly to the parents, to be used at a public, private, or parochial school of their choice. Vouchers, now supported by a wide array of people across party lines, would bring an element of choice and free market competition to the failing monopoly of the public schools. Good schools where parents want to send their kids would thrive; bad schools that parents want to flee would be eventually driven out of business. The UFT and the other teachers' unions consistently back liberal politicians who fight against school choice, such as New York Senator Charles Schumer, to protect their monopoly and block any reforms that might purge bad teachers and bad schools from the system. They cling stubbornly to their belief that the solution to bad schools is ever more federal money—both to the failing schools and to various federal and state education bureaucracies, with no market accountability for teacher performance. Hillary agrees wholeheartedly.

The hidden headline behind that appearance with the UFT leadership: Hillary's campaign, down in the polls, had been ransomed to a special interest group that depends on big government for its existence.

Hillary's education-focused kickoff shouldn't have come as a surprise—she had named education as one of the most important pillars of her campaign at almost every stop of her fall pre-campaign "listening tour" of New York. "When she comes here to the Senate of the United States, she will be the education senator," enthused Massachusetts Senator Ted Kennedy in October 1999. The occasion was an education briefing for Democratic senators, where the First Lady was the star guest speaker. The accolades came pouring out for Hillary's work for "the children." "The children" has long since become one of Hillary's main political props.

Bill and Hillary carefully cultivated their pro-education image during the 1992 presidential campaign, with Hillary promising voters that her husband would be "a real education president," one-upping George Bush who had campaigned himself under the same moniker. A few years later, in *It Takes a Village*, she wrote that "our commitment to education will determine whether we graduate to a new era of progress and prosperity or fail our children and ourselves." Today it's hard to find a profile of Hillary that doesn't mention her dedication to improving our schools.

Sloganeering about education is easy. Everyone loves children. Everyone wants better schools. Campaigning as the "education congressman" or the "education mayor" or the "education dog catcher" is how politicians transmit to voters that they "care"—about children or education or Mom and apple pie. Hillary tells us she wants to "fight for the children," but she's vague on exactly how. However, to fix a failing system, you have to understand how it got to its sorry state to begin with. Hillary obviously doesn't, for she aligns herself solidly with the same groups—the educrats and teachers' unions—that are directly responsible for dumbing down our schools and for introducing the worst educational fads, such as bilingual education, anti-intellectual multiculturalism, and politicalization of the curriculum. Thus, Hillary's education philosophy is actually antireform, and her invocation of "education" for "our children" is another trap—an Education Trap holding our public schools and many universities captive to incompetent and self-serving special interests.

Over the years, Hillary has supported policies that cede significant control of education to lobbyists, unions, gendercrats, and radical feminists. This isn't popular, so for political cover she has paid lip service to principles like "accountability" and "standards" without defining what they mean to her in terms of policy. In fact her policy plans are to leave public school students and their parents at the mercy of the same social science "experts" and "education professionals" who helped wreck the schools in the first place—and to fund them even more heavily to do what they have always done, which is to protect their fiefdoms and sinecures in the education and diversity industry. Hillary wants us all to be even more dependent on these experts. The deal is simple: more taxpayer dollars to these interest groups in exchange for their generous campaign support. Hillary and her allies then denounce those who question their agenda as "Christian fanatics" or right-wing kooks, and brand truly innovative reform that would help break the grip of special interests on education as "anti-child" or "anti-teacher" or "anti–public education."

Hillary, to put it bluntly, is a hypocrite. She advocates an education system for others that is very different from the system that encouraged Hillary herself to excel. Back when she was a young girl attending the public schools of Park Ridge, Illinois, an incompetent teacher could actually be fired. A core curriculum—history, composition, literature, math, and science—was the foundation of every young child's education. Hillary's parents instilled the value of hard work and discipline in their daughter. They set an example for their children: Hugh Rodham put himself through Penn State University by working in coal mines and factories. Dorothy Rodham returned to school to get her college degree as an adult. After being a star pupil in elementary and middle school in quiet Park Ridge, Hillary attended the elite public high school Maine East, making the honor roll and racking up numerous academic awards. (In high school, she once wrote a seventy-five-page term paper!)

It's true that in those years the educational system had some drawbacks that feminists have rightly criticized. At the high school level, girls were still steered into home economics and boys into shop. And even at the elite Wellesley College, which Hillary attended, students were instructed in the proper way to pour tea and subjected to an annual "marriage lecture" offering tips on such fascinating subjects as how to entertain your husband's boss. Nevertheless, Hillary's Wellesley education also gave her a solid academic grounding, even as campuses across the country roiled with Vietnam War–era political unrest. In the late sixties, Wellesley professors didn't rant against the oppressiveness of Western civilization and didn't tell women that studying the works of "dead white males" was beneath them; the curriculum was quite traditional and the academic standards were rigorous.

American education began to go bad in the years after Hillary graduated from Wellesley, and that decline had its roots in the muddled ideas of Hillary's generation. They tolerated poor standards because they were afraid of looking "racist" or "sexist" or "elitist" in defending traditional norms. And they allowed fuzzy feel-good politics to pervade nearly every discipline outside the chemistry lab or the physics workshop.

To get the flavor of these ruinous changes, you need only visit Hillary's alma mater. Today, Wellesley is a bouillabaisse of diversity workshops, sensitivity training, and cheerleading for various trendy causes. There's a pervasive distrust for the core subjects Hillary mastered as a student. Multiculturalism and classes on such weighty matters as the cultural significance of Madonna are in; traditional academics are out.

As is sadly the case at most colleges across the country, a Wellesley student's introduction to political correctitude starts early. At freshman workshops, students are encouraged to look inward for unconscious sexist, racist, or homophobic feelings. Writing in *Heterodoxy* magazine, Alyson Todd, Wellesley '93, described her orientation day and concluded that "you have to be a victim to fit in at Wellesley." When Todd—whose ethnic background includes Irish, English, Dutch, German, French, and Italian ancestry—described her cultural identity as simply "American," the other women in the workshop greeted her with "icy stares and stony silence." Undoubtedly, a savvy Wellesley student can still find some excellent professors. But she has to navigate a faculty that includes people like Peggy McIntosh, who scoffs at traditional standards of "excellence, accomplishment, success, and achievement" as symptoms of white male "vertical thinking." McIntosh instead extols what she calls "lateral thinking," which she claims is more "inclusive" and supposedly more congenial for women and people of color. In her schema, no answers are right or wrong, no one's work product is better or worse than another's. Such judgments would be "vertical," i.e., male. To be sure, many professors would reject this muddled thinking. But the fact that it can be taught at all shows that at Wellesley and elsewhere there has been a discernible shift away from objective standards and criteria toward a less judgmental, "no-fault" learning process. That's a shame, because it deprives students not only of academic rigor but of healthy competition.

The erosion of educational standards begins long before a student reaches college. Today a disturbing number of students are graduating from high school without solid foundations in core subjects. In 1998, the Department of Education reported that our twelfth-graders were not keeping up with the rest of the developed world in important subjects such as mathematics and science. This study was the focus of the 1998 bipartisan report "A Nation Still at Risk." The facts are frightening and remain so today, especially given the importance of education in an ever more competitive global economy. American twelfth-graders scored near the bottom among twenty-one nations—nineteenth in math, sixteenth in science. Our advanced students fared even worse when compared to the best from other countries: They were at the bottom of the heap in physics. And it's not because foreign students are such geniuses that American kids rank low. It's that our kids aren't required to learn what they need to know. Since 1983, more than ten million of our high school seniors have made it to twelfth grade without having learned to read at a basic level. More than twenty million of them couldn't do basic math. And twenty-five million of them didn't know the essentials of American history. This sad state of educational affairs was documented in the 1987 book *What Do Our Seventeen-Year-Olds Know?* by researchers and educators Chester Finn and Diane Ravitch, who found that forty-three percent of high school seniors could not place World War I between 1900 and 1950 and that more than two-thirds did not know in which half-century the Civil War took place.

Given these fundamental deficiencies in American education, it's inevitable that students arrive at college unprepared. "A Nation Still at Risk" reports that colleges must now devote significant resources to offering new students remedial education. Some thirty percent of today's entering freshmen need remedial courses in reading, writing, and mathematics; at the sprawling California state university system, that figure jumps to more than fifty percent. Even the supposedly best and brightest are in trouble: A 1993 survey of incoming freshmen at Ivy League schools revealed that three out of four did not know that Thomas Jefferson had authored the opening words of the Declaration of Independence. The late Richard Marius, director of the expository writing program at Harvard, lamented to *The New York Times* that today's freshmen are so "woefully deficient" in reading and writing that a remedial course is needed to get them to the level where their peers started out a generation ago.

Hillary Clinton could have performed an invaluable service for America's girls and young women (not to mention boys and young men!) if she had used her platform as First Lady to push real reform of American schools. Instead, through her husband's presidency and her own Senate campaign, Hillary has cynically played politics, catering to rich, established, and politically powerful interest groups like the teachers' unions and the education bureaucracies, which waste enormous amounts of taxpayer money developing avant-garde educational theories and programs that hurt, not help, education. These groups built the current failed system and they contribute big money to Democrat coffers to keep it that way.

Interestingly, when it came to the education of her own daughter, Hillary didn't trust her usual allies and supporters. She didn't deliver Chelsea to the clutches of a unionized public school in Washington, but to the top private school in town—Sidwell Friends. It's a great school, to be sure, precisely because it has rigorous academic standards and doesn't let politics distort education. But what about the thousands of other girls in Washington, condemned to the system that Hillary's daughter escaped? They don't have the money for private schools. And Hillary has fought tooth and nail against the voucher programs that would give these poor D.C. kids the same kind of opportunity she could buy for Chelsea.

My views on education reflect my experience, first as a public school student in Connecticut and later as a college undergraduate at Dartmouth. At the Glastonbury schools, I learned to respect traditional teaching methods: They gave me a chance to transcend the world of my mother, a bright and loving woman who never had the chance to go to college. At Dartmouth, I learned to challenge the new left-wing orthodoxy that was preaching tolerance but was actually stifling criticism from anyone who disagreed with the dominant liberal views on race, sex, and academic standards.

My high school was a microcosm of what once made American education great. Glastonbury, Connecticut, is a suburb of Hartford, and many of my classmates' parents worked in the insurance industry or, like my father, for one of numerous defense contractors in the area. It certainly wasn't a rich town, like the New York suburbs of Greenwich or Darien. It was the "middle class" of America's collective imagination. Like almost everyone who lived there, I was a product of the local public schools. In fact, you were seen as different if you went to private school—an outcast, a misfit, or maybe a Catholic. But the public schools we attended were great schools. I began taking Spanish in the fourth grade; Miss Clarke, my fourth-grade teacher, was so dedicated and creative she actually made me sorry when the school week ended. In junior high I was able to study Russian starting in the eighth grade, taught by a wonderful Russian emigre named Mrs. Kovaleski, whose accented voice still echoes in my head: "Laaaara, I vish you vould keep still!" My English teacher, Mrs. Stanhope, had us study the Bible as literature. Can you imagine an assignment like that passing the ACLU police today? (My paper was on "Insects of the Bible." Not my finest hour, but I tried.)

High school was tracked into a "high ability" group, a middle track, and "remedial." In many school systems today this kind of classification would be a no-no, deemed harmful to "self-esteem." But it allowed kids with determination, whatever their backgrounds, to have a chance to excel at levels that challenged them. I was from a family where few relatives had gone to college. We didn't have much money and never took vacations. But that didn't present any special obstacles—or confer any special breaks. I was able to take the hardest courses I could handle—chemistry, physics, calculus, advanced placement English. I had to work hard to get good grades, but I graduated in the top fifteen in my class and won early admission to Dartmouth.

My most vivid memories are of sports—my field hockey team was ranked number one in the state and I was starting pitcher on our fast-pitch softball team. While it is certainly true that girls' sports were underfunded at the time, we didn't sit around and moan about it. Girls could play soccer, volleyball, basketball, tennis, run track, and swim. We weren't victims at Glastonbury High, and the school certainly didn't treat us as if we were.

I stopped by my old high school in May 1999 to see if things had changed. Many of the same teachers were there, but so much else about the school was transformed. The most striking thing, superficially, was how slovenly the boys were dressed, in jeans so baggy they were falling off their butts, and how provocatively the girls were dressed, in micro-miniskirts and spaghetti-strap tops. One of the chemistry teachers I talked to despaired that teachers were powerless to enforce academic standards now. Yes, there were still exceptional students and teachers at Glastonbury High. But I had the sad feeling that my old school was slowly sinking into an enforced mediocrity, where high achievement was tolerated, but not prized as it once was. One by one, the old teachers were retiring, and I feared that when the last of them was gone the educrats would be in full control.

My years at Dartmouth taught me that real education wasn't just about hard work and good study habits. It was about critical thinking—challenging received ideas and conventional wisdom. And I must admit, my friends and I did that with a vengeance—in ways that brought the national media trekking to Hanover to see what these crazy right-wing kids were up to. My real education took place largely at a student-run weekly newspaper called *The Dartmouth Review*. By the time I arrived on campus in the fall of 1981, the *Review* had already been written up in *Newsweek* for its renegade conservative style. It was an amazing time: Ronald Reagan had just become president, liberals were on the run, and there was an opening for a band of student iconoclasts to question what was happening to academic standards under the prevailing liberal orthodoxy at Dartmouth and most universities.

So we began exposing intellectual hypocrisy. After Native American activists convinced Dartmouth to ban the school's popular Indian mascot as "racist" and offensive, we at the *Review* had the Gallup organization poll nearly 300 Indian chiefs and leaders across the country. It turned out that eighty-nine percent thought the Indian symbol should be reinstated. To demonstrate the absurdity of the college's funding of the Gay Students Association based on the sexual preference of its membership, we formally petitioned the Committee on Student Organizations to fund the newly formed Dartmouth Bestiality Society. We used the same wording as the gay students had in their petition and we nearly got funding, failing by just two votes!

Then came the real fun—and problems. Responding to student reports about the lecture-hall antics of music professor William Cole, I audited his first class of the semester in January 1983 to see what the fuss was all about. The class was called "American Music in the Oral Tradition." Professor Cole wasted most of the class rambling about his political ideas. The main assignment was to keep a daily journal, which could be about anything, and Professor Cole said he would give the students a copy of the final exam early in the semester. The class was widely known as a "gut"— an "easy A." The class I went to was packed with almost 150 students and Cole lived up to his advance billing. So I wrote about it for the *Review*, lavishly quoting from Cole's "lecture," which I had taped. Two days later, early on a Saturday morning, he showed up at my dorm, irate and demanding that I come to his class and apologize. When I didn't show up the next Monday, he went on a vicious tirade, calling me a "motherf***ing c***sucking reporter," and indignantly canceled the class indefinitely. At the next faculty meeting, he received a standing ovation.

We offered him a full page in the newspaper to respond, but he instead sued me and the *Review* for libel, seeking $2.4 million in damages. How many people do you know who have been sued for $2.4 million at the age of nineteen? Soon, First Amendment lawyers and Dartmouth alumni rallied to our cause and years later the suit was settled. Oh, I forgot to mention—Bill Cole was an African-American who played the race card with finesse, both in class and with the Dartmouth administration. This meant that even professors who thought Cole was an embarrassment to Dartmouth were afraid to side with the *Review* and against academic incompetence. The *Review* dared to keep reporting on Professor Cole and others on the faculty who were using their classrooms to advance their pet political causes. That's what I really learned at Dartmouth: to stand up for what I believed in—academic standards and the First Amendment. The Cole experience stayed with me, because really for the first time I felt like I was thinking for myself, regardless of whether other people liked my views or not.

I went to college at a time when, due to the labors of Hillary Clinton's generation, academic standards and curricular excellence were not a general norm but a controversial political cause to be fought for. But Hillary and I do have something in common: We both benefitted from an old-fashioned, rigorous, fad-free public education. It's too bad that Hillary didn't draw on this legacy when she made education one of her priorities. The right starting point would have been for Hillary to think honestly about her own life, so strikingly documented in *It Takes a Village*, and about the traditional educational values that allowed her to succeed.

What Kind of Education Reform Does Hillary Want?

We all know that Hillary Clinton cares about education. Deeply. But what exactly is she crusading for? Thirty-four years after she walked out the door of Maine East High School, how would she actually seek to rebuild the nation's public education system? In her July 1999 speech to the National Education Association (NEA), Hillary used the right reform buzzwords, calling for "risk-taking and personal responsibility." She even supported charter schools, a concept pushed by conservatives for years that is finally making headway with liberals. But her bold words are belied by a hodge-podge of federal spending schemes—for more teachers, school moderniza-tion, loan forgiveness, teacher development programs.

Hillary saved some of her strongest language to attack the school-choice initiatives many feel are the only way to improve the quality of pub-lic education. This approach, giving parents vouchers they can use at private or parochial schools, would add competition and accountability to the public system. But Hillary said of voucher supporters: "I believe they are dead wrong. There is simply no evidence that vouchers improve stu-dent achievement." She told the assembled unionized teachers that vouchers "divert much-needed public funds . . . and have weakened the entire system." She left out the real problem a voucher plan would cause for her friends in the audience, who run the nation's largest teachers' union: It would threaten their monopoly over public education. (By the way, the NEA gave her their 1999 "Friend of Education Award." Need I say more?)

Of course, the Clintons would argue that they do support choice. In that July 1999 NEA speech, Hillary talks about increasing schools' accountability by giving parents "public" choice options. For example, the education spending bill for fiscal 2000 will include $134 million to help school districts meet a new requirement—that parents must be given a choice to transfer their child to another public school if their school is deemed "failing" by the state. But there are several problems with this so-called "choice" feature. First, it applies only to schools that serve poor and otherwise disadvantaged students. Second, the education bureaucracy, rather than parents, gets to decide whether a school is failing a child. And third, it uses the predictable liberal approach to reform—throw federal money at the problem.

Hillary and the president actually worked hard to defeat a 1999 bill that would have created a true choice for parents and children. That bill, crafted by House Republican leader Representative Dick Armey of Texas, contained a lot of interesting ideas. It would have established a five-year pilot program designed to create a national school choice option for elementary school children trapped in failing public schools. Governors would declare "academic emergencies" at chronically underperforming schools, making students eligible for academic relief funds, with state participation purely voluntary. Those funds would give parents up to $3,500 a year to cover the costs of tuition and other fees to attend any qualified school in the state. But the measure was defeated in the House, thanks to active lobbying by the White House. And a year before, the Clintons and congressional Democrats had killed a voucher program for the District of Columbia—one that would have given poor kids in the District a chance to escape the appalling schools there and follow the Clinton's daughter, Chelsea, to a private or parochial school. Supporting such programs, argues Hillary, would gut the public schools. Poppycock.

Hillary's alternative, big-spender approach to reforming public education ignores the fact that our per-capita spending on education is already higher than in virtually all industrial countries in Europe and Asia, yet our students lag behind on international tests. Within the United States, the District of Columbia spends more money per pupil per year than any other state—$9,500—yet its students are near the bottom of the heap on standardized tests. Nationally, per-pupil spending on education doubled from 1965 to 1985, yet during the same decades educational standards went down the drain. Meanwhile, a 1998 Harvard study reported that Catholic schools, while spending only about a third as much money per pupil as the public schools, do a far better job of educating kids from the most disadvantaged backgrounds.

Behind her education rhetoric, what real-life accomplishments does Hillary have to show for all her years of crusading? Well, it's true that as First Lady of Arkansas she played a central role in the "education reform" that the Clintons touted in the 1992 campaign. Appointed in 1983 by her husband to chair the Education Standards Committee, Hillary threw herself into the effort. She held public hearings over the next two years in each of the state's seventy-four counties and worked relentlessly to win public backing for a reform package, one that would be financed by the biggest tax hike in the state's history.

Yet the Clinton reforms achieved only modest success. They brought Arkansas schools in line with the rest of the country by such measures as student-teacher ratios, course requirements, the length of the academic year, and attendance requirements. While these seem like reasonable reforms, it is not clear that they actually helped students much. In 1988, Arkansas fourth-graders were only in the top thirty-eight percent in the nation on standardized reading tests and in the top thirty-three percent on math tests; by 1995, they were barely in the top fifty percent. Older schoolchildren also fell further behind their peers in other states in reading and math skills.

The real scandal, ultimately, is not how children in Arkansas fared under the Clintons—it's what has happened to children all across America. At a time when our country is exploding with new technology and wealth, our students are starving for quality schools that promote learning and demand results. Today, parents are told by educrats that too much homework can make a child stressed out, create an environment with too much pressure. That would have gotten a laugh from our great-great grandparents who were struggling to educate their kids amid the real hardships of the nineteenth century. The following items are from a test that eighth-graders had to pass to be admitted to a Jersey City high school in 1885:

- Define algebra, an algebraic expression, a polynomial. Make a literal trinomial.
- Write a homogeneous quadrinomial of the third degree.
- What is the axis of the earth? What is the equator? What is the distance from the equator to either pole in degrees? In miles?
- Name four Spanish explorers and state what induced them to come to America.

Can you imagine the howls of cultural bias if public school students today were measured by their performance on a test with such questions?

Spanish explorers might be judged too "Eurocentric." The algebra question might be "anti-girl," since for years they were not encouraged to study math.

At the dawn of a new millennium, many of our public schools offer, not equal opportunity for excellence, but equal mediocrity for all. According to results released in 1995 by the National Assessment of Education Progress, only one-third of our seventeen-year-olds can be called proficient readers, while practically half of all fourth-graders and one-third of eighth-graders do not meet minimum standards of reading competency. The title of a recent book by Charles J. Sykes, *Dumbing Down Our Kids*, says it all.

It's true that, as Hillary bragged in her 1999 speech to the NEA, reading scores have improved somewhat since 1994. But it's too early to cheer for the Clinton-Gore education reforms: First of all, the improvement was only among eighth-graders, but not among fourth- or twelfth-graders. And second, even those gains may have been partly a statistical mirage: It turns out that more students classified as learning-disabled or having limited English proficiency had been eliminated from the testing pool.

The main problem isn't lack of funding for computers and other teaching tools, as Hillary and her allies sometimes argue. This crisis is about values. From grade school to graduate school, American education has been hijacked by people whose view of the purpose of schools is very different from that of most parents. Impart knowledge? Promote good citizenship? How dull and reactionary. This new breed of educators has something more exciting in mind: transforming American society, which they regard as mired in oppression and prejudice. They cling to the utopian vision of the sixties that Hillary embraced. They are attentive to every imagined sign of bias (even insistence on correct use of English can be branded racist) and hostile to the idea of a meritocracy where people succeed through determination, effort, and hard work. They believe that self-esteem is an entitlement, rather than something to be earned. These new educators disdain teaching techniques that "impose knowledge" on students by requiring them to memorize facts—regarding this as mere rote learning. Instead, they favor less rigid and more "creative" ways to learn. "Telling a youngster what is important to know is said to be oppressive" is how

William J. Bennett describes their dislike of fact-based learning in his book *The Educated Child*.

The new education fads claim to promote critical thinking, but they have the opposite effect. Critical thinking requires facts, just as true creative work is impossible without a solid foundation of knowledge. By undermining the core base of knowledge—the things all students should know in common—the educrats leave students floating in an amorphous world of half-understood concepts where, if an idea feels good, it must be true. What happened at Valley Forge? What are the Federalist Papers? How did the Battle of Midway change the history of the world? Memorizing the answers to questions like these may not be fashionable today but without the answers students can't appreciate or understand their world. Today's education bureaucracy wants to foster a creative "process of learning" through "skills-building." Their mantra is "learning how to learn." So why do their students fare so badly compared to the rest of the developed world? Something is not working.

What happened a few years ago in Brookline, Massachusetts, an affluent town that has always prided itself on its excellent schools, may have been an extreme example of these trends, but it was hardly an aberration. In the summer of 1990, parents in Brookline got an unpleasant surprise in the mail: a letter informing them of planned changes in the curriculum of Brookline High School. Advanced Placement European History, for example, was to be shelved—and replaced with timelier fare such as The Urban Experience, Women and Society (which promised to examine "how gender, race, and class act as personal and social forces") and The World in Crisis. According to the teacher handbook, student grades would be based on how well they "organize[d] mock civil-rights demonstrations," "create[d] banners and press releases" and crafted a "policy statement on whether to be violent." On this last question, the course textbook, *A Terrorism Reader*, was careful to address all sides. A section called "Opposing Viewpoints" featured an article by master terrorist Abu Nidal and a response by former U.N. ambassador Jeanne Kirkpatrick. "As these two represent the most radical of their positions," the handbook matter-of-factly explained, "they need to be put in context."

On that occasion, outraged parents thwarted the revolutionary fantasies of leftist teachers and intimidated school officials. Parents protested, crashed school board meetings, and went to the media. While champions of the new curriculum attacked the opposition as "vigilantes" and "brownshirts," the parents prevailed: The hard-left The World in Crisis course was dumped, and the popular Advanced Placement European History class restored to its rightful place. But this incident shows the mindset at work in the education establishment—an establishment that many parents do not have the savvy or the resources to resist.

Ship of Fools: The Educrats at Work

Hillary's loyalty to the NEA goes way back. Five years before she won that "Friend of Education" award, she gave the keynote address at an NEA annual convention in New Orleans. She opened her speech by warmly thanking the union's leaders for their "commitment to making this country be what it should be for our children." Yet the NEA's leaders, through their policies, have made clear that they're also committed to preserving their own power base and promoting a liberal political ideology.

The NEA has 2.4 million members and an annual budget of $200 million—not counting its political action committees and foundations. It is also a major contributor to the Democratic Party. (Although thirty percent of teachers describe themselves as Republicans and another twenty-eight percent as independents, ninety-nine percent of the NEA's political donations go to Democrats.) In 1996, the NEA had 405 delegates at the Democratic National Convention, a contingent larger than the delegation of any single state except California.

Forbes magazine has noted that "the rise of the modern NEA has exactly coincided with what critics have called the 1963–80 'Great Decline' of the

American education." It shouldn't be hard to figure out why: The NEA has a flair for backing every fad that has contributed to the Great Decline, from questionable teaching techniques to the blatant politicalization of schooling.

While the NEA is staunchly pro-choice on abortion (can somebody tell me what that has to do with the mission of a teacher's union?), it is vehemently anti-choice when it comes to voucher programs. For a long time, it even fought against charter schools—independently operated public schools that are exempt from many government regulations. In recent years, the NEA has ostensibly softened its position, perhaps because it didn't want to seem adamantly opposed to all school choice proposals. But according to former assistant U.S. secretaries of education Chester Finn and Bruno Manno, the teachers' unions "pay lip service to the charter concept but hedge with so many conditions and restrictions that resulting schools tend to resemble conventional public schools." In California, the state chapter of the NEA has been pushing a law that would require all charter-school teachers to join the union that represents the public-school teachers in their district. And it's not exactly as if there was a chorus of charter-school teachers complaining about inhuman exploitation in sweatshops. In fact, as the *Bergen* (New Jersey) *Record* reported in a 1997 story, many teachers who have switched from conventional public schools to charter schools say that for the first time they are actually looking forward to going to work.

The NEA also staunchly defends some of the inanities that have left public education a shambles in the first place—such as bilingual education, a misnomer for programs in which children are taught in their native language, usually Spanish, while being doled out crumbs of English. Originally meant to ease children with limited English into an English-speaking environment, bilingual education has morphed into a language ghetto where kids languish for years, including some Hispanic children who actually speak better English than Spanish. Virtually every study has found that programs in which immigrant children receive special language aid, or are taught in simple English until their proficiency improves, work

far better. The current system of bilingual education is opposed by prominent Hispanic educators like Jaime Escalante, the math teacher whose
success in the barrio was recounted in the film *Stand and Deliver*, and is
even under attack in the left-wing magazine *The Nation*. Yet Hillary,
trapped by her teachers' union friends and their vested interest in the program, steadfastly supports it.

Another pet cause of the unions is "outcome-based education (OBE)."
Sounds good, but in practice what started as a laudable effort to judge
schools on the performance of their students has turned away from serious measurement of outcomes in core subjects. Evidently, the educrats
were uncomfortable with the idea of being evaluated in terms of their students' achievement, so they softened the criteria. Instead of middle-class
achievements in English and science, today's version of OBE stresses
squishy "outcomes" like "thinking skills" and "cooperative learning"—and
political goals such as concern for "the global environment" and "respect
for the dignity, worth, contributions and equal rights of each person,"
according to a 1995 article in *Forbes*. When these loose goals are criticized, the NEA responds in Clintonian fashion, by attacking the critics as
"anti-teacher."

The NEA champions other causes that seem worthy at first glance but
turn out to be more dubious on closer examination. In late 1999, for
instance, the union issued a call for an ironclad ban on hiring teachers
who were not fully accredited by the National Council for Accreditation of
Teacher Education (NCATE). "No waivers. No exceptions. No excuses,"
NEA president Bob Chase declared dramatically. That seems to make
sense: Who wouldn't want to bar unqualified teachers from the classroom?
Except that it turns out "uncertified" hardly means "unqualified." Studies
by scholars at the University of Missouri and the University of Massachusetts show that whether or not a teacher is certified by the NCATE has
absolutely no impact on the students' performance. As *The New Republic*
noted, "The NEA isn't really after higher student achievement, it's after
higher teacher salaries, which it believes the certification requirement will
bring."

What's more, the NEA insistence on universal certification could be not only useless but harmful. Requiring prospective teachers to sit through NCATE certification programs—which, in typical educrat fashion, are heavy on politically correct rhetoric about "diversity" and "equity" and light on anything to do with academic content or excellence—could actually scare off some excellent math and science instructors. The NEA's notion of "quality" means that if Albert Einstein came back to life and wanted to teach physics in a public high school, he would be turned away. The bipartisan signatories of the 1998 manifesto "A Nation Still at Risk" take a very different view of the issue. They point out that "[O]ne good way to boost the number of knowledgeable teachers is to throw open the classroom door to men and women who are well-educated but have not gone through programs of 'teacher education . . .' "—such as scientists who have worked for NASA or for IBM, journalists, or former public officials.

The NEA jumps into politically correct fads, too. Take the primer they endorsed in 1999 for school principals and teachers on "Sexual Orientation and Youth." It was basically a propaganda pamphlet, endorsing the opposition of gay rights groups to conservative efforts such as reparative therapy and transformational ministry, aimed at encouraging people conflicted about their sexual orientation to resist homosexuality. "Sexual orientation develops across a person's lifetime—different people realize at different points in their lives that they are heterosexual, gay, lesbian, or bisexual," opined the pamphlet. It noted the "unanimity of the health and mental health professions on the normality of homosexuality." Now, whatever you think about homosexuality—and on this one I tend to side with the libertarian wing of conservatism—you have to wonder why our teachers and principals should be proselytizing about it at all, especially since there are no transformational ministries or reparative therapy centers operating in public schools. But that's the NEA's style.

Just look at the NEA's 1998–99 resolutions, a laundry list of "progressive" causes: environmental education (including participation in Earth Day events), multiculturalism, "Violence Against and Exploitation of Asian/Pacific Islanders," national health care and other social welfare entitlements, even an end to the production of nuclear weapons and "State-hood for the District of Columbia." Oh, yes, "Excellence in Education" got smuggled in there, too—but it's allotted less than half as much space as "Racism, Sexism, and Sexual Orientation Discrimination."

The hijacking of American schools is a disaster for everyone, but most of all for America's daughters. Why? First, because the education establishment singles out girls as a victim class and encourages them to feel aggrieved, to see every slight and setback, every obstacle and frustration as a sexist assault. Second, because the dumbing down of education is a betrayal of everything our feminist foremothers fought for at a time when women and girls were denied equal educational opportunities.

Who's Really Shortchanging Girls?

As we saw in the previous chapter, the alleged inequities that girls suffer at the hands of a male-dominated educational establishment are one of the causes championed by the False Sisterhood of radical feminists. But here, as in so many other areas, their rhetoric misstates the facts and belittles the true gains women have made in America. In fact, reading their tendentious reports, you can't but wonder if their real mission is to produce a stream of bad news and foreboding that justifies their existence. This gender-equity elite is part of Hillary Clinton's loyal constituency; it includes one of her staunchest allies in the Clinton Administration, Health and Human Services Secretary Donna Shalala, who earned plaudits from *Ms.* magazine during her tenure as chancellor of the University of Wisconsin at Madison.

Once, the crusade for equal educational opportunities for girls and women was a noble and much-needed cause. A hundred and fifty years ago, when college presidents rhapsodized about the joys of molding boys into splendid, clear-thinking young men, women were largely excluded from the benefits of education. Instead, they were steered toward learning more "appropriate" skills: singing, dancing, embroidering, being a hostess.

Even in the twentieth century, as more and more women set aside their embroidery and entered the public world, they continued to encounter barriers to their educational aspirations. As late as the 1950s, teachers and guidance counselors would sometimes talk girls out of pursuing a degree in a nontraditional field such as science. Only a third of the girls in the top forty percent of high school graduates, compared to two-thirds of the boys, pursued a higher education. And two out of three college women dropped out before graduating—usually to get their M.R.S. degree.

Even in my own lifetime, discrimination in education against women and girls was a reality. When I was a child, many top colleges still excluded women—including my future alma mater, Dartmouth, which didn't admit women as full-time students until the mid-1970s. At other schools, a woman had less of a chance of being admitted than a man with lower grades and test scores. There were quotas restricting women's access to medical schools and even prohibitions against female students taking courses such as auto mechanics or criminal justice or enrolling in science and math clubs. Girls were just one percent of all high school athletes, and fewer than 32,000 competed in college sports. Young women had few athletic scholarships available to them; they got a mere two percent of the total athletic budget.

If the early feminist crusaders were alive today, they would give women hugs and say, "Well done!" All around us, girls and young women are on the ascendancy in what were once thought male domains—winning science contests, excelling on debating teams and on the soccer field—and generally pulling ahead of the supposedly stronger sex in just about every index of scholastic achievement. Girls dominate high school honor societies and academic clubs, and are now more likely than boys to take geometry, chemistry, and trigonometry. Boys still outnumber girls in advanced placement physics, chemistry, and calculus, but girls are catching up fast. By 1994, they made up more than forty percent of the total enrollment in these courses. At the highest level of junior achievement in math and science, girls are now winning forty percent of the prestigious Intel/Westinghouse Science Talent Search Awards, given to ten high school seniors each year. To see the best that has been achieved by women's battle for opportunity, one has only to look at young women like Natalia Toro, who in 1999, at the age of fourteen, became the youngest-ever winner of the top Intel prize for a research project on subatomic particles that could make a major contribution to high-energy physics.

At the college level, too, the progress has been amazing. In 1971, women received forty-three percent of all bachelor's degrees, forty percent of the master's degrees, and just fourteen percent of the doctorates. By 1996, the figure had grown to fifty-five percent of the bachelors, fifty-six percent of the masters, and forty percent of the doctorates. Women professors—hardly represented at all on major faculties two decades ago—now occupy fully one-third of all faculty positions.

But the painful paradox is that just as women and girls made a giant leap forward, the standards of education in America took a giant step backward. Among the worst offenders are the champions of so-called "gender equity" who are trying to bring back what Harriet Beecher Stowe dubbed "the pink-and-white tyranny," this time with a feminist face. Two groups that won't take *yes* for an answer are the American Association of University Women (AAUW) and the Wellesley College Center for Research on Women. Their reports on the mistreatment of the American schoolgirl—*Shortchanging Girls, Shortchanging America* (1992) and *How Schools Shortchange Girls* (1992)—set off a frantic search for ways to remedy what they described as the systematic discrimination of girls in the classroom. The media responded with alarmist headlines and muckraking books. "School is still a place of unequal opportunity, where girls face discrimination from teachers, textbooks, tests, and their male classmates," cried the lead of a front-page article in *The New York Times*.

In reality, it was a false alarm. In her 1994 book *Who Stole Feminism*, philosophy professor Christina Hoff Sommers demolished the central claims of *How Schools Shortchange Girls*—that girls are routinely ignored by teachers, discouraged from classroom participation, degraded by sexist textbooks, and demoralized by gender-biased tests. Indeed, she showed that one of the report's most striking and widely quoted contentions—that boys call out answers in class eight times as often as girls do and that girls who call out are rebuked by teachers—was based on two liberal scholars misrepresenting their own research. Myra and David Sadker, leading "experts" on gender equity in education, cited a 1981 article they published in a now-defunct teachers' journal called *The Pointer* to support the eight-to-one "call-out" ratio favoring boys. But when Sommers looked up the article, she found that it said nothing at all about call outs but focused on what could be described as bias against *boys*—teachers disciplining boys more harshly for the same misbehavior. The article noted that "boys, particularly low-achieving boys, receive eight to ten times as many reprimands as do their female classmates."

Sommers also demolished the claims about chronically low self-esteem among girls. *Shortchanging Girls, Shortchanging America* had purported to document a precipitous "plunge" between the ages of nine and twelve. But after examining the study's raw data, Sommers found that the sole basis for these claims was that fewer girls than boys chose "always true" as the response to the statement "I am happy the way I am." The AAUW never mentioned that the gap shrank drastically when "sort of true" responses were included, and virtually disappeared when "sometimes true/sometimes false" was added to the equation. Or that no reliable study has ever established a link between so-called "self-esteem" and achievement.

The AAUW has tried to depict Sommers as a gadfly with a grudge against their organization, but the group's claims have been questioned by plenty of others. Critics point out that while teachers may talk to boys in the classroom more than they do to girls, the gap is small and the extra attention that boys get is mostly negative. That is to say, they're reprimanded more often—both because they're more likely to act up and because girls are more likely to get away with misbehaving. The AAUW and the Wellesley College Center have some valid points. They are right to be concerned that girls still lag behind in science and math. But most of their proposed "solutions" are likely to make the problem worse, by promoting the same kind of clouded thinking that has already made a mess of our educational system. It's a world view shared by Hillary's allies at the NEA, UFT and the other acronyms symbolizing steadfast adherence to the status quo.

Despite their flawed evidence and their tendentious arguments, the AAUW reports on the state of girlhood—uncritically received by the press—resulted in action on Capitol Hill. The Women's Educational Equity Act, discussed earlier as an example of False Sisterhood, created a full-time gender-equity bureaucracy within the Department of Education for the purpose of "promoting and coordinating women's equity policies, programs, activities, and initiatives." It also boosted the already growing cadre of gender professionals nationwide. Wisconsin, a state that never saw a "progressive" policy it didn't like, may offer a preview of things to come. There, the educrats have devised a model lesson plan to stamp out sexism in the heartland, by means of a board game to be played on class time by elementary school students! It's called Equity Feud: A Game for Overcoming Stereotypes. Believe it or not, this one is really being used in public school classrooms. In the game, kids get points for items like this:

- "You have talked your parents into ordering a subscription to *Ms.* magazine. Take one Free from Stereotype card."
- "You are a female. You are interested in women's liberation and do something about it. You decide to join the National Organization for Women (NOW). Take one Free from Stereotype Card."
- "You are male. You have just become the first boy on the school cheerleading squad. Congratulations. Take one Free from Stereo-type card."

An accompanying "Parent's Guide" advises Mom and Dad to "support only those candidates who support equal opportunity for girls and women" and urges that you "write your elected representatives in support of the Equal Rights Amendment."

Hillary Clinton didn't invent this absurd game and the inane gender obsession it represents. But the educational climate that produces these howlers was created by her friends and allies—who resist any attempt to restore a measure of common sense.

In colleges and universities things only get worse. At my alma mater, Dartmouth, students in the introductory women's studies class Sex, Gender and Society are assigned the writings of Charlotte Bunch. She proclaims that "women interested in destroying male supremacy, patriarchy, and capitalism must, equally with lesbians, fight heterosexual domination." Another assigned author is Marilyn Frye, who asserts that "heterosexuality, marriage, and motherhood" are "the institutions which . . . form the core of antifeminist ideology." Sure, one can steer clear of these loony gender warriors, but they help create a mood on campus that pits men against women.

I won't embark on a lengthy catalogue of the follies of academic feminism, already amply documented by a number of female scholars who worry that young women's energies are being diverted from real learning and their minds filled with tripe. Sommers and women's studies defectors Daphne Patai and Noretta Koertge have documented some of the nuttiest abuses—from preoccupation with vacuous topics like witchcraft, the glories of body hair, and women's menstrual cycles to the displacement of scholarship by political activism and the exploration of feelings. Requirements in some courses include "performing some 'outrageous' and 'liberating' act outside of class and then sharing feelings and reactions with the class," keeping a journal of "narratives of personal experience, expressions of emotion, dream accounts, poetry, doodles, etc.," and forming small in-class consciousness-raising groups.

Unfortunately, this kind of "thinking" has even infected the elite law schools. They should be teaching students to discern specious arguments, but that's not so easy when the curriculum includes such lovelies as Feminist Legal Theory. In a law review article, one professor rapturously reports that the materials used in her class include "poems, essays, cases, letters, slides of paintings and buildings, cartoons, things students bring in, including a bag of dirt from one student's garden." Another proudly quotes from a student's journal: "Everybody sort of schlepps along when we do cases and, you know, legal stuff, but then when we shift to a CR [consciousness-raising] sort of mode, everybody perks up and the energy level just soars." Tell it to Judge Judy, honey. She'll throw you out of court.

Ultimately, it's easy to laugh off the strange rants of the gender-equity elite, and their fallacious arguments about girls' disadvantages in education. But by standing alongside these feminist educators, Hillary gives legitimacy to their charges. The more girls are told that they suffer from stereotyping and discrimination, the more likely they'll be to blame others for their missteps in school. Women really have gone far beyond that limiting self-image, and Hillary should be ashamed of herself for not challenging the prophets of false victimization.

Who Owns Education?

Hillary's Education Trap is dangerous because there's no escape from her vision of public education for millions of children—those whose parents can't afford to pay the taxes that support public education and pay tuition for a private school. As businessman Ted Forstmann, who runs the Children's Scholarship Fund, notes: "Ninety percent of American children attend government-run schools. But think of what this would mean in any other industry. Any system that can demand . . . a ninety percent market share surely qualifies as a monopoly." The good news is that parents and concerned citizens are taking steps to turn things around.

Some parents have simply opted out—taking the radical step of schooling their children at home. Every morning, as many as 1.2 million American children get their lessons right at home with Mom (or, in more than ten percent of the cases, Dad). It is interesting that in all her pronouncements about how moms and dads can help in their children's education, Hillary has never mentioned home schooling, despite its impressive track record.

Nationwide, average achievement test scores for home-schooled children place them in the top twenty percent of all children in their age group. Rebecca Sealfon, a thirteen-year-old home schooler from Brooklyn, New York, won the National Spelling Bee in 1997 by spelling "euonym"— a word so obscure that it's not even in the *Oxford English Dictionary*. (It means "good or beautiful name.") The same year, another home-schooled girl, ten-year-old Alexandra Rose of Woodbridge, Illinois, became the first child to present a research paper at a prestigious scientific conference on insects. The scientists were so impressed they invited her to do a presentation at the Natural History Museum of the Smithsonian Institution in Washington, D.C. No self-esteem building needed, thank you.

While home-schooling parents have developed extensive support networks, theirs is still a daunting task. Not all parents have the patience and discipline for it, and many can't or don't want to sacrifice a second income. Home schooling should be an option, but parents shouldn't feel forced into taking on this very difficult mission. The fact is, if public schools were what they should be, the number of children schooled at home would be a fraction of what it is today.

Charter schools provide another option, and they may be the hottest trend in education. Although they receive public funds, they are run by parents and teachers and operate outside the normal education bureaucracy. Unless they fulfill their commitment to achieve "superior results," their charter won't be renewed after the initial funding period, usually five years. Charter schools can hire nonunion teachers and set their own rules, from longer school days to a more challenging and stimulating curriculum.

Because they meet such an obvious need, charter schools have become enormously popular. In 1990, charter schools didn't exist. In 1992, there was one in the whole country. By 1997, when twenty-five states had enacted laws allowing charter schools, there were more than eight hundred, with about two hundred thousand students enrolled in them. Forstmann in 1999 counted seventeen hundred charter schools. Charter schools typically attract more dedicated teachers and succeed because parents are integrally involved in the education process. Parents who send their children to charter schools often put in several hours a week volunteering at the school—as classroom helpers or even doing menial tasks that, in public schools, are left to overpaid janitors.

The heroes of the charter-school movement are parents like Jim and Fawn Spady of Seattle. Fawn, who had put her marketing business on hold to be a full-time mother, wanted to get involved in her daughter's public school. However, she found that the school administrators were, as she put it, "happy to have me do bake sales, but nothing that involved academics." Jim and Fawn put their children in a small, nonreligious private school, but they were also concerned about people who could not afford such a choice. So they drafted a proposal to allow charter schools in Washington State—mortgaging their house and spending over $200,000 of their own money to put it on the ballot. They encountered a hysterical, well-funded campaign from the Washington Education Association, the state chapter of the NEA, which claimed that this "radical, untested initiative" would destroy public schools. While initial polls showed high levels of voter approval, the initiative ended up losing by a 2:1 margin.

Despite the opposition, charter schools continue to grow. And, contrary to the educrats' scare tactics, they are not merely succeeding by skimming off elite students from public schools. A majority of kids in charter schools come from poor families. According to one study, nearly one-fifth of them are black and thirty percent are Hispanic; nineteen percent speak limited English, one in five is disabled, and many have learning or behavioral problems. As a 1997 article in a Florida newspaper put it, "Charter schools may be a reform movement led by conservatives, but the benefits reach minorities and the disadvantaged."

Hillary and her friends in the educrat establishment point to their support for charter schools as proof that they are in favor of school choice. In her July 1999 speech to the NEA, Hillary urged the group to continue supporting the charter school movement because "parents do deserve greater choice within the public school system." But of course that support only goes so far—because the more a charter school turns away from card-carrying union members for its hiring pool, the more groups like the NEA will push back.

Good for Hillary for supporting charter schools. But why not go an extra step? Meaningful choice would enable a parent who doesn't have the money for tuition at Chelsea's Sidwell Friends to use the tax money allotted for her child's education at any school, public or private. And as we've seen, Hillary and the education lobby virulently oppose this kind of real choice.

The education establishment has good reason to be scared: Support for vouchers is growing. In a 1998 Gallup poll, fifty-one percent of all Americans—up from forty-three percent just two years earlier—favored allowing parents to send their children to any public, private, or parochial school with the government paying all or part of the tuition. Support for school choice among African-Americans—especially in urban areas—is very strong. Among blacks and other minorities, sixty-eight percent supported parents' right to choose a private school at public expense. These figures make perfect sense, since in communities like the District of Columbia minority children are the ones often forced to endure poorly performing schools.

As of 1999, voucher programs have been implemented in Milwaukee (where six thousand of the city's 107,000 students in kindergarten through twelfth grade attend private schools with publicly funded vouchers), and in Cleveland, where the program covers four thousand of 77,000 students. So far, the evidence suggests these programs work well. The typical response from the teachers' unions and the rest of the anti-choice crowd is that the trials have been too small to really tell us anything. But, as liberal journalist Matthew Miller points out in *The Atlantic Monthly*, "That's a nervy case to make when it is union opposition that has kept the trials small."

The anti-voucher forces are trying to frighten parents and stem the tide of support for this innovative reform. Hillary, for example, charges that vouchers drain funds from public schools. That's simply untrue. When Cleveland spent $10 million on a school voucher plan, the money didn't come out of the city's $600 million public education trough—it was provided on top of that budget, just to keep the teachers' unions happy.

Another argument against choice is that in a voucher system, private schools will drain public schools of the talent pool—leaving public schools with the most disadvantaged students. Again, this contention is without merit. A study by Harvard University's Program on Education Policy and Governance found that applications for a privately funded voucher program in Washington, D.C., came disproportionately from poor and single-parent families. Why did these parents want to send their kids to private schools? Simple: They were looking for higher standards, a better curriculum, and safer hallways.

Parents are beginning to resist other schemes hatched by the education "experts." Take bilingual education, which is now on the retreat in many parts of the country thanks mostly to the efforts of concerned mothers and fathers. A 1996 study revealed that four out of five Hispanic parents wanted their children to be taught in English (sometimes called the "immersion method"), instead of Spanish. From Brooklyn, New York, to Dearborn, Michigan, to Los Angeles, California, immigrant parents have rebelled against the bureaucrats who would keep their children in Spanish-speaking classrooms—filing lawsuits to have their children released from bilingual classes, staging protests against plans to introduce bilingual programs, even keeping children at home to force schools to start using English. These protests caught the eye of computer entrepreneur and maverick social activist Ron Unz and ultimately inspired him to launch the English for the Children initiative in California, or Proposition 227. It would abolish mandatory bilingual education for children from non-English-speaking households and introduce "sheltered English" programs, in which the teachers would use simple English at first and then move on to higher levels.

Initial polls showed sixty percent of Hispanic voters in favor of Proposition 227. The militant Hispanic activists, the teachers' unions, and the bilingual-ed "experts" who saw their gravy train riding off into the sunset were beside themselves. They cried "racism" and "immigrant-bashing"—even though Unz had earlier opposed an initiative denying tax-funded services to illegal aliens. The scare tactics managed to sway many Hispanics and a majority of them ended up voting against the initiative. But it still carried the day. The result? Only ten to twenty percent of eligible parents have exercised the option of placing their children in traditional bilingual classrooms—even though, in places like the People's Republic of Berkeley, teachers and school officials have been actively encouraging them to do so. And, by the summer of 1999, children with limited English proficiency showed dramatic progress in reading. There is no proof, as yet, that this was due to the curtailing of bilingual education. But the cause-and-effect relationship seems pretty clear.

Despite the overwhelming evidence that the billions in federal money spent on bilingual programs was largely wasted, Hillary has remained in her customary lockstep with the NEA, consistently favoring bilingual programs that allow immigrant children to take core classes (math, science, civics) in their native language while taking a separate English course or courses for a limited time period during the day. In a 1998 speech to the National Council of La Raza, Hillary intoned, "We cannot cut off bilingual education plans and the extensive opportunities they provide for children." Addressing a school near Jerusalem in December 1998, where Jewish and Arab children learn side by side, she again used this opportunity to praise bicultural and bilingual education: "If all children could have this experience, we would be that much closer to peace, where we would respect and look at each other as individuals, and not classify people according to the group from which they come." As indecipherable as her position may be, isn't it bilingual education, as traditionally practiced in the United States, that "classifies people according to the group from which they come"? But Hillary is not alone. Even Texas Governor George W. Bush, the Republican presidential candidate, supports a limited bilingual program, although one that "teaches English as soon as possible."

As for school vouchers, Hillary is, as we already know, openly hostile to the idea. She has fulminated against school choice on the campaign trail in New York State, trotting out the tired charge that voucher proponents want to give up on the public schools. In 1999, addressing the NEA convention in Orlando, Florida, while receiving her Friend of Education award, she assailed Florida's proposed voucher plan and repeated the canard that the Milwaukee and Cleveland programs have siphoned money away from already underfunded public schools.

Hillary Clinton, the "friend of education," is in the end just another friend of the educrat industry. In Hillary's world, the government and its experts know best. Moms and dads have to help the experts raise their children, but making the important decisions is not up to them. The way to escape the trap that Hillary and the bureaucrats have set is to take control: Visit your school, talk to your kids' teachers, challenge ideas that don't make sense to you—and if you decide your local public school can't be freed from forces of mediocrity, demand that politicians provide a real alternative. Hillary has given passionate speeches about educational opportunity in Third World countries where girls are, to this day, denied equal access to schooling. But what about the miseducation, or noneducation, of millions of children at home? In America, girls and women have achieved equality in education, but given the current state of the school system, it is rather like gaining equal access to the first-class cabins on the *Titanic*. Girls are indeed shortchanged in the classroom. But the reason for this has precious little to do with discrimination. It has everything to do with the educrat industry whose grip on our children Hillary is helping to maintain.

If Hillary had really wanted to be an "education Senator," maybe she would have announced her candidacy at a school like H. D. Woodson High in Washington, D.C.—not at the offices of a teachers' union. Woodson is in the far reaches of the northeast portion of the nation's capital, surrounded by decrepit public-housing projects. I visited there to do my then-weekly television commentary for *CBS News* about an exceptional teacher named Suzie Kay. I nearly drove past the school, since it looks far more like a warehouse. Kay's class was atypical, namely bright and hopeful, with political figures on the wall and a blackboard filled with words of encouragement. The students loved her, but their accounts of her colleagues were dramatically different. Some other teachers at Woodson don't teach at all, preferring to just sit behind their desks and read, sometimes actually keeping their backs to the students. Looking out on a class-room of graduating seniors, I found many of them looking angry, like they had been let down. Except for a small percentage who had been in Kay's class, or had been able to attend some charter-school classes, most felt trapped. They knew it. I knew it. And Hillary should know it, too. But she's in a trap of her own making: She has made her bed with the teachers' unions and the education bureaucrats, and now she must lie in it. Her political funders and allies aren't offering a solution to the problem—they're the purveyors of the problem. Like too many teachers at Woodson, Hillary simply turns her back.

If you are a young woman who is just embarking on her work life after college or high school, you will find yourself facing yet another potential Hillary Trap. Just when you're safely out of the hands of the educrats, another army of would-be saviors is waiting to tell you that you can't be trusted to make your own choices, that without help from the government, the experts, and the feminists you will be a perpetual helpless victim—this time in the workplace. You're being set up for the Work Trap.

3

The
Work Trap

The first career woman in the White House. The symbol of the modern working woman. A First Lady with her own ambitions and a mind of her own. We've gotten used to these plaudits, which have been bestowed on Hillary Rodham Clinton ever since she moved to Washington. Hillary's image as a role model for women with independent aspirations is one of the reasons she has become a heroine for the sisterhood. But just how good a role model for working women is she, really?

As a graduate of Wellesley College and a star student at Yale Law School, Hillary Rodham was poised to embark on a brilliant career in the seventies, when all doors were at last opening to women. Yet ten years later, she could be found in Little Rock, Arkansas, doing legal work for Jim McDougal, a crooked savings and loan operator and real estate developer (and the Clintons' business partner in the infamous Whitewater land scheme). According to a much-repeated story told by McDougal, Hillary's husband, the Governor, stopped by McDougal's office one day, all sweaty from his morning jog, and urged McDougal to throw some business Hillary's way since she was having trouble bringing clients into the Rose Law Firm.

Since I'm well aware of the Clinton Scandal Fatigue Syndrome, I will not rehash the mind-numbing details of Hillary's involvement in McDougal's ventures: Madison Guaranty, a corrupt savings and loan institution; and Castle Grande, a scam in which near-worthless land was sold at inflated prices to buyers who got government-backed loans from Madison Guaranty and then usually defaulted. Suffice it to say that, using her political connections and her influence, Hillary helped grease the wheels of the bureaucratic machine for McDougal as he bilked taxpayers out of millions of dollars. Eventually, as First Lady, Hillary would have to fall back on the time dishonored "dumb blonde" strategy to explain this away: She claimed that even though she was a senior partner at Rose, she did only low level research for Castle Grande and never noticed that it was a swindle.

One has to wonder if Hillary ever paused to reflect on the sad irony of her position: a Yale Law School graduate and former Watergate impeachment lawyer turned legal fixer in a small southern state, tied to the apron strings of her husband's political career. Hillary had cut short her own promising career in Washington in 1974 to follow Bill to Arkansas, to the chagrin of many friends. (Yes, there was a method to her madness: her Arkansas boyfriend would someday be president, she effused to her coworkers at the House Judiciary committee.) It was through his recommendations that she got a teaching position at the University of Arkansas Law School and then, in January 1975, a job at the Rose Law Firm. It just so happens that the Rose firm did a lot of business with the state—so the fact that Hillary was married to the state Attorney General and then the Governor was probably not irrelevant to her hiring and promotion.

As First Lady, Hillary's public career remained tethered to her marriage just as much as it had been for any traditional political wife. First, she tried to create a position for herself as an unelected "co-president" and took on a high-visibility role as chair of the task force on health care reform. But health care reform became the biggest debacle of Clinton's first term: This government effort to commandeer one seventh of the national economy, shrouded in bizarre backroom secrecy, did not sit well with the American public. Hillary's popularity ratings took a dive, and she beat a hasty retreat to the conventional First Lady role of issuing warm and fuzzy platitudes on women's and children's issues . . . while exercising influence behind the scenes.

A truly revolutionary move for a career woman would have been to hold a job outside the White House—as Elizabeth Dole planned to do if Bob Dole had won the presidential race in 1996. While Liddy took a leave from the presidency of the Red Cross to campaign for her husband, she announced that she'd be her own person in her own job after election day whether he won or not. Elizabeth Dole is a decade older than Hillary, and she received much less societal encouragement in forging an independent career. Yet in many ways Dole is a far better model of the modern liberated woman. An official with the Federal Trade Commission when she married Bob Dole in 1975, she served in two Cabinet posts: Secretary of Transportation under President Reagan and Secretary of Labor under President Bush. None of those appointments had anything to do with her marriage. She put her career on hold several times to help her husband, but never molded her career around his.

I look at Hillary through the eyes of a working woman a generation younger who's trying to make good choices about work and personal life. Like Hillary, I've been lucky. I won a scholarship to Dartmouth, went on to law school at the University of Virginia, clerked at the Supreme Court of the United States, and worked at a high-powered law firm. Now I host a cable television program. To an outsider, it might look like I have it all, but I've learned that success comes at a price. Every day, just like millions of other women, I have to make choices about how much time to devote to work, and how much to save for myself, friends, and family. At times I've set the wrong priorities and made bad choices—but I've never seen myself as a victim. The mistakes are mine, and in a strange way I'm proud of *them*, too.

The peculiarity of Hillary Rodham Clinton's career underscores the paradox of her position as a symbol of the liberated woman. It turns out that she's not so liberated after all—she's as dependent on her husband as any 1950s housewife. But there's a more intriguing lesson here. Like millions of women, Hillary has made life choices that limited her career but suited her life and her marriage, given the choices she had made. And that's fine, too. It's not necessarily "unliberated" or self-sacrificing to make such choices; on the contrary, putting career second may be exactly what you want or need at a particular time. You can choose a life that combines the satisfaction of home and family with the rewards of working outside the home—or not. (Who says a high-pressure, full-steam-ahead career is always more fulfilling than a lower-key, more flexible one?) You just have to be realistic about the trade-offs, like not achieving the same power or prestige as someone who's given her career everything she's got.

Hillary, on the other hand, has demanded to be treated as the equal of women and men who have paid their political dues and made a career for themselves as public servants. In some crucial sense, she does not seem to have grappled with the reality that choices, including her own, have consequences. This denial is at the heart of the Hillary Trap. In much the same way, when addressing the larger issues of women's work and women's lives, Hillary—and all the Hillarys of the world—either pretend that the personal decisions that account for many of the differences between men's and women's status as workers don't exist, or insist that women should be able to make those choices without having to face any trade-offs. In so doing, they often obscure the truly exciting good news: As we enter a new millennium, young women in America have a spectacular array of options and opportunities. Thirty years after an era when the notion of equal job opportunities for women was widely regarded as a joke, we have made stunning gains in almost every field, exercising our talents in formerly masculine domains and charting our own paths in the marketplace. In education, as we saw in the preceding chapter, we have already caught up with men and in some areas are pulling ahead. We can do the same thing in the workplace—as long as we're honest with ourselves about our goals, and are prepared to work like hell to achieve them.

In a sense, Hillary's instincts are conservative in the worst sense of the word. The policies she advocates have far less to do with helping women's advancement today than with protecting the agenda (and the jobs) of the social set that was fashionable back when Hillary was in college and grad school. Those liberal true-believers now run government programs, activist groups, and trade unions. Like everyone else, they don't take too kindly to the suggestion that they have become dysfunctional and an obstacle to progress.

The Working Woman as Victim: Bogus Problems, Bogus Solutions

Given Hillary's belief in the power of women, it's odd that she so often describes them as victims. Maybe that's because, deep down, she feels victimized herself—by the way she has allowed her own career to be suppressed and subverted by her husband. This is the Work Trap that Hillary has fallen into. If you are forever the victim, you're always looking for someone else either to help you or to take the blame for your misfortune. Portraying today's confident and successful women as victims requires some pretty strenuous mental gymnastics. So, inevitably, Hillary and her allies have had to resort to half-truths and misleading statistics that hide and distort women's progress.

What an opportunity Hillary has missed. The truth is, young women thinking about their careers would love to have a role model they could trust. Recent surveys had shown that only about one in twelve teenage girls envision a future spent primarily at home. A mere 1 percent of college freshman women pick "homemaker" as a vocation. But what is Hillary's message to those women? In 1995, on one of her Third World tours as a global champion of women, Mrs. Clinton gave a speech at the Lahore University of Management Sciences in Pakistan, calling for more protection of women's rights and praising the hard work of women worldwide. This is what she had to say about women in America: "In my own country, I have seen single mothers who are raising children alone while holding down several jobs. I have seen women professionals bumping against the glass ceiling, unable to fulfill their own potential in their professions."

What's missing from this picture? Not just married moms raising their children at home. Where are the women who are marching toward parity with men in law and medicine, invading male bastions like investment banking, taking senior posts in corporations, and opening their own businesses? In Hillary's world, the American working woman isn't a self-confident achiever—she's a damsel in distress, with Uncle Sam as her knight in shining armor.

On April 7, 1999, the First Lady hosted a roundtable discussion at the White House to observe Equal Pay Day, a creation of the National Committee on Pay Equity, and an event that the feminists probably hope will someday supplant Valentine's Day in our cultural consciousness. It's supposed to stand for the extra three months and seven days a woman has to work to equal a man's annual pay. Flanked by her husband (whose personal efforts to make the workplace friendly for women are fresh in our memory) and Labor Secretary Alexis Herman, Hillary deplored the "long-time inequity" faced by working women who, she said, "still bring home only about seventy-five cents for every man's dollar."

"We know that women who walk into the grocery store are not asked to pay twenty-five percent less for milk," Hillary declared. "They're not asked by their landlords to pay twenty-five percent less for rent. And they should no longer be asked to try to make their ends meet and their family incomes what they should be by having twenty-five percent less in their paychecks." But wait a minute. Are women really paid seventy-five (actually, seventy-six) percent of what men earn for the same work? Should we conclude that, as National Organization for Women president Patricia Ireland has asserted, every time a woman earns a dollar, "someone"—some awful man—"is pocketing twenty four cents"? Let's examine this proposition carefully.

At the Equal Pay Day roundtable discussion, Hillary got guffaws from the audience by describing a cartoon in which six men in suits sit around a conference room table: "And one of them announces, gentlemen, we must cut our expenses in half, so I'm replacing each of you with a woman." Very funny, but think for a minute about the real-life implications of this. If the pay gap really is just malicious discrimination, and not simply a matter of individual job performance and job experience, why wouldn't cost-conscious businesses just dump as many male employees as they could to replace them with cheap but just as good female labor? Surely not even Hillary Clinton and Pat Ireland think that venal capitalists put male bonding over profits!

Hillary-endorsed feminist agitation about the supposed pay gap is a classic example of denying that choices have consequences. The "seventy six cents" figure refers to the earnings of all women working full time compared to all men working full-time. It doesn't take into account the fact that even in our post-feminist world, men and women choose to work in different jobs. That's why feminists have had to come up with schemes like equal pay for "comparable work"—the notion that an army of gender bureaucrats should be in charge of deciding which predominantly male or predominantly female jobs are "comparable" as to skills and training. It comes down to a bunch of well-paid academic hairsplitters devising ways to compare apples and oranges. A 1999 resolution passed by the National Organization of Women offers two examples: bookkeeping is "comparable" with truck driving, and data entry with welding.

One thing that should be immediately obvious is that traditionally male jobs tend to be far more physically arduous and dangerous. A bookkeeper or data entry clerk who makes a mistake can get chewed out by the boss; a welder or truck driver who makes a mistake can end up injured or even dead. Part of the reason people (women included) choose bookkeeping and data entry is that they're willing to settle for less pay in exchange for more pleasant working conditions, shorter hours, and a less high-pressure atmosphere. Part of the reason people get paid well for hard labor like welding (work on which the integrity of buildings and people's lives depend) is that employers have to pay well to get and keep good workers in such jobs.

Moreover, men take time-outs from employment for less than two percent of their working lives, compared to fifteen percent for the average working woman, according to a 1984 study by the Census Bureau. If you suspend and restart your career a lot, you're just not going to have the same pay vector, whether you're a man or a woman. Even full-time women workers typically put in eight to ten hours a week less than men do. Those simple facts account for much of the pay differential between women and men.

The fact is, when you look at the salaries of men and women in *really* comparable jobs, you find patterns that defy easy labeling. Here are some interesting statistics provided by the 1997 Salary Report in the January 1997 *Working Woman*:

- Women pharmacists at chain drugstores outearn men by $1,500 a year. However, male hospital pharmacists are $3,000 ahead of their female counterparts.
- In academia, male deans of arts and letters and chief financial officers are ahead of women by a $3,000-to-$9,000 margin. However, female deans of arts and sciences and chief administration officers earn $6,000 to $9,000 more than men with the same title.
- Female engineers with six years of experience earn about as much as men. Women with seven to nine years of experience are $6,500 behind. At ten to fourteen years, they earn $600 a year more.

Clearly, whatever the reasons for these disparities, they can't be easily blamed on discrimination; reality is far more complicated.

In the 1995 briefing *Free Markets, Free Choices: Women in the Work-force*, Pacific Research Institute policy analysts Katharine Post and Michael Lynch report that distinguished economists who've studied gender and earnings—including former Congressional Budget Office director June O'Neill—conclude that once you take into account factors like age, education, and continuous time spent in the workforce, the pay gap virtually vanishes. Even feminist economist Suzanne Bianchi-Sands, executive director of the National Committee on Pay Equity and one of the luminaries who attended Hillary's Equal Pay Day event at the White House, concedes in her 1996 monograph *Women, Work and Family in America* that women earn less than men at least in part due to "different choices about schooling, jobs, and family." As Post and Lynch point out, "While it is simply common sense that people who work more earn more, these inconvenient facts are often absent from 'factual' presentations on discrimination."

But don't bother Hillary Clinton with inconvenient facts! At the equal pay roundtable discussion, the First Lady sneered that "there are still those who claim that this is a made-up problem, that any wage gap between men and women can be explained away by the choices women make." (Charter members of the vast right-wing conspiracy, no doubt.) In Hillary's world, technicalities like economic and statistical analysis are always trumped by dogma. All you have to do is assert that "the gap between men's and women's salaries . . . can best be explained by one phenomenon: the continuing presence and the persistent effect of discrimination."

If you still buy the notion that women's personal choices and priorities have nothing to do with the gap between men's and women's salaries, here's one academic study you might want to consider. Scholars Joy Schneer of Rider University and Frieda Reitman of Pace University, experts on the barriers facing women in management, in 1993 analyzed the effect of family status on the earnings of men and women with MBA degrees in the *Academy of Management Journal*. Single women earned nearly the same salaries as single men. In the DINK (dual income, no kids) category, women were behind men by a slim six-percent margin. The real gender gap was among the married with children: MBA moms made twelve percent less than MBA dads in dual-earner families and a whopping 29 percent less than fathers with stay at-home wives.

There's no denying that, historically, institutional discrimination and societal prejudice kept women out of high-paying, high-level jobs. Until recently, both women *and* men generally agreed that a woman's primary vocation was homemaking and that if she worked outside the home, it should be in a job that could accommodate her family and fit into the traditional feminine sphere of nurturing, caring for children, and being a helpmate to men: nursing, teaching, or secretarial work. Few young women saw any point in investing a lot of time and money into job training when they expected their financial security to come from their husbands. In a 1968 survey, for instance, only about thirty percent of girls and young women ages fourteen to twenty-one thought they would be working at the age of thirty-five. But by the time their generation reached that age, in fact, seventy percent of them worked.

In the three decades since then, new doors have opened for women. Social attitudes have changed. Young women's expectations have shifted fast and dramatically. Gallup Youth Surveys show that most girls of my generation who were teenagers in the late seventies expected to work—though they mainly named traditional "feminine" occupations as their likely fields. But by the late eighties, teenage girls' and women's top three career choices were medicine, business, and law. In 1971, over a third of bachelor's degrees awarded to women were in education while only three percent were in business management. By 1996, education was down to twelve percent and business up to seventeen percent. Women also flocked to the nation's medical and law schools.

Has women's new commitment to work paid off? You bet. The wage gap has been steadily narrowing for twenty years; progress was especially dramatic in the eighties, which Susan Faludi and other feminists have dubbed "the backlash decade." Look at the earnings of men and women from different age groups. In 1993, women aged twenty to twenty-four earned ninety-five percent of what their male peers were making. For twenty-five to thirty-four-year olds, the ratio was eighty-three percent; for women over forty-five, sixty-seven percent. Amazingly, the media some-times manage to spin these statistics as bad news for women. A *New York Times* headline sounded the alarm: "Age Found to Widen Income Gap for Sexes." Shouldn't it have been, "Young Women Closing the Wage Gap Fast"?

To make the case for government protection of women in the work-place, the White House held a press conference in October 1994, hosted by then–labor secretary Robert Reich, Al Gore, and Hillary Clinton, to announce with great fanfare the results of a survey entitled "Working Women Count!" from the Women's Bureau of the U.S. Labor Department.

"Work, Job Inequity Remains the Rule, Women Say," cried an anguished headline in the Memphis, Tennessee, *Commercial Appeal*. What exactly did the survey find? A majority of working women weren't happy with their pay or opportunities for advancement, and a lot of them were stressed out. News flash! If men had been surveyed, do we think a majority would say, "Work is fulfilling, life is easy, I have more time than I know what to do with!"?

In March 1995, the Labor Department released the widely publicized report of the federal Glass Ceiling Commission. Needless to say, its conclusions were gloomy: "At the highest levels of business there is indeed a barrier only rarely penetrated by women." The claim that only five percent of senior executive posts in American corporations were held by women was trumpeted as a dramatic symbol of the "glass ceiling."

But wait a minute. In an article titled "Holes in the Glass Ceiling Theory," *Newsweek*, not normally known as a mouthpiece of the vast right-wing conspiracy, pointed out that the five-percent figure was based on data from 1989–1990. And even that represented a substantial increase from the mid-eighties, when women made up only about 1.5 percent of senior executive ranks. "Measured against a decade ago," Harvard economic historian Claudia Goldin was quoted as saying, "five percent seems like progress indeed." Indeed! More than triple the numbers in only five years—and during the Reagan administration to boot. What's more, the magazine reported, the progress continued at a brisk pace: A survey by the Korn/Ferry executive search firm in 1992 found that nine percent of executive vice presidents in the Fortune 1000 industrials and the Fortune 500 service corporations were women.

Richard Cohen, the liberal *Washington Post* columnist, was also among the skeptics. Though the editorialist made an obligatory nod to "America's traditional sexism and racism," he questioned the report's assumption that the disparity between the overall proportion of women in the labor force and the proportion of women in executive suites was sufficient proof of pervasive discrimination: "Could it be that women choose to go into other fields? Could it be that some of them . . . interrupt, abandon or curtail their careers so that they can raise children? Could it be that some choose to give their husbands career primacy? To say no to any of those questions is to defy common sense and the evidence all around us."

It wasn't so long ago that agencies of the federal government were admired for their relatively objective and depoliticized data-gathering efforts by career bureaucrats. Under the Clinton administration, however, academic studies are spun to say whatever the Clintons want them to say; reality seems to pose no obstacle.

Staying willfully ignorant of how women set their own priorities is part of the Work Trap that Hillary promotes and exemplifies. According to Schneer and Reitman, fourteen percent of all women who received MBA degrees from 1975 to 1980 were not in the workforce by 1987 and nine percent were working part-time; among those employed full-time, twenty-four percent had spent some time out of the workforce. By contrast, ninety-eight percent of male MBAs held full-time jobs, and eighty-eight percent had been continuously employed. In a later study, Schneer and Reitman found that women managers who take a break from their jobs for as little as nine months usually end up paying a price. Six years after going back to work, those women earned seventeen percent less than equally qualified women with no career interruptions and were much less likely to have risen to the level of upper middle management or higher (forty-four percent vs. sixty percent). If you think that's due to sexism, consider this: According to Schneer and Reitman, men's careers suffer even more from employment gaps. Now, you might say this comparison is irrelevant because few men take time off for child rearing. But again, it's a matter of choice and personal priorities. Women who interrupt their careers when their children are young could go back to work a lot sooner than they often do; but to some women, spending a year or two at home is a privilege, not a punishment. A choice, not an oppression imposed upon them from above. And for women, if not for men, taking time off to start your family is regarded as a valid reason for interrupting a career—which may be why the data show that women suffer less from career breaks.

In fact, far from bumping into a glass ceiling, women these days are actually outpacing men with similar backgrounds on the corporate ladder. Before you roll your eyes and write me off as an apologist for the patriarchy, consider a 1993 study by Rebecca Yates, associate dean of the University of Dayton School of Business Administration, and Professor Roy Adler of Pepperdine University. Yates and Adler calculated that it takes an average of twenty-five years to climb all the way from an MBA degree to a senior executive position with a Fortune 500 company. They also found that while only 2.6 percent of MBA degrees went to women in 1968, women accounted for 7.5 percent of upper-echelon executives at the Fortune 500 companies twenty-five years later. That means a woman with an MBA was three times as likely to make it to the top ranks as her male counterpart! But leave it to the feminists to shoot the messenger bearing the *good* news.

Add women lawyers to the victim roster: In January 1996, the American Bar Association's Commission on Women in the Profession came out with its report "Unfinished Business: Overcoming the Sisyphus Factor." Sisyphus, I'll explain for the benefit of the casualties of our public education system, was a guy in ancient Greek mythology who got on the wrong side of the gods and was sentenced to an eternity of pushing a huge boulder up a hill. Every time he would get near the top, wham! the boulder came rolling down.

Hillary Clinton, presented with an advance copy of the ABA report, hailed it as a milestone in fairness for women: "Equal opportunity for women in the law is important to all of society," she declared. No shock that Hillary should love "Unfinished Business." After all, it was practically her baby, or at least her grandchild—a follow-up to the first report submitted by the Commission on Women in the Profession in 1988, when the commission was chaired by . . . you guessed it, Hillary Clinton.

The original report, "The Status of Women in the Legal Profession," glumly predicted that "time alone is unlikely to alter significantly the underrepresentation of women in the law firm partnerships, judicial appointments and tenured faculty positions" without a special effort to root out sexism. The ABA's "Unfinished Business"—surprise, surprise—validated that prognosis. Though the report announced that its purpose was "to chronicle and celebrate the progress of women lawyers," it had remarkably little to say about progress and less to celebrate. (Its tone was about as upbeat as a chronicle of the Great Depression.) It grudgingly acknowledged that the proportion of women in the legal profession had grown nearly eightfold between 1971 and 1995, from three percent to twenty-three percent, and that women were approaching half of the total enrollment in the nation's law schools. However, the report's real focus was a dire litany of the perils supposedly lying in wait for women: "pay inequities, skewed opportunities for advancement, sexual harassment, and hostility to family needs."

This grim picture was based on data like this: In 1995, women were twenty-three percent of all practicing attorneys but only thirteen percent of partners in large law firms. The report's conclusion? "Clearly, advancement opportunities are artificially limited." Is this so clear? Female attorneys are more likely to be younger and less experienced than men on average. In 1985, women made up just thirteen percent of all attorneys. Moreover, women lawyers are more likely to go into the public sector or the in-house legal departments of corporations, where the schedules are less punishing than at private law firms. In 1994, fifty-five percent of junior corporate counsel positions were female, a survey found. The report itself says that "women often base their choice of work environments on how that environment can accommodate their personal needs. They seek an environment that allows for an integrated family life and career [and] has a relatively flexible structure . . . These priorities influence women's choice to work solo or in a small firm, academia, government, corporate or the non-profit sector." But that didn't stop the ABA from concluding that if women on average prefer a certain type of work environment, then, by golly, law firms should be required to create it for them.

Biased, politically correct reports like this bend over backward to manufacture conclusions like: "Using the same criteria to evaluate men and women frequently undervalues the contributions of women." Huh? Equal standards make everything unequal? We're approaching Orwell here, on the order of War Is Peace and Slavery Is Freedom—or at least high confusion. Hillary's friends at the left-leaning ABA want women to have their flexible low-pressure workplace and still get the same pay and the same number of law-firm partnerships as men cultivating aneurysms in a high pressure cooker.

If you want to climb the conventional ladder of success, then you should set your priorities accordingly. If you opt for a less-demanding career to make more time for your family, that doesn't necessarily mean you're "sacrificing" your career fulfillment for marriage and motherhood. A career with a less-hectic pace can be more satisfying, not less. Quite a few women—and a growing number of men, too—have found that law didn't become personally rewarding for them until they struck out on their own or joined a smaller firm, ditching the dog-eat-dog politics of big law firms. The same is certainly true in business and many other fields.

It's fine to have high expectations for ourselves and our daughters. But there's a big difference between high expectations and an unrealistic sense of entitlement, whether you're male or female.

Is sex discrimination in the workplace a thing of the past? Of course not. There are still a few men out there who take a dim view of women's abilities or feel threatened by strong, capable women. While bias-in-the-workplace litigation has turned into a lucrative racket for unscrupulous plaintiffs and attorneys flacking bogus claims (read Walter K. Olson's eye-opening book, *The Excuse Factory*), some claims of discrimination are credible and truly egregious. Overt discrimination and subtle career barriers still exist—you might be excluded from an "old boys' network" or face the challenge of balancing career and a hectic personal life. The question is, what do we do about this? Is everything a matter for the police, the politicians, and the plaintiffs' attorneys? Or are some things just personal?

You know what my answer would be: Personal choices don't necessarily require political responses. But to Hillary, the answer is: Ever more laws. Ever more lawsuits. More affirmative action. More federal edicts demanding that all businesses make a "family-friendly workplace," whatever that's supposed to mean. More roundtable discussions and fancy lunches and weighty proclamations about all the lovely things that ought to happen—right now!

Why don't Hillary's answers make sense? Because her "remedies" often do more harm than good.

Take the civil rights laws. Some of them have, without a doubt, helped open doors for women in education and in the workplace. Today, however, looking to these laws—or ever-newer spin-offs of them—as the main answer to women's problems in the workplace lures us into the trap of exaggerating the obstacles we face (which can undermine our confidence and poison our relations with our male coworkers) and seeking salvation from the government rather than relying on our own energies. Some claims of discrimination are such obvious ploys they only give women's fight for equality a bad name.

Take the case of Joanne Flynn, a former vice president at the Wall Street firm of Goldman Sachs, who saw a promotion she wanted go to one Doris Smith—that's right, another woman. Smith went on to fire her. Flynn then claimed in a lawsuit that the men at the firm were on a vendetta against her because she had once fired a male subordinate, and Smith had been brought in as a cover for a sexist plot against her at the firm. Never mind that nearly a quarter of the vice presidents and associates at Goldman Sachs by that time were women. Flynn's allegation of bias included her claim that a former partner in the firm once characterized her in conversation as "a treacherous bitch." Let's see. If someone doesn't like you and tells someone else so, is this personal, or is it political? Juries often ignore the distinction. Amazingly, a jury found that Flynn had been discriminated against because of her sex—though federal judge Kimba Wood threw out the verdict, citing "complete absence of evidence" to support it.

In many cases, sex discrimination laws have become the last refuge of the incompetent, who are seeking to score in litigation lotto after they've struck out in life. Even the most groundless civil rights suits are so costly to deal with employers often prefer to settle or pay off potential litigants. A few years ago, a *New York* magazine cover story on what to do when you lose your job quoted one attorney who said, straight out, that if you're a woman or a member of any other group protected based on race, ethnic origin, religion, and so forth, you should immediately call a lawyer to file a discrimination complaint. Such charges, he said cheerfully, don't need to have merit—the threat of suit alone will give you leverage in extracting severance pay and other goodies. (Anyone still wondering why people tell nasty lawyer jokes?) This isn't civil rights litigation, it's a legalized shakedown. And the victims, in many cases, are other women—the business owners.

When Jo Ann Bass, the owner of Joe's Stone Crab, a popular Miami Beach restaurant, got a letter from the Equal Employment Opportunity Commission informing her that she was being investigated on charges of discrimination against women, she might've wondered if it was April Fools' Day. Jo Ann was, after all, the recipient of a number of awards for her leadership on behalf of women in business. Women made up most of her managerial staff. Like many upscale eateries, Joe's—a local landmark founded in 1913 by her grandfather—traditionally featured tuxedo-clad male waiters. Women were never formally excluded, Bass said, and in fact, no woman had ever complained. It was just the EEOC that was bent out of shape.

When Jo Ann consulted a lawyer, he advised her to settle. That was in 1992. By 1998, she had spent about a million dollars on the case. "It's a case of right and wrong," she told a reporter. "Why do I go after this? Why do I keep on going? Because it's right. It's trying to prove a right will overcome a wrong."

After learning about the investigation, the management of Joe's Stone Crab made more of an effort to hire female servers. By 1997, when the case went to trial, its wait staff was twenty-two percent female. But federal judge Daniel Hurley decreed this wasn't good enough. Based on the local labor pool, he said, the numbers should have been higher—31.9 percent, to be precise. He found no deliberate wrongdoing but pronounced the restaurant guilty of "unintentional discrimination." So Jo Ann Bass was ordered to pay a total of nearly $155,000 in back pay and benefits to four stand-ins whom the EEOC trotted out as victims of discrimination at Joe's between 1986 and 1991. Three of them had never even tried to apply for a job at the restaurant—supposedly because they had heard it didn't hire women.

Judge Hurley then decided to put himself in charge of the annual hiring sessions at Joe's for the next five years: The court together with the EEOC would approve the placement and wording of all help-wanted ads for wait staff, supervise job interviews, and set hiring criteria. Ironically, the first year this was done, the proportion of waitresses applying to Joe's actually went down slightly. And as it turns out, 31.9 percent proportionality at Joe's is going to be really tough to get to—after all, stone crab trays can be as heavy as forty pounds. So unless Jo Ann Bass wins on appeal, the government may be doing her hiring for her for many years to come.

Does Hillary ever stop to ask herself: Why is the government doing such absurd stuff? What is all this accomplishing apart from massive taxpayer expenditure and massive harassment of good citizens? Alas, as she has advised us, Hillary can't be bothered with the plights of unfairly targeted "undercapitalized" women entrepreneurs when social utopias of proportionality enforced by big government dance like sugarplums before her.

It's not just as entrepreneurs that women are hurt by abuse of discrimination laws. Frivolous lawsuits confirm the worst stereotypes about women: conniving, manipulative, always ready to cry victim. If bosses and coworkers feel that they have to walk on eggshells because a woman could drop the nuclear bomb of a sex discrimination suit, it doesn't make for very collegial relations. And what about the burden that out-of-control lawsuits impose on us all, by clogging up the courts and driving up the cost of business? Remember, every time you buy a car, a computer, or a dress—or have dinner at a restaurant—you're paying a litigation surcharge.

We've barely touched on the biggest breeding ground for litigation run amok in the civil rights laws: sexual harassment. Like discrimination laws in general, harassment laws were created to protect women from being sexually assaulted on the job or coerced into sex by threats of retaliation.

Today, thanks to feminist "consciousness-raising" and a series of bad court decisions advancing the radical edge of feminist dogma, we now have an avalanche of cases in the courts vying for the title of Wackiest Sex Harassment Lawsuit. A former manager at a real-estate development company in Cincinnati won $250,000 because some men made a few sophomoric off-color jokes at business meetings. She never realized how upset she had been by this behavior, however, until shortly after she was fired for attaching a page with the company president's signature to a document he hadn't read. Thankfully, a federal court of appeals eventually came to its senses and struck down the award. In another case, two female nurses in Santa Rosa, California, sued the hospital because the head nurse—also female—had an earthy sense of humor and (horrors!) liked bawdy birthday cards. Rather than go through a lot of legal rigmarole, the hospital settled.

Such stories sound like jokes or isolated cases, but they're not. Sexual harassment training seminars now commonly warn men that smiling or "staring" at a woman can get them in trouble if she decides to take offense. So working men have started to avoid getting too close to women colleagues. I've heard a number of men comment after sitting through harassment workshops that the only way to be safe was to never talk to a woman at work. In a 1997 *Washington Post* poll, about a quarter of men said that they had sometimes or often avoided interacting with women at the office or at work-related social events. Twenty-eight percent avoided mentoring or giving career advice to women out of fear of sexual harassment suits. A partner in the law firm where I used to work told me that he's reluctant to travel with female associates: "I don't want any problems!" he said. Once again, special protections intended to help women end up limiting their opportunities.

Another of Hillary and her pals' pet projects is the "family friendly" workplace. But these programs are a mixed blessing. Negotiating time off, shorter hours, or flexible schedules, tailored to both employers' and employees' particular needs, can be just great—and employers are often happy to work flextimes out, even if the state isn't breathing down their necks to do so, especially if they want to keep good workers. But one-size-fits-all government policies have their price too. Apart from the cost to society of maintaining a big expensive bureaucracy, and to businesses of being constantly on guard against the threat of costly lawsuits, even the most career-minded females in Hillary's world are inevitably stigmatized as potentially less-than-dedicated mommy trackers. And if small mistakes can trigger litigation land mines, you can bet that employers will find ways not to hire so many potential time bombs in the form of women. Ironic but true—regulation often tends perversely to create disincentives for the very behavior the law is trying to encourage, and incentives for behavior the law is trying to crush! A 1994 *Wall Street Journal* survey found that some family-friendly companies (like Johnson & Johnson) were in fact the least "woman-friendly" as defined by women's actual presence in the executive suites, far behind the female representation at some companies with skimpy family policies (like PepsiCo or Sara Lee).

What's true for companies is also true for countries. American feminists often tout Sweden, with its generous family policies, as the working woman's new utopia. In fact, when it comes to women's professional achievement, the Swedish paradise lags far behind these benighted States. According to a 1995 *Wall Street Journal* report, women hold only seventeen percent of managerial jobs in Sweden (including a measly eight percent in the private sector!), compared to nearly forty-five percent in the United States. A study published the same year in *American Sociological Review* showed that Swedish women managers are far more likely than their oppressed American sisters to be clustered in low-level positions with no real authority.

As this example shows, government-mandated special accommodations may backfire on the very women they're supposed to benefit. Women can simply become too expensive to employ in career-track positions. Of course, they are protected by sex discrimination laws; but commentators are already beginning to notice the big holes suddenly forming in the safety net as companies increasingly farm out work to independent contractors not covered by regulations instead of continuing to hire employees that are.

Yet Hillary's enthusiasm—for all her talk of women achieving economic self-sufficiency—is reserved for what the government can do for working women. "If we provide economic security for women, that will ensure the strength of families," Hillary declared at the Summit on Women's Security hosted by the Women's Foundation of Colorado in 1995. But who exactly is "we"? As an editorial in the *Denver Rocky Mountain News* pointed out:

> *Surely the First Lady understands that no official entity can "provide economic security," if by "provide" she means "guarantee," other than by dipping ever more deeply into the pockets of working Americans, male and female alike. What political leadership can and should do is improve the legal and economic framework within which able-bodied women (and other Americans) can provide for their own security.*

If you ask me, the editorial writer was way too optimistic: I'm not at all sure Hillary understands anything of the sort. But she should. The real key to progress isn't what Hillary can do for women, but what women these days can do for themselves.

Women's Opportunities, Women's Choices

At Hillary's 1999 "Equal Pay Day" event at the White House, the First Lady honored four women who had sued their employers for sex discrimination. Who didn't get invited? The thousands of women who have fought sexist bosses without a stitch of help from the feds—that is, by becoming bosses themselves.

Maryles Casto kept getting passed over for promotions at the travel agency where she worked in the mid-seventies. Finally she decided to strike out on her own. By 1992, she was running a company with annual revenues of $70 million and had 145 people working for her. Of her former boss, Casto told *Fortune* magazine, "I knew I was better than he was. So I beat him at his own game."

Erica Swerdlow thought she had an ideal work-family arrangement. While pregnant, her boss at S&S Public Relations in Illinois told her she could work from home three days a week and bring the baby to work the other two. Unfortunately, as Erica told *The Wall Street Journal*, things didn't turn out that way: Mr. Sensitive Boss pressured her to come back to work a month early and then started needling her with snide remarks like "Oh, the mother's here!" and "What do we owe this honor to?" whenever she came in. On a few occasions, she was reduced to tears. But Erica had the last laugh. After she left S&S in 1993, she and her husband, Brian, launched EBS Public Relations with an office in their basement and $10,000 in the bank. Five years later, EBS was one of the Midwest's leading public relations firms specializing in the high-tech information industry, with thirty employees, a second office, and annual revenues of $2 million a year—projected to reach $5 million by 2000, higher than those of her former firm.

You might argue that stories like this show that there is still a need for tough enforcement of antidiscrimination laws or affirmative action programs. But you would be wrong. For one thing, a lot has changed in the twenty-five years since Maryles Casto left the company where she couldn't get ahead. Many women who become entrepreneurs today are motivated less by gender-based obstacles in the workplace than by nonconformity and a desire for true independence.

I'm quite willing to admit that sexist bosses do exist—and probably always will. But let's face it: No court or government agency can transform a major jerk into a nice and supportive boss. To the extent that there may be a "glass ceiling" in some sectors of the economy, the best solution is the one offered by Alexandria Johnson Boone, head of the Cleveland-based public relations and advertising firm GAP Productions, in her testimony before the 1994 hearings of the federal Glass Ceiling Commission: "The quickest and surest way to an economic structure free from the glass ceiling is for women and minorities to start their own businesses." But the commission did not see fit to include that recommendation in its final report—perhaps it doesn't leave Hillary and her do-gooder friends enough to do.

Casto, Swerdlow, and Boone are just three of nearly eight million American women who own nearly a third of the nation's businesses today. Their share of the economic pie is likely to keep expanding, since women now launch small businesses at twice the rate of men and have a lower rate of failure than men who do. American women entrepreneurs already employ more people than the Fortune 500 together do worldwide. Women-owned business revenues are growing nearly twice as fast as total business revenues. True, most women-owned businesses are in the service sector and have a traditional feminine flavor—from restaurants to interior decorating—but the growth rates of women-owned businesses in nontraditional sectors like manufacturing, construction, computers, and transportation are higher than in those traditional categories.

Do female entrepreneurs exist in Hillary's world? Indeed they do—as beneficiaries of government largesse. While addressing a symposium on women's economic empowerment at the U.N. Conference on Women in Beijing in 1995, Hillary Clinton deplored the hardships women face when trying to get credit to start a business and bragged that "our Small Business Administration is already making more loans than ever to women." Well, a seed loan from the SBA may be all fine and well (Susan McDougal was certainly pleased to get hers and to plunk part of it, illegally, into the Whitewater development), but most businesspeople appreciate government getting off their backs even more. About half of women business owners surveyed in 1995 said that government was making things worse for them. You'll never hear Hillary talk about those women—the ones who aren't held down by a glass ceiling, but are choked to death by red tape:

- Judy Hopper, a bakery owner in Evanston, Illinois, was hit with a $13,000 fine by the Occupational Safety and Health Administration (OSHA) after a surprise inspection brought on by a disgruntled ex-employee's complaint about unsafe conditions in the kitchen.

The complaints all turned out to be false, but the inspector dug up a few regulatory lapses anyway. The bakery's thirty-three workers hadn't been given OSHA data sheets on the chemicals they were exposed to on the job—specifically, dishwashing detergent and bleach. No fire evacuation route was posted, though the bakery was on the first floor with four clearly marked exits. No injury log had been kept, though the most serious injury ever to befall any of Hooper's employees was a cut finger. After Hooper and her husband fixed these "hazards" at the cost of about $100, OSHA agreed to modify the sanction to a $5,500 cash fine—about one tenth of the bakery's annual profits—and $7,500 to be spent on safety improvements dictated or approved by OSHA.

• Anita Cragg, the owner and president of Space Coast Management Services, Inc., in Florida, bought a housing subdivision planning to build new homes. In 1993, federal investigators from the U.S. Fish and Wildlife Service spotted two Florida scrub jays—a bird protected under the Endangered Species Act—flying onto the property and ordered construction halted as a hazard to land "suitable for occupation by scrub jays." Neither federal investigators nor an independent environmental engineer could actually ever find any scrub jay nests on the lots. After eighteen months of trying to fight the government, though, Cragg realized her quest was hopeless and agreed to a "compromise": To compensate for any possible loss of scrub jay habitat, she would buy four acres of land off-site for every homesite her company developed. She had to fork over more than $100,000 for the privilege.

Hillary isn't personally responsible for the high-handed dealings of every government agency, of course—though one can legitimately wonder what kind of entrepreneur-unfriendly policies she would pursue if elected to the Senate. (Remember, this is the woman who once told the students at the Arkansas Governor's School that she would trust big government over big business any time!) But these women's stories are worth recalling when Hillary brags about all that government does for women, which is like congratulating the mugger for his generosity after he lifts your wallet but hands you $5 for cab fare.

Despite the bureaucratic hurdles, millions of women are succeeding in the new economy. The Internet is creating a whole new range of opportunities for women who like the freedom and flexibility of working from home. The other day, I opened *The Washington Post*. Instead of the usual hand-wringing about the tribulations of oppressed women, I found a story about a "housewife with no business experience and no venture capital" who grew her company into a multinational force in a single year. Sandy Kleppinger of Leesburg, Virginia, was searching for educational software for her kids and stumbled onto eBay, the world's largest online auction house (whose CEO happens to be another woman, Meg Whitman). Soon, she decided to try her hand at selling software online. In the first seven months of 1999, she made over $40,000 in profits as the head of her solo business, Sandy's Finds.

There are lots of other ways women are taking their destiny into their own hands. Doctors may choose less consuming specialties like pediatrics instead of surgery; lawyers setting up solo practice rather than going for the partnership in a big firm; managers opting for positions with less pay and less authority. Women who make such trade-offs may seem to have less power in some conventional sense, but they may actually have more power over their own lives—and not only more time with their families but more career satisfaction as well. Yet Hillary and her friends trot out data showing such trends as evidence of "pay inequity" and "glass ceilings."

This point was illustrated by a remarkable story in *Fortune* magazine in 1995 about the "midlife crises" experienced by some executive women— the kind where you look around the oak-paneled office and ask, "Is this all there is?" The women profiled were the trailblazers who stormed male-dominated corporate bastions in the seventies. They hadn't hit any infamous glass ceiling. On the contrary, many of them were riding an express elevator to the top only to find that they wanted to get off. Some deliberately put the brakes on upward mobility, refusing prestigious promotions and staying in lower-level but more enjoyable jobs. Others bailed out of the corporate world altogether.

There are some famous examples of such transitions. Brenda Barnes made headlines and caused a lot of feminists to reach for the Maalox when she resigned as CEO of PepsiCo-North America in 1997 to devote more attention to her three children; she then became, in the words of *Fortune* magazine—which still rates her as one of this country's fifty most powerful women in business—"the most sought-after female board member in America." Patty Stonesifer, senior vice president at Microsoft, resigned for a job that allowed more time for a personal life. She now serves as president and cochair of the Bill and Melinda Gates Foundation, one of the world's largest philanthropic organizations.

It's possible that women on average tend to be more interested than men in having a personal life as well as a career. In the words of former labor secretary Lynn Martin: "Women are more aware of what's on the gravestone, which is not 'I worked for IBM.' " Or perhaps they just have more freedom to have a life. Getting fed up with the rat race isn't just a woman thing, of course. In one recent survey, reports the *San Diego Union-Tribune*, forty-three percent of female managers said they'd ditch work altogether if they had the money to live comfortably—but so did thirty-five percent of their male counterparts. Men who would like to explore new paths are often tied down by fear of social disapproval and by their role as breadwinners. As the *Fortune* article about executive women at midlife reported, some men even tell their therapists that their wives won't let them leave high-paying jobs. So maybe it's *men* who are really in need of liberation! Until then, we women should count our blessings and rejoice in the choices we do have. True, the outcome of some of these choices may mean fewer women at the top of the workplace hierarchy, numerically. Are feminists going to tell these women to sacrifice their personal and professional fulfilment just to stack up more female bodies on the upper rungs of the corporate ladder?

No one forces women to tailor their careers to families. It's their choice. Mothers like it when men share in parenting, but two thirds of them still feel the woman ought to be the primary caretaker, according to a 1987 study titled *The Motherhood Report*. Only one in four strongly endorsed fifty-fifty parenting. Pepper Schwartz, a sociologist whose 1994 book *The Peer Marriage* sings the praises of families with no gender-based division of roles, concedes ruefully that egalitarian arrangements often crumble as soon as the first baby arrives. Not because Daddy balks at changing diapers, but because Mommy balks at turning Baby over to Daddy! Besides, to most of us, a guy who'll trade his briefcase for a baby bottle doesn't seem like terribly good marriage material. Try asking a young woman training for a lucrative profession such as law or medicine if she'd be willing to support a nonworking spouse, and with few exceptions the answer will be a resounding *no*. In fact, chances are, she'll tell you that she would prefer a mate who is at least as successful in his field as she is in hers. Many scientists believe that the desire to "marry up" is ingrained in women by millennia of evolution, when women needed men with resources if their children were to survive.

I'm no expert on evolutionary biology, but it seems to me that the fact that women get pregnant and have the babies has something to do with their role as mothers. Even Hillary, her trial lawyer friends, and the NOW Legal Defense Fund haven't yet figured out a way to sue Mother Nature. Sorry, feminists, but I don't think we'll ever see a society where men are pushing half the strollers and women are running half the corporations.

This doesn't mean that I think all women should be pushing strollers. No way! Plenty of women lead perfectly happy lives without children and without regrets. Others are happy with fifty-fifty parenting. "I have found someone who cares for my one-year-old daughter like she was their own, shares my toddler's every triumph and disaster . . . and doesn't tire of me calling to check up on her," writes Sarah Stapleton-Gray in *The Washington Post*, appreciatively, of her husband. "We have avoided the feelings of guilt associated with letting others take care of [our] child, or the feelings of isolation some have experienced when staying home full-time with their children, by sharing our daughter's care."

Many women, including many pioneers hailed for shattering the "glass ceiling," are also leaving caring for the home and the kids to willing husbands these days. Connie Duckworth, now a top executive at the Goldman Sachs investment firm and a mother of three, had just had her first baby when she was offered a big promotion that required frequent travel. After a year of juggling work and child care and leaning heavily on the grandparents, she and her husband, a money manager, decided that one of them would have to quit—him. Carleton Fiorina, who made headlines when she took over as president and CEO of Hewlett-Packard in 1999—the third woman to lead a Fortune 500 company—also had the advantage of a supportive man at home. When the pace of her career got too hectic, Frank, formerly a senior executive at AT&T, took early retirement at forty-nine so they could spend more time together.

The moral of these stories? Women who want to change the division of labor in the family so that they can have children and fulfill their ambitions can just do it, without any help from NOW, the Department of Labor, or Hillary. If you're willing to make the same sacrifices for your careers that men have always made, and if you have the talent, you'll rise just as high.

But you won't get ahead by whining and asking Big Sister to shield you from every slight and every naughty word. The protection of the law should be a last resort, not the first. Sometimes, women can just develop a thicker skin. Remember that everyone, male or female, has to put up with a few things on the job they don't like. At other times, confronting some total jerk directly can be way more effective than filing a complaint—and will win you more respect, too. Anyway, if you giggle at a guy's dirty jokes, never letting on that you're upset, how do you justify hitting him later with a harassment charge? It's just hypocritical, and gross opportunism.

Instead of Anita Hill, we ought to pick role models like Susan Estes, who became the chief of the government-bond trading division at Morgan Stanley Dean Witter & Co. in late 1999, at the age of forty, with a salary estimated at $1.5 million a year. According to the *Wall Street Journal*, Estes managed to climb to the top from a basically secretarial position in a male dominated, macho industry "by balancing confrontation and accommodation, shrugging off slights and occasional blatant sexism while pressing to change a recalcitrant industry." One day in 1987, she was one of two women among the firm's fifty bond traders. Her male colleagues gathered around the TV set, ogling a cute blond meteorologist on CNN and making lewd remarks. Unfazed, Estes wrote down every word they said and then, with a sly smile, got up and read these comments aloud for the entire office to hear. The culprits laughed but their faces were red. After she did this a few more times, the men at the office realized that they sounded like a bunch of cretinous jerks, and stopped.

More recently, Estes overheard a fellow broker she traded with assert that the only way a female assistant could get ahead at his firm was by granting him sexual favors. Outraged, she went to her boss and got permission to stop doing business with the man. It cost him tens of thousands of dollars in commissions. And that worked way better than sensitivity training: When Estes relented and ended her boycott three years later, she found that he was a changed man.

On the other hand, an industry like bond-trading may never become hospitable to the very sensitive. It's an extremely high-pressure, competitive environment where nerves get frayed, tensions have to be released, and verbal one-upmanship is inevitable. As Estes has learned, you have to be able to take it and dish it right back. If you're not comfortable with that, then you'd probably do well to consider looking for another field. Remember, it's not just women who have to make such choices. Not all men are comfortable in a locker-room atmosphere either.

One thing is clear: You can't eat all the cake you want and still be able to wear that slinky black dress. Want to succeed in traditionally male domains? Then be prepared to make the same sacrifices men have made. (The authors of the ABA report on women in law seem to assume that working sixty-five hour weeks and missing family events aren't sacrifices for men, but that sounds to me like reverse sexism.) Want to protect your turf as Mom and see your daughter take her first steps? Then be prepared to make accommodations that might slow down your career.

This message would do young women a lot more good than the self-pity and gender-oppression rhetoric they currently get in college or from stuck-in-the-sixties types like Hillary. Teaching women to see themselves as victims and to rely on the government to solve all their problems can only undermine them, by discouraging them from making the right (and often difficult) choices and setting their priorities in order.

So how can we take full advantage of the options and opportunities in today's marketplace, without falling into the Hillary Trap of denying that choices have consequences? Besides being realistic about balancing work and family, women must focus on competence first and gender last. Carleton Fiorina, the CEO of Hewlett-Packard, seems to have it just right. After she was selected to run one of America's most important technology companies, she told reporters, "I hope that we are at a point that everyone has figured out that there is not a glass ceiling."

Hillary Clinton must have thought to herself, what is Carly smoking? Ms. Fiorina clearly does not live in Hillary's world. In Hillary's world, the experts know best, working women are victims no matter how successful, and women who don't fit the "progressive" mold are naive and misguided. Their studies and advice scream out: "You need our help." But the real joy of work is that we're on our own, free to succeed or fail based on our talents and ambition. We're not in Hillary's Work Trap—we can choose. We know discrimination still exists, but we don't let that paralyze or intimidate us. We don't have to call in a government task force to decide how many hours we want to work, how ambitious we want to be at different stages of our lives, or how to balance our personal lives and careers. Those decisions can be painful, because nobody can have everything at once. But we can at least be more honest than Hillary is about the choices we make, and their consequences.

But in spite of all the evidence that women are thriving, Hillary and friends are still determined to ride to the rescue. And, since many of the challenges we face in the workplace have to do with the work-family dilemma, they are convinced that the government should not only help us advance at work but also help manage our family lives. Often, as we will see in the next chapter, this "help" does little more than lead women into yet another corner of the Hillary Trap—the antigun trap.

4.

The
Antigun Trap

It's not just in the workplace that Hillary Clinton's view of the world traps women in a dependency culture that actually limits our power and self-reliance. Hillary also urges women to entrust themselves to Big Brother (or Big Sister), in an area that may be the most important of all: our personal safety.

Hillary can sound passionate and almost convincing when she talks about violence against women. It was a central theme in her speech to the U.N. Conference on Women in Beijing in 1995. She declared that "if women are free from violence, their families will flourish" and spoke movingly of "women whose lives are threatened by violence" around the world.

But Hillary's idea of combating this scourge is to tell women to dial 911 and hope for the best. Or attend a workshop. Or write your congressperson. And, of course, support gun control. At a May 1999 Mother's Day event at the White House, Hillary urged Americans to "stand behind political leaders who are brave enough to buck the gun lobby."

Yet all these solutions, instead of helping women fight back, draw them further into the Hillary Trap. The hidden message is: Women can't protect themselves on their own. They need politicians, police, and sweeping restrictions on gun ownership.

Of course we need an effective court system and a reliable police force. But that doesn't mean we shouldn't do all we can to help ourselves. If you have the courage to stop and think for yourself, you can see that Hillary's agenda is as demeaning to women as men telling us to stay in the house and lock the doors, honey—this is a man's job.

Hillary is hardly an exception. Her view of guns, as we'll see, is shared by virtually all of the "sisterhood" that claims to speak on behalf of women. Almost all feminists urge women, in the most melodramatic terms, to stay away from the evil of guns, and also champion measures that would deny us the choice to use our best means of defense.

Why this antigun fanaticism? It's puzzling, even by the standards of Hillary's world. One answer must be that, consciously or not, the feminists really don't want women to be so self-reliant that they won't need Hillary's governmental "village" to look out for them. They'd rather see women as a "protected class" than as people who can fight their own battles, using the same weapons as men. Another answer is that Hillary's sisterhood would rather dream of a better world, where nobody has guns and no one is ever faced with violence, than deal with the world that actually exists. This immature desire to "have it all" in an imaginary world and avoid making hard choices in this one is a recurring aspect of the Hillary Trap.

Sorry, Hillary, but I'd feel safer with a Smith & Wesson. If that makes me a gun nut in your eyes, so be it. In fact, I freely confess that until I moved into the quasi-communist District of Columbia, I was a proud gun owner.

In my early teens, my father taught me how to shoot and also taught me about gun safety. But I didn't buy a gun of my own until my second year as a law student at the University of Virginia. I was making frequent trips to Washington, D.C.—a two-hour drive through poorly lit rural areas, often after dark, with computer equipment needed for my part-time job and law school work. After several stories of female drivers being run off the road, robbed, and worse, I began to worry about my safety. My room-mate (a male classmate), who also traveled often with expensive gear in his car, told me he had gotten a concealed carry permit and asked if I had thought about it. I hadn't. But when I thought about it, it made a lot of sense. I got a permit, went to a gun store in Charlottesville, Virginia, and bought a little .38 Brazilian-made Taurus 5-shot, which I kept in my car. While I never had occasion to use it and could not legally carry it in the District of Columbia, I felt better just knowing it was there.

I got rid of my gun shortly after graduation. My boyfriend's yellow Lab Lobby had chewed up my leather shoulder holster. And besides, I was moving to the gun owner's nightmare known as the District of Columbia.

I didn't think much about my gun-owning past—until it was dredged up in order to portray me as an extremist, maybe even a loony.

It all started with a voice, sweet as congealed syrup, on my answering machine. It was *Vanity Fair*'s Marjorie Williams, whom you may remember from the False Sisterhood chapter—a fortysomething feminist with a tou-sled sandy crop and deceptively kind eyes. Guess what, she crooned: She'd been assigned to do my profile. She was so looking forward to meeting me. She just knew we'd have *soooo* much to talk about.

When the piece eventually appeared, it portrayed me as part of a dis-turbing trend: a new generation of blonde, right-wing female pundits run-ning amok in the nation's capital. And what did Williams seize upon as evidence that I wasn't ready for prime time? She mentioned worrisome rumors that I had once owned—gasp!—a handgun. None of my friends were willing to confirm this bombshell, so Williams was reduced to punc-tuating her piece with nudge-nudge, wink-wink references: "The gun, whether it existed or not, has clearly been a useful way of drawing atten-tion." The title of the *Vanity Fair* story was "Laura, Get Your Gun."

Among the *Vanity Fair* set, which largely overlaps with Hillary's social world, the mere fact that a woman has owned a gun becomes a kind of shorthand: She's unstable—a crazy gun-toting chick, a powder keg ready to blow at any moment. For Hillary and her friends, a woman who carries a gun to defend herself is no better than the violent men who threaten them. She can't comprehend that a gun could ever be a lifesaving tool that women might find indispensable to guarantee their safety. That's part of the Trap—another aspect of the tunnel vision that, in the name of supporting women, actually makes them more vulnerable.

In the real world, guns can be a "women's issue" all right, but not in the way Hillary and the sisterhood mean it. We have seen how women are taking charge of their lives in education and on the job. Increasingly, they are also taking charge of their own protection. And here, a gun can be a woman's best friend—even the ultimate declaration of independence.

Hillary's answer to the issue of women's safety, predictably, is impersonal and bureaucratic. She would take choices out of the hands of individual women and put them into the hands of "experts" who supposedly know best. And, of course, she wants more laws and federal programs to comfort the victims and research the social ills motivating all those robbers, rapists, and murderers. This urge to legislate isn't just a liberal response, alas. As we saw earlier, Republicans proudly helped pass the legislative monstrosity known as the Violence Against Women Act. This much-hailed 1994 bill ladled out $5 billion for counseling and consciousness-raising while earmarking not a penny for self-defense initiatives. Four years later, the politicians who served up this slab of gender pork are still congratulating themselves for their sensitivity. Yet laws like this do nothing to help a woman in that terrifying moment when she hears the footsteps of an attacker in a dark parking lot and has nothing but her fists and desperate screams to defend herself.

The one message you won't hear from Hillary is what I consider to be the ultimate feminist declaration of independence. Instead of wallowing in the horror of men's violence and women's vulnerability, we can do something about it. We can really take back the night, and not by clutching a clove-scented candle at a campus rally. We can be victorious fighters instead of torch-bearing sob sisters. We can actually stop men from hurting us.

Guns are not the only way for a woman to protect herself. If she can fend off a predator with a front kick to the groin or use her car keys to gouge a rapist's eyes out, more power to her. However, defending yourself in these ways puts a woman closer to her attacker and requires physical strength and psychological readiness to engage in direct combat. Even then, a woman is in danger if she's outnumbered. The truth is, when you face a stronger opponent, there's no equalizer like a gun.

Hillary may not explicitly tell us it's wrong for women to defend ourselves with guns. During her "listening tour" of New York State in the summer of 1999, she deplored gun violence, invoked children, and lashed out at the National Rifle Association; but when asked an inconveniently straightforward question—was she against gun ownership?—she dodged it and just talked some more about stronger gun legislation.

Yet the so-called gun control movement, whose standard-bearer Hillary has become, is indeed permeated with extreme antigun ideology. Handgun Control, Inc., chairwoman Sarah Brady and her husband, James—with whom Hillary shared the spotlight at the 1996 Democratic National Convention—believe that "the only reason for guns in civilian hands is for sporting purposes." They propose a national licensing program under which self-defense would not be accepted as grounds to allow a civilian to own a gun. Only sportsmen would be licensed.

Comedienne Rosie O'Donnell, popular daytime talk show host and well-known Friend of Hillary, takes an equally extreme view. When actor Tom Selleck appeared on her show in May 1999 to plug his new movie *The Love Letter*, Rosie suddenly shed her Queen of Nice persona and started berating her astonished guest because he had done an ad for the NRA. "There's no reason, in my opinion, to have guns," Rosie pronounced. Sure. Not when you can afford a limousine to chauffeur you around and a home in a safe neighborhood with an expensive security system.

At the same time that Rosie O'Donnell was using Tom Selleck for verbal target practice, Hillary Clinton turned a White House Mother's Day event into an occasion to assail the gun lobby and to call for the passage of new gun control laws, "measures that we know will save lives."

Of course, this was less than three weeks after the horrific massacre at the Columbine High School in Littleton, Colorado, when the gun-bashing bandwagon was a pretty crowded vehicle. But there were a few things Hillary, like her fellow antigun crusaders, forgot to mention. For instance, that the killers, Dylan Klebold and Eric Harris, had already broken eighteen existing gun laws, so it's not clear why they wouldn't have been able to circumvent new ones. Or that two other recent school shooting sprees were stopped by gun-wielding civilians (assistant principal Joel Myrick in Pearl, Mississippi, in 1997 and restaurateur James Strand in Edinboro, Pennsylvania, in 1998) who disarmed and subdued the shooters before the police arrived. People fighting back—with guns! Those are the stories Hillary Clinton would never tell to a White House audience or on the Senate campaign trail.

Consider the tale of Josie Simms Cash, a thirtysomething mother of two working as a delivery woman for Palermo's Pizza in Rockville, Illinois. Josie had a queasy feeling when she pulled up to make her second-to-last delivery one night in 1997. It was the west side of town, a not-so-great neighborhood where Palermo's drivers had sometimes had their wallets swiped and their pies plundered. When Josie knocked on her customer's door and got no answer, the queasy feeling grew. As she turned to head back to her Honda Civic, four men emerged from an alley. Josie knew she'd been set up. One of the men, gun drawn, hissed at her to turn over her money. But when Josie lifted up her cardboard boxes, the hoodlum was in for a rough surprise—and I don't mean anchovies. "He saw I had a gun," Josie told me. "He said: 'Bitch, why you pull a gun on me?' I said, 'Why you pull one on me? I'm trying to work!'" Cursing under his breath, Josie's attacker fled. (Unfortunately, the story doesn't end there. When Josie conscientiously went to the police to report the incident, she was the one who ended up being handcuffed and carted off to jail: She had violated a state law making it a felony to carry a concealed weapon.)

In Hillary's world, the fight-back heroines are Sarah Brady and Carolyn McCarthy, who turned into antigun crusaders after their loved ones became victims of gun violence. I'd rather recognize Suzanne Gratia Hupp, whose parents were among the twenty-three people gunned down by George Hennard at Luby's Cafeteria in Killeen, Texas, in 1991. Hupp, a chiropractor, also channeled her grief into a political cause—except that her crusade was for a law allowing citizens to carry concealed weapons. The day of the tragedy, the thirty-one-year-old woman was in the café dining with her parents. When the shooting began, she reached into her purse for her .38-caliber special, only to realize that she had left it in her car: She was carrying the gun illegally and feared that she could lose her medical license if she got caught with it in the restaurant. "The handgun, which the government denied me, might have saved my parents' lives as well as those of the other innocent victims who lost their lives that day," Hupp said a few years later, announcing her campaign for the Texas state legislature. "It was then that I realized that someone needs to take a stand for average, law-abiding citizens."

Take back the night? I like the approach of Gina Cushon, a diminutive Memphis resident in her mid-forties, who shot and killed a "totally berserk" drunk who had broken through her screen door and lunged at her and her mother. (Like Josie, Gina found herself on the wrong side of the law, charged with handgun possession and, initially, second-degree murder.) Gina, a registered Democrat, later reflected: "People who say guns are bad are lucky enough never to have been in a situation where someone has kicked down your door and threatened the life of your son and your sixty-five-year-old mother."

Dorothy Cunningham and Marty Killinger would certainly agree. The seventysomething housemates were relaxing in their Moses Lake, Washington, home one crisp winter evening in early 1997 when they heard a knock on the door. A young man was asking if he could use their telephone. Before Dorothy could say yes, he and three of his friends had forced their way in. When she picked up the phone to dial 911, she realized that the line had been cut. But instead of meekly surrendering, Dorothy grabbed her Luger and aimed it at the men. The foursome howled with laughter, but their mirth quickly stopped when she fired four shots over their heads. "I told them to get out or I'd kill them," she told reporters afterward.

All four ran off and were later arrested for burglary and attempted rob-

bery. The talk show circuit clamored for Marty and Dorothy, whom the county sheriff dubbed "pistol-packing grandmas." When a CNN interviewer asked what they thought of the label, Dorothy declared, "I love it." Marty, grandmother of eight, chimed in: "I think it's great. My kids are thrilled to death at what we were able to do. We're both strong people. They just picked on the wrong old ladies."

Let's say it again: Owning a gun and learning to use it can save a woman's life. Most criminals target people they think are easy prey: unaware, unprepared, and—most important—unarmed. In a survey of two thousand convicted felons conducted by the National Institute of Justice, sixty percent said they worried more about armed victims than about being nailed by the police; eighty-five percent reported that "smart criminals" will try to find out if their prey is armed before making a move. Our culture wasn't always as squeamish about female self-defense. Our pioneer foremothers knew that if they heard the thunder of hooves when they weren't expecting company, it was time to reach for the family gun. An illustrated book called *Hands Off!* by Major William Fairburn, which sold for seventy-five cents in 1942, recommended serious, violent defensive moves—like throwing a punch in the face—against any man who threatens a woman.

What advice are women actually getting about staying safe in the elite, feminist world that Hillary symbolizes? Has feel-good gender politics overwhelmed the practical realities of self-protection?

To find out, I contacted two prestigious university campuses in the Washington, D.C., area and got all their literature on campus crime. Georgetown University's materials decry "gender violence" and discuss numerous activities to "raise awareness about violence and sexual assault," including a performance art piece and a Take Back the Night march for torch-bearing survivors to recount their victimization. There's a full-time sexual assault services coordinator, and a "point person for all students recording incidents of unwanted sexual advances." But not a word on how to fight back.

The Georgetown Sexual Assault Services brochure with the promising title "What You Can Do to Reduce Your Risk of Sexual Assault" tells you to

"trust your intuition," restrict your activities, "beware of selfish and aggressive comments or behavior" while socializing, and—oh yes—"make contributions to . . . the Women's Center" in your community. Instead of showing women how to thwart an attacker, *The Georgetown Guide to Surviving Sexual Assault* offers touchingly multicultural victim testimonials, with chapter headings like "I Am a Deaf or Hard-of-Hearing Survivor," "I Am a Black Survivor," "I am a Latina Survivor," "I am an Asian or Asian-American Survivor," "I am a Lesbian Survivor," and so forth. The authors implicitly impugn women's physical competence: "It's not your fault," they soothe. "Even physical resistance may not have prevented the assault." They also point out that while "it is not uncommon after a sexual assault to want to purchase a weapon," women really aren't up to the task. "Weapons can foster dependence on an external object for protection or can be taken away and used against you."

The University of Virginia, where I attended law school, doles out more of the same. The University's sexual assault education office, run out of the campus Women's Center, takes a rather broad view of male violence. Its list of abusive behaviors includes everything from "withholding sex or affection," "giving mixed signals," and "ignoring or minimizing feelings" to "rape with murder," and (my personal favorite) "kills/maims the family pet." To its credit, UVA discusses self-defense, but its view of self-defense is pretty broad as well: It encompasses "verbal resistance" (i.e., hurling invective), "positive self-talk," and "becoming aware of the facts about violence against women." Indeed, according to the brochure, you might already be a self-defense pro and not even know it: "Self defense is actually practiced by many women at many levels on a daily basis. We assert ourselves with individuals who verbally harass us . . . we write letters to protest images of violence against women in print or in films." Take that, you knife-wielding thug.

UVA's approach is not atypical. These days, women who want instruction in self-defense have to navigate a feminist minefield. Outfits like Rage, Ready!, Women Defending Ourselves, and F.I.S.T. (Feminists in Self-Defense Training) masquerade as self-defense trainers but mostly

traffic in "progressive" ideology and group therapy. They're selling self-defense through defenselessness.

Donna Chaiet, head of New York–based Prepare, proclaims that her program explores "links between feminist theory and the antigender violence movement." Each class begins and ends with students forming a circle and doing a "feelings check." Boxes of Kleenex are passed around as women share tearful stories of child abuse, date rape, and harassment. "Self-defense isn't about teaching violence," says Chaiet. "The idea is to empower yourself from the inside."

Lori Dobeus, head of the San Francisco–based Women's Safety Project, suggests "broadening the notion of self-defense": "[I]f you believe in pacifism, your response doesn't have to be physical at all . . . You may not want to answer violence with violence." Instead, she advocates "positive self-talk." While being raped, "you tell yourself, 'This is not my fault. I don't deserve this. This person is wrong.'" Braver souls may even want to voice such uplifting thoughts aloud: "You can look your rapist straight in the eye. While the rape is occurring, you can say, 'I don't consent to this.'" That'll show him.

The pacifist belief that by resorting to violence in self-defense we become morally indistinguishable from our attackers pervades the antigun movement and provides much of its philosophical base. The Reverend Allen Brockway condemns armed resistance in the magazine of the Board of Church and Society of the United Methodist Church. Reverend Brockway rejects the traditional doctrine that it's not only lawful but moral to use deadly force to repel robbers, rapists, or other felons whose acts threaten great bodily harm, maiming, or death. (Indeed, the maxim "a man's home is his castle" first came up in early English cases that upheld the use of deadly force against burglars and arsonists.) Rhetorically posing the question "Is the Robber My Brother?" he answers, "Yes." True, he concedes, a burglary victim or a woman accosted by a rapist "is [not] likely to consider the violator to be a neighbor whose safety is of immediate concern." However, "criminals are members of the larger community no less than are others. As such they are our neighbors or, as Jesus put it, our brothers . . . [Though violent criminals act wrongfully,] it is equally wrong for the victim to kill, save in those extremely rare circumstances when the unambiguous alternative is one own's death."

While such an extreme pacifist interpretation of Christian brotherhood has never been accepted by the vast majority of established churches, Reverend Brockway is certainly entitled to his beliefs. However, these aren't just his personal views—it would be interesting to ask Hillary Clinton if she agrees with them!—but attitudes that have a lot of influence in the antigun movement. One of this country's foremost antigun groups, the Coalition Against Gun Violence, formerly the National Coalition to Ban Handguns, operates under the aegis of Reverend Brockway's Board of Church and Society of the United Methodist Church and has its national office in the Methodist Board's Washington building. The Board was the NCBH's official fiscal agent until 1976, when gun rights groups' complaints to the Internal Revenue Service threatened the church's tax exemption.

You'd think the feminists would be pretty upset when a clergyman solemnly advises women that it's their Christian duty to submit to rape rather than imperil the life of their "brother" the rapist. You'd think they'd be yelling about patriarchal religions abusing women (and on this occasion they would have a point). Well, think again: Feminists buy these arguments lock, stock, and barrel. Betty Friedan has told *Health* magazine that "lethal violence even in self-defense only engenders more lethal violence" and denounced the trend of women buying guns as "a horrifying, obscene perversion of feminism." Many feminists believe that violence is "male" and that women who choose to defend themselves—especially with guns, those phallocentric tools of evil—are being co-opted by our male-driven, testosterone-soaked culture of violence. So until we achieve the feminist utopia in which sexism, ageism, ableism, and all the other "oppressions" have vanished and all conflicts are somehow resolved peacefully, women will have to cringe in submission and think positive thoughts. Some feminism.

The case against women owning guns would collapse if it weren't for

some powerful myths that are repeated shamelessly by gun-control advocates and lazy reporters. Many of them have been used by Hillary and her
friends over the years. Let's look at some of them and the faulty research
that underlies them:

*MYTH No. 1: Resisting a criminal with a gun is more dangerous than
giving him what he wants or trying to reason with him.*

FACT: According to the latest data from the U.S. Department of Justice's National Crime Victimization Surveys, one in four victims who
resists with a gun sustains an injury—slightly below the injury rate for all
victims of violent crime and much lower than the injury rate for those who
attempt to defend themselves without a weapon (fifty percent). In his
1991 book *Point Blank*, criminologist Gary Kleck of Florida State University gives a more detailed breakdown of statistics from national studies and
provides data on the rates of injury to victims of robbery and assault.
Here's who got hurt:

12 to 17 percent of victims who resisted with a gun;

26 percent of victims who submitted;

40 to 49 percent of those who screamed;

25 to 30 percent of those who tried to reason with the attacker;

25 to 35 percent of those who resisted passively or sought to escape;

29 to 40 percent of those resisting with a knife;

22 to 25 percent of those using some other weapon;

51 percent of those resisting bare-handed.

MYTH No. 2: Guns are not effective or practical for self-defense.

Poppycock, says Professor Kleck, who has devoted his career to
researching the effects of an armed citizenry on criminal behavior—and
who embarked on this research seeking to show that guns in private hands
were dangerous. Far from being a right-wing dittohead, Kleck is a lifelong

liberal Democrat, a card-carrying member of the ACLU and Amnesty International who has run afoul of the National Rifle Association for advocating moderate gun-control measures like background checks for retail gun purchases.

Kleck has conducted what is widely regarded as the most comprehensive, ambitious, and methodologically sound study of the protective benefits of firearms in America. His dramatic findings, summarized in the 1997 book *Targeting Guns: Firearms and Their Control*, reveal that guns are successfully used in self-defense 2.5 million times per year. That's five lives protected every minute—or, to put it another way, seventy-five lives protected for every life lost to a gun. And the really good news is that the vast majority of these incidents did not involve pulling the trigger: brandishing a weapon was enough to cause the perpetrator to flee. Defensive gun use not only protects countless lives, it prevents injuries and psychological trauma, averts property damage, and saves on medical costs incurred when victims are maimed or injured.

Consider the experience of the state of Florida. In May 1987, Governor Bob Martinez signed a bill implemented in October of that year, drastically curtailing restrictions on civilian-owned weapons. The state's four hundred local gun control laws were repealed. Another provision liberalized restrictions on carrying concealed weapons. Gun-control partisans shrieked that there would be blood in the streets. The *Daytona Beach Evening News* predicted that issuing a million-plus permits would "turn Florida into the Wild West." The gun-control lobby gave dire scenarios of hot-tempered gun owners mowing each other down over trivial disputes.

What actually happened? Homicide drastically decreased in Florida. John Lott, professor of criminology at the University of Chicago, in a comprehensive study of Florida's experiment in lifting gun controls found that out of the nearly 444,000 Floridians who filed concealed carry licenses from 1987 to 1997, a mere eighty-four had their permits revoked for handgun-related felonies. The majority weren't violent assaults but for comparatively minor offenses, such as carrying a gun—perhaps inadvertently—into official gun-free zones like courtrooms or airports. As of 1992, not a single unlawful killing had been committed by any Floridian licensed to carry. The large-scale acquisition of handguns by ordinary citizens in Florida had served only to deter criminal attacks. In Orlando over the eight years since the ordinance was passed, aggravated assault and burglary dropped twenty-five percent while rape plummeted an astounding ninety percent.

Is Florida an anomaly? Hardly. Over the past decade or so thirty-one states have enacted concealed-carry laws whereby applicants can carry a concealed handgun if they can prove they are law-abiding, responsible adults with firearms training. The number of licensees varies from state to state but generally runs from one percent to ten percent of the eligible population. A "guesstimate" based on figures available from seven of these states suggests that at least two million concealed-carry weapon licenses have been issued among these states.

In a monumental scholarly review, Lott tracked the experience of three thousand counties that adopted legislation allowing citizens to carry concealed weapons in the 1980s and 1990s. The results are summed up in the title of his provocative 1998 book: *More Guns, Less Crime*. In the years following the passage of these laws, murder rates dropped 8.5 percent, rapes dropped five percent, aggravated assaults seven percent, and armed robberies two percent. Lott found no increase in accidental deaths in those counties. Had similar right-to-carry laws been adopted across the country in 1992, he calculated, approximately 1,570 murders, 4,177 rapes, and over sixty thousand aggravated assaults a year could have been prevented.

According to criminologist Don Kates, fewer than two percent of handguns and well under one percent of all guns are ever involved in even a single violent crime. Criminal gun violence is concentrated within a very small subset of gun owners, most commonly people who buy guns from friends or get them by theft. Thus, gun regulation will never control gun violence unless it targets these "nonretail" transactions. How do you pass a law to control that?

Common sense, history, and the best scholarly research tell us that more guns owned by law-abiding Americans equals less crime. Yes, it is really that simple. Criminals are cowards with weapons. They rob because they know few will resist. They rape because they know they can easily overpower their victims. Take away their advantage, ratchet up their risk, and suddenly criminality isn't quite so attractive a vocation anymore. Lawful gun ownership makes everyone safer. In a community where citizens take the responsibility to defend themselves and their families, nongun owners benefit, too: They get to "free-ride" off the message being given to criminals that there is nothing in this town worth risking your life for. Here's another interesting fact that shows that guns do deter crime: American crooks, unlike crooks in other countries, tend to steer away from "hot" burglaries—burglaries committed when the resident is at home. Surveys of incarcerated felons show that this is due not to shyness or good manners, but to fear that the owner may be armed. In Canada and Britain, where gun control is strict, such burglaries are far more common.

MYTH No. 3: If you have a gun in the home, you are far more likely to die from a gun accident or kill someone you know than to use the gun in self-defense.

Some of the worst statistical demagoguery on the gun issue has to do with the understandably wrenching subject of child fatalities. Handgun Control, Inc., likes to use an advertisement picturing a dimpled toddler capering about with a pistol. In her Mother's Day speech at the White House in 1999, Hillary declared that "every day in America we lose thirteen precious children to gun-related violence." What she didn't mention is that a lot of these "precious children" are not adorable tots but teenage gang members shooting each other. In 1986, urging Congress to adopt stringent antigun measures, Dr. Joseph Greensher of the American Academy of Pediatrics asserted that one child under fifteen is killed in a firearms accident every day (a claim also repeated by Sarah Brady). In fact, this overstated the real figure by about fifty percent. At the time, the latest available figures from the National Safety Council, for 1983, showed not 366 gun-accident deaths in that age group but 243. For 1986, the figure was 234. It's also worth remembering that guns cause a mere fraction of the nearly ten thousand accidental child deaths that occur every year.

Despite all the panic-mongering, the risks of a fatal gun accident in the home are fairly remote. According to the National Center for Health Statistics, all firearm accidents (many of them related to hunting) kill about twelve hundred Americans annually. A tragedy, to be sure—but one dwarfed by accidental poisoning, which kills about nine thousand, and accidental drowning, responsible for nearly four thousand deaths every year. Drowning in swimming pools is one of the leading causes of accidental fatalities among young children. So, shall we ban swimming pools? Gun-control advocates will scoff that you can't compare handguns and swimming pools. And maybe they're right. A swimming pool is a nice thing to have, but it won't save you from being robbed, raped, or murdered.

It's also important to look at the context in which these rare gun accidents occur. Studies by Kleck and other researchers show that people whose recklessness causes accidental gun deaths (either directly or by allowing guns to fall into the hands of children) are not, by and large, respectable average citizens. Rather, they disproportionately tend to be involved in other accidents, violent crime, and heavy drinking. In other words, if you are a responsible, safety-conscious person and you get a gun, it's not going to suddenly transform your home into a dangerous place.

Nearly every claim about the calamitous consequences of guns in households can be traced to one Dr. Arthur Kellerman, an emergency room physician and passionate antigun crusader. His most influential contribution to the gun debate was a 1986 article, published in *The New England Journal of Medicine*, in which he contended that a gun owner is forty-three times more likely to kill a family member than to kill an intruder. Arguably one of the most irresponsible and misleading studies ever to emerge from the academy, the Kellerman article has been seized upon by advocacy scholars and antigun lobbyists as proof that handguns are an imminent public-health hazard and that the protective function of handguns is an illusion.

What's wrong with Dr. Kellerman's study? First of all, you don't need a Ph.D. in statistics to consider his definition of the "protective" uses of firearms a wee bit narrow. In his eyes, the only defensive gun episodes that count are ones in which the victim shot *and killed* an assailant. But, as Gary Kleck has demonstrated, ninety-eight percent of the time when a gun is used successfully in self-defense it is not fired. It is enough for the victim to display the weapon or even simply to mention that he or she is armed. This is especially true for female victims, who are usually set upon by unarmed assailants. (Bureau of Justice Statistics reports show that only six percent of rapes, for instance, involve a gun-wielding perpetrator.) Women are therefore often able to deter violence without ever firing a single shot.

If Dr. Kellerman's definition of successful self-defense is too narrow, his definition of deaths caused by "handguns in the home" is much too broad. Among victims of fatal "gun accidents," the doctor counted not only men who were shot and killed by battered wives or girlfriends acting in self-defense, but, incredibly, a gun owner's family members who were cut down by an intruder's weapon. As Professor Lott has shown, family members actually killed by the homeowner's gun account for no more than four percent of the gun deaths cited in Dr. Kellerman's study.

In fact, under a double-barreled assault from his peers, the good doctor himself abandoned his ludicrous claim. After doing some further calculations, Dr. Kellerman says he has hit on the real number: guns in the home are 2.7 times more likely to kill a household member than an intruder, not forty-three times. (Oops! I hope Doc is more careful when he does his rounds in the ER.) Yet the 2.7 figure is just as bogus. It still fails to take into account all defensive uses of guns except ones in which the weapon is fired and the criminal is killed. Yet the myth that guns in the home are a danger to the owner is touted by the pillars of the medical establishment: the Centers for Disease Control, the American Medical Association, Physicians for Social Responsibility. For the public-health mavens, political expediency matters more than unbiased scientific inquiry. Dr. Mark Rosenberg, head of the CDC's National Center for Injury Prevention and Control, has openly told *Rolling Stone* magazine that he "envision[ed] a long-term campaign . . . to convince Americans that guns are, first and foremost, a public-health menace." The web site of Physicians for Social Responsibility, citing the Kellerman study, exhorts all doctors to "educate people that a gun does not offer protection, and actually puts them at greater risk of injury or death."

We can only guess at how many women have been dissuaded from even thinking about a gun because they have been misled into believing that it's likely to leave their child dead or permanently disabled.

MYTH No. 4: Guns in the home are likely to cause arguments between friends and relatives to escalate into homicide, since most killings are the result of such arguments and not of criminal attacks.

FACT: The culprit here is a set of FBI data on homicide between acquaintances and family members whose definition of "friends" is overbroad and misleading. Reading over the FBI's numbers, you're likely to come away with the impression that handgun owners risk turning their homes into the O.K. Corral, as minor disagreements become deadly shoot-outs. And antigun groups exploit this perception. "Most homicides do not derive from criminal or premeditated attacks," asserts the Washington, D.C.–based Violence Policy Center in its antigun handbook *Female Persuasion*, citing the ubiquitous Dr. Kellerman. "They are often the result of arguments and usually occur between people who know one another and are often related to one another. They turn deadly because of ready access to a firearm."

I guess it goes something like this: See Jane scratch new minivan. See Jane tell husband, Dick. See Dick lose it. See Dick shoot Jane.

When most of us think friends and family, the mental images we conjure up are like those sepia-toned commercials for discount phone rates: our chatty college roommate, our kindly grandmother, the gravelly voice of dear old Dad crackling over the wire on our birthday. Better not get a gun or else we might explode in a murderous frenzy and it's bye-bye Grandma. The problem is "people who know one another" often refers to situations far removed from those Norman Rockwell images, such as shoot-outs between rival drug dealers or gang members. And even family murders include cases in which wives shoot their husbands after years of abuse.

MYTH No. 5: *It is dangerous for a woman to carry a gun, since the gun is likely to be taken away by an assailant and used against her.*

FACT: This sexist, retrograde claptrap may be the most potent myth of all. Not a scintilla of statistical evidence supports the contention that a woman's armed self-defense usually fails or results in her disarmament. According to sixteen years' worth of data from the National Crime Victimization Survey, in no more than one percent of defensive gun use is a gun taken away by a criminal. Far more often, the armed victim emerges unscathed. Women who resist violent attack with a gun are two and a half times more likely than their unarmed sisters to escape serious injury, the survey's data showed. Men, it should be noted, also benefit from carrying a firearm, though not as dramatically as women.

You won't hear this from the likes of Bill Ritter, a Colorado district attorney who testified against liberalizing that state's concealed-carry laws: "A person who uses a handgun to protect himself is three times as likely to be the victim and to be injured than a person who doesn't." (As we already know—see Myth No. 1—this assertion is disputed by federal statistics.) Or from Gena Holden, executive vice president of the National Criminal Justice Association, who intones that "for the average citizen, being armed is dangerous."

The media have played a major role in perpetuating gun myths. Mainstream reporters are stuck in a time warp, unable to wean themselves from their aging Rolodexes and clinging to shocking claims that have been discredited—even, as in Dr. Kellerman's case, retracted by the original authors. The story of an epidemic of inadvertent domestic mayhem is too sexy to be abandoned. "Statistics show guns in the home kill family and friends forty-three times more often than burglars," reported ABC's *Prime Time Live* in April 1997, the reporter's creamy brow furrowing in concern. In a 1996 article, ominously titled "Guns Pose One of the Biggest Threats to Families," Gannett News Service warned that "one recent study showed that the gun is forty-three times more likely to injure you or a family member than an intruder." In the September 1993 issue of *Esquire*, writer John Berendt berated the NRA for "paving the way for ladies' guns, neglecting to mention that . . . a gun kept in the home is forty-three times more likely to kill a friend or family member."

Meanwhile, the scholarship and the astonishing findings of respected researchers like Gary Kleck, John Lott, and Don Kates go virtually unmentioned in all the oceans of ink and jillions of pixels devoted to the subject of guns and crime in America.

Why do reporters keep peddling quackeries and suppressing facts? Why do they play up relatively isolated tragedies like school shootings while giving little attention to the thousands of incidents every year when people save themselves, their families, or a bystander with the help of a gun? Consider eighty-five-year-old Alberta Nickles. In January 1997, while inside her Muskegon, Michigan, home, an ex-con out on bail awaiting trial broke in, ransacked it, and threatened to rape her. She went to the closet, took out her handgun, and shot him dead. Nickles's story had pulse-pounding drama, a courageous victim, and a surprising outcome. But the incident was barely noted by the media. The heroism of Joel Myrick and James Strand, the armed civilians who were able to stop school-shooting rampages, went virtually unmentioned in the coverage of those incidents. Even the rare stories that acknowledged Myrick's and Strand's role usually left out the fact that they used firearms, saying instead that they "persuaded" the shooters to surrender. Maybe by using the power of positive thinking?

Is there a vast left-wing conspiracy determined to screen out stories that paint gun ownership in a positive light? Unlikely. Newsrooms are too frantic to be that calculating and the reporters I know are too hungry for gritty human-interest stories to reject them on ideological grounds. But an unconscious bias, both political and cultural, is surely at work. The people who filter the news—network TV producers and correspondents, editors and writers at major newspapers and magazines—are mostly people who live in Hillary's world. They are overwhelmingly liberal in their political allegiance (eighty-nine percent of them voted for Bill Clinton both in 1992 and in 1996). They tend to live in metropolitan areas; relatively few come from families that had a gun in the home or have close friends who own guns. For the most part, these journalists are quite simply mystified by the phenomenon of gun ownership, just as they are mystified by Monster Truck competitions, home schooling, weekly Bible studies, and professional bowling. For them, these cultural oddities are simply off the radar screen—until, of course, a gun tragedy occurs.

Moreover, because most media hotshots have so little experience with guns, they treat gun owners and the NRA as interchangeable. In fact, only ten percent of all gun owners are NRA members. (Bias commingled with ignorance results in distorted reporting. Once, as I sat in a TV studio waiting to go on the air, I watched the anchor interview a policeman who favored the Supreme Court's decision striking down part of the Brady Bill. As the officer coolly deflected her hostile questions, the exasperated anchor finally blurted out, "Sir, are you a member of the NRA?" "No," responded the bemused guest, "and I never have been." Throwing the rules of office diplomacy to the winds, I recounted the incident to the producer and inquired: "What would happen to me if I asked a liberal guest who supported abortion whether she was a member of Planned Parenthood or NOW?" Silence. The producer, to his credit, conceded the point and agreed that the exchange was unfair and that it's the sort of thing that fans public suspicions about liberal bias in the media.

Most gun owners are neither fanatics nor crazed survivalists crawling around in fatigues with greasepaint on their faces. They are perfectly ordinary people, generally well-educated and living in middle- to upper-income households. Surveys show that as a group, they are no more psychologically deviant, racist, sexist, or violence-prone than nonowners.

Yet the stereotypes persist. "[T]he typical private weapon owner is often depicted as a virtual psychopath—unstable, violent, dangerous," comments James D. Wright in the 1983 book *Under the Gun: Weapons, Crime and Violence in the United States.*

Okay, part of the blame has to be laid at the feet of the NRA. While much of the criticism of that organization is shrill and reflexive, some is justified. The NRA's opposition to seemingly reasonable gun regulations scares a lot of people, and especially women. Trigger locks and limits on the number of guns people can buy at one time make intuitive sense. A 1990 *Time* magazine survey found that eighty-seven percent of gun owners supported a waiting period and background check for handgun buyers, and nearly three out of four supported registration for all handguns and semi-automatic weapons—all of which are at odds with the NRA's position. When you hear that the NRA opposes beefing up the ridiculously easy licensing procedure for federal gun dealers, most people understandably say: Wait a minute, that's not for me.

As with the abortion-rights movement, whose infatuation with partial-birth abortion has alienated many of its former champions, the NRA's intransigence on gun-control issues can leave even supporters scratching their heads. But as Don Kates points out, this not-one-inch position needs to be viewed in the context of the equally shrill extremism of the antigun zealots (which is habitually overlooked by the media). "It is this discourse," he writes, "which convinces gun owners that gun control is not a legitimate social imperative aimed at criminals, but an expression of moral or ethical hatred directed at them."

The good news is: Women are finally beginning to see through the facile antigun propaganda and to think for themselves about self-defense. Women are among the fastest-growing segments of the gun-buying public. In 1997, between twelve and fifteen million women owned a gun for self-defense. Those numbers are on the rise, particularly in states that have liberalized their concealed-weapons laws. In Connecticut, the number of women holding state gun permits leapt by forty-six percent between 1992 and 1996—from 10,625 to 15,516. Firearms instruction courses nationwide are booming with women enrollees. Even designer gun accessories for women are flying off the shelves—hideaway purses, fancy leather thigh holsters, and pastel carrying cases, to name just a few.

Yet the Hillary school of feminism persists in its strident, knee-jerk opposition to gun ownership. When the NRA unveiled its "Refuse to Be a Victim" campaign aimed at recruiting women members, the feminists were driven into a froth. "A cynical effort . . . to build political power and make money by playing to the fears of women," declared law professor Susan Estrich in a *USA Today* column. "The NRA wants more members; the manufacturers want new buyers . . . and more women may end up dead." Even as feminist protestors shouted down NRA executive director Tanya Metaksa while she was on tour promoting her book *Safe, Not Sorry*, the National Organization of Women passed a resolution that "Guns are killing us, not protecting us." Women's magazines, always a reliable repository for squishy junk science, jumped happily into the fray. "It's not the firearms in the street you most have to fear," honked Joy Horowitz in *Harper's Bazaar*. "The one at home is much more likely to kill you or your child." A bit of sisterly advice, Joy: Do your homework, or stick to tips about how not to chip that pedicure.

To the feminists, female gun owners are not gutsy role models but pitiable dupes of NRA puppeteers. Marlene Wenograd, a "gun control specialist" for the League of Women Voters, wrings her hands over the new line of dainty ladies' handguns: It's "absolutely dreadful," part of a "national push" to corrupt innocent females. And what about target-shooting, now one of the fastest-growing sports in Beverly Hills? "A backdoor way of getting women into guns," ominously warns Susan Glick of the Violence Policy Center. Sponsors of shooting competitions for women are not hailed for breaking down traditional stereotypes but met with scorn and indignation. If all proceeds are donated to charities such as battered women's shelters, that makes it even more insidious: "The idea is to link it to a charity, so women will be more drawn to it," Glick laments.

A particularly revealing antigun diatribe appeared in the May/June 1994 *Ms.*, a special issue devoted to the evils of America's gun culture. Its centerpiece was a long, fervid article by Anne Jones titled "Living with Guns, Playing with Fire." Jones was most incensed that pro-gun forces had stolen the feminists' empowerment rhetoric and were talking about firearms ownership as a woman's choice.

Jones admitted that she had once been a gun owner herself and that it had come in handy when she was investigating a murder for a potential book. But she'd put her piece away. "It wasn't a gun I needed," Jones wrote. "It was courage." (How about courage *and* a gun!)

I'm not saying that every woman should go out and buy one of those sherbet-hued pistols advertised in *Women & Guns* magazine. (Though if they had one in lime green . . .) Some women—like some men—will always be uncomfortable around firearms and will never feel sufficiently confident to use one effectively. If you have a gun and fumble around with it, that is dangerous. A woman may also have deeply pacifist convictions like those of Reverend Brockway—that it's better to be raped, hurt, or even killed than to take the life of a fellow human being, no matter how vile.

I strongly believe that every woman who is concerned about personal safety should at least learn the real facts about gun use for self-defense or general security purposes. Protecting oneself is a health and safety issue—and women should be encouraged to take it as seriously as monthly breast self-exams. Women should familiarize themselves with the gun laws in their states. A majority of the states will issue concealed-carry permits to people who pass a background check and who can certify that they passed the required safety course. Women deserve to have good information on the subject so they can make their decisions about self-defense on the basis of facts, not hype. Pro-gun forces and gun manufacturers will sometimes act irresponsibly or sound extreme in their zeal to safeguard the right to bear arms. But to demonize all those who believe in gun rights as part of the "culture of violence"—the way Hillary Clinton does—is to take away an important choice that can give women true independence and empowerment, the very things modern women (and Hillary) are suppose to treasure.

Do I wish we lived in a world in which no one needed a gun? Sure I do.

Is that likely to happen anytime soon? No. As long as human nature is what it is, crime will be with us, and the police cannot be there for us twenty-four hours a day. It's a reality that Hillary and her sisters may want to wish away, just as they would wish away the fact that the needs of our families sometimes conflict with the demands of our careers. But wishing will not make it so. Sometimes, whether it's balancing work and family or ensuring our physical safety, we have to make difficult decisions, such as accepting the awesome responsibility that comes with owning a deadly weapon. As long as many of us need to protect ourselves, no one should deny us that basic right—or try to frighten us out of exercising it.

Breaking out of the Hillary Trap means dealing with the world as it is, and in that real world a lot of us sisters would rather be armed and deadly than nice and defenseless. Lady, get your gun!

5.

The
Sex Trap

When people remember Hillary Clinton's time as First Lady, it won't be for her failed efforts at health care reform or her tortured explanation of her $100,000 cattle futures bonanza. They'll remember Hillary as the blindly loyal wife of a philandering husband. They'll recall her defiant defense of her husband on the *Today Show*, after the allegations of his relationship with Monica Lewinsky first surfaced. The charges against her husband were politically motivated, she said—the work of a "vast right-wing conspiracy." Later, after the humiliating disclosure that her husband had left behind what was politely termed "DNA material" on Monica's blue dress, Hillary retreated into what commentators called a "dignified silence."

"They are going to work this out," predicted First Brother Roger Clinton on CNN's *Larry King Live*. "I think Hillary's going to be the doggoned one to come to the forefront and save the day." And so she did, as she had so many times before during the marriage. She not only stood by her husband, she stood up to his detractors and helped coordinate his legal defense. The picture the nation saw was of a wronged wife—betrayed by her husband, but determined to rescue their political partnership by warding off and discrediting his critics. Their marriage was under assault and she wouldn't give up the fight no matter what—she wouldn't give them the satisfaction.

People remarked on how "together" she seemed during the early days of the Monica scandal. But why shouldn't she have been? After all, Hillary had the role of aggrieved but devoted wife down pat. Before Monica, there had been Gennifer. And before Gennifer, who knows how many others? Monica testified that Bill told her it was "hundreds"; Clinton biographers agree that the numbers were, at the very least, well into the double digits. And all the while, Hillary played her part.

We have already seen how the Hillary Trap keeps women from achieving true independence in the public world: in politics, education, the workplace, and protection from crime. But does Hillary, who was once hailed as half of the only truly egalitarian First Couple in American history, serve as a good model for modern women who seek empowerment in their personal lives? No. Once again, she offers women a false promise of equality and self-reliance that turns into a reality of a new dependence, sometimes more humiliating than the old kind.

Hillary, supposedly the savvy feminist, could not have contrived to paint a more desolate portrait of the state of modern womanhood. We'll never know for sure what she said to her husband in private during those excruciating weeks of Monicagate. But we know the message she sent us: Women of America, accept your victimhood. You're trapped. Whatever your accomplishments in life, you're bound to the man who brought you to the dance. Never mind shattered trust, broken vows, serial cheating, a lifetime of explanations and denials. Your fate is to accommodate and accept—and gracefully, please! That was the most poignant part of Hillary's ordeal: The way the country rallied around her as she played the role of noble victim. As late as November 1999, focus groups conducted by *ABC News* about Hillary's U.S. Senate bid revealed just how much the public admired the way Hillary had carried herself. Participants used words like "nervy" and "dignified" to describe her performance. For all the applause for women's advancement, America still loves a victim, especially when she bears it stoically.

How ironic that Hillary should have reached the height of her popularity at the nadir of her marriage. She assumed the most traditional and demeaning role assigned to women—and predictably, the public responded with sympathy. *How does she go on? So selfless! She's doing it all for Chelsea. She looks so tough on the outside, but deep down her heart must be breaking.* These were the kinds of comments people used to make about women in the fifties and sixties when wives didn't have any option but to stay with their dirty rotten scoundrel husbands. America seemed more comfortable with Hillary caught in her Sex Trap than with Hillary, the independent woman.

"He couldn't protect me, so he lied," sighed Hillary in her notorious 1999 *Talk* magazine interview about Bill's trysts with White House intern Monica Lewinsky. In the same interview, she hinted that her husband's lifelong compulsive philandering was related to his being "scarred by abuse" as a four-year-old. Apparently his mother and his grandmother had quarreled and vied for his affection. Who could say otherwise? Both women were dead and couldn't give their side of the story. Media moderates like ABC's Cokie Roberts called Hillary on this armchair justification of her husband's disgusting behavior, and she "clarified." But the message was sent. Don't blame the cheater—he's a victim, too. Individual responsibility was irrelevant. The interview encapsulated Hillary's no-fault worldview perfectly.

Hillary's fallback was to maintain that her relationship with her husband was a private matter. In her *Talk* interview, she lamented how sad it was that in Washington, "we sort of strip away everybody's sense of dignity, of privacy." But would Hillary have allowed "privacy" to shield a Republican who admitted getting oral sex from a young, vulnerable intern in a government office? No, she would have been leading candlelight vigils against workplace harassment! Besides, Hillary, like many feminists, has deplored the tendency to see spousal abuse as a "private" problem. Yet extramarital affairs are often seen as a form of psychological abuse in domestic violence literature, harming not only the spouse but the children, too.

Infidelity on the Clintonian scale should be every woman's concern. Hillary had a chance in her bully pulpit to do more for American women than "female-friendly" government programs ever could. She could have drawn a line in the sand: "Bill, you've humiliated me for the last time." Instead, Hillary's example lures women into believing that willful blindness is okay. Message to wives: What you pretend you don't know won't hurt you.

You would think that by the final years of the twentieth century, our society's view of philandering husbands and wronged wives would have evolved—playing around was no longer considered a tacit male prerogative. Women, with their new financial independence and assertiveness, had more freedom to leave degrading marriages devoid of loyalty, trust, or respect. But quite a few stayed put.

So why do women—even privileged, savvy women like Hillary—continue to tolerate serial betrayal? Of course, as my married friends point out, forgiveness is part of any successful marriage. Walking out might not always be the best response to infidelity—especially when small children are involved. But there's a big difference between forgiving a "slip" that is followed by genuine contrition and firm resolve not to transgress again and habitually turning a blind eye to unrepentant, chronic philandering. Some wives stay with unfaithful husbands out of fear and financial dependence. Others have more opportunistic motives—they don't want to relinquish the social status and power in the community their marriage provides. Others worry about breaking up the family. Hillary's reasoning probably involved a combination of all three.

There's something else going on here, too. Our culture's views of sex and marriage have changed. The barriers to women's equality have been swept away, but so have many of the norms that used to restrain bad behavior. In pre-1960s America—in contrast to supposedly more sophisticated cultures—men who had extramarital affairs were seen as dishonorable, even if their faults were treated with more indulgence than female infidelity (at least as long as the straying husband was discreet). In the new, anything-goes world that Hillary's generation helped create, flings on the side are no big deal and carry no penalty. Some feminists, as we'll see, have even tried to convince women that empowerment lies not in insisting on fidelity from their husbands, but in equal-opportunity self-indulgence. Using "judgmental" words like "immorality" came to be seen as old-fashioned, unhip, and unliberated.

Old-fashioned, yes, but is this looser view of commitment and sexual fidelity making women stronger, happier, more independent? In Hillary's case, the answer is clearly no. "Here's a woman who was the primary breadwinner for her family, Yale Law School educated, by some accounts certifiably brilliant," columnist Robyn Blumner noted in bewilderment during the Monica follies. "[Y]et she remains her husband's most vehement supporter while the country snickers into its sleeve over Bill's sexual 'peccadillos.'"

Many commentators, including Hillary Clinton's biographer Gail Sheehy, have dubbed Hillary her husband's "enabler." I'm not trained to make a psychological diagnosis, but whatever you call this behavior, it's a big step backward for women. To put it simply, Hillary has succeeded in making the country safer for infidelity. By letting Bill get away with it time after cheating time, Hillary shows millions of young women across the country that it's okay, that some things are more important than trust and honesty. Whatever Hillary may personally think of adultery, her unflagging allegiance to our commander in cheat put her squarely in the role of the doormat wife of the olden days, who knows of her husband's affairs but chooses to look the other way. Suddenly, adultery with girls scarcely out of their teens, and lying about it under oath, was just another lifestyle choice. I wish I had a dollar for every time I heard a pundit or one of my male friends say, *"Hell, who wouldn't lie about having an affair under oath?"* The same folks branded me "narrow-minded" and "judgmental" when I said Congress should toss him out of office for his behavior and that Hillary should toss him in the street. *Wait a second,* I thought, *I'm on her side in this one!*

Despite the blandishments of feminists and women's magazines who argue that adultery can be a fortifying tonic for women—*Try it, you'll like it!*—most women value strong and stable families far more than the "right" to get away with sleazy sex on an equal footing with men. Surely, equal opportunity was about having a fair shot at an education and a job, not an equal right to act like a ball of slime. Feminism wasn't supposed to be about making cheating safe for married men (or women). Yes, sometimes married men and women will fall in love outside their marriages then separate, divorce, and remarry. But a lot of what goes on out there today is a kind of "sport-adultery." Now that women have arrived on the doorstep of equality, it's more important than ever that we try not to fall into the trap of tolerating, justifying, and yes, enabling promiscuous behavior by our husbands, brothers, sons, fathers, or even our girlfriends—or of engaging in such behavior ourselves.

My own parents' marriage was fraught with difficulties—my father's alcoholism (which he has bravely struggled with his entire life), money pressures, and the frustration and arguing that these problems spawned. Neither of my parents were blameless, but I believe with great certainty that my mother was always faithful. It would never have occurred to her to cheat, and in that sense she lived up to the values of the Depression and World War II generation.

"You can maybe forgive one mistake, one dalliance," she once told me over hot cocoa during my college break, "but don't *ever* let anyone—including your husband—take away your self-respect by forgiving too much, too often." We didn't talk all that often about what it was that held their marriage together, but in looking back one thing was clear: My father respected my mother because she didn't tolerate b.s. from anyone—especially the man that enjoyed her cooking, cleaning, and child-rearing. Bottom line: My mother, at five feet tall and with only a high school degree, would rather have worked two jobs and move into an apartment than live with chronic infidelity. She stood her ground and taught me to, also. In my eyes, that makes her a stronger woman and a better feminist than the fifty-two-year-old Hillary Clinton of today, who chose not to use her prestigious law degree when it could have helped her most—to support herself without Bill.

At some point, women who tolerate repeated infidelity just seem stupid. Wait, you say, Hillary is no dumb blonde. She was well-educated, at all the right schools! Well, her resume didn't rescue her from the Sex Trap. She reduced herself to rationalizing her husband's lecherous behavior in *Talk* magazine. That mind-boggling performance compelled even liberal *Washington Post* columnist Richard Cohen to comment that "we can only conclude that her husband strayed partially because he craved intellectual companionship." It all started to look like the battered wife syndrome—a woman wronged repeatedly and harshly not only keeps coming back for more, she expresses the belief that by staying with her abuser she can help him get better. Think back to Hillary's very first appearance on national television in 1992, when she sat demurely by Bill's side holding his hand for the *60 Minutes* cameras to help him quash the Gennifer Flowers revelations. You just have to cringe. That was the voice of America's new strong, highly educated woman?

Hillary's role in managing "bimbo eruptions" was nothing new. As Joyce Milton writes in *The First Partner*, "For several years—probably since 1989, when she decided to back Bill's run for president—Hillary made a deliberate decision to adopt the posture of a defense lawyer." She was well aware that her husband cheated, but reflexively sided with him, displacing her anger at Bill's betrayal of her onto the women. How satisfying to vent her rage at women who romped with Bill by demonizing them as lying tramps. Milton also reports that "campaign aides who happened to overhear her and Bill discussing the 'bitches' who were making his life miserable were shocked by the level of vitriol. Hillary had almost worked herself around to believing that Bill was the sexual harassment victim, beset by predatory females."

What's really going on here? Misty-eyed Clinton allies rhapsodize that their love is real, their respect mutual. Others take the more cynical view that Hillary has stayed in the marriage out of pure self-interest—for the power and the status. In other words, she's a traditional wife who ignores her husband's catting around because he's a good provider. Bill's more than a paycheck—he's her ticket to political power. Either way, Hillary is no model for modern womanhood. She's either a dupe who loves her man so much she's willing to sacrifice all dignity for his sake, or a Machiavellian who craves power so much she'll do anything to keep it.

Other Clinton watchers speculate that the pair made some kind of "deal" years ago. Early on, after Bill felt another woman's pain a bit too literally one too many times, they may have agreed to stick together strictly for political purposes. These cynics think, Hillary said, Take your spoils, so long as you give me mine in the form of influence. Clinton defenders argue that such an "arrangement" is actually a sign of strength—after all, Hillary's doing all this with her eyes wide open and knows just what she's getting in the bargain.

But isn't this the opposite of "empowerment"? *Hey, girls, siphon power off your husband no matter what a skunk he is! Then reap a share of his lime-light!* Bask in your husband's reflected glory and in the glamour of your victimization by him, as a substitute for making it on your own. Well, if that's how it's supposed to be, why did feminists fight so hard for women's advancement in education and the workplace in the first place? If Hillary has made such a deal, I wish she'd just come out and say so. It'd at least have the bracing effect of honesty—a commodity in short supply at the White House.

Hillary demands to have it both ways: all the trappings of power of the East Wing (not to mention those convenient Air Force One flights to New York during her "listening tour") and the role of noble martyr. Hillary kept a conspicuously chilly public face toward her errant husband. In *Hillary's Choice*, biographer Gail Sheehy writes that Hillary barely spoke to Bill for eight months. Interestingly, the First Lady's spokeswoman later denied this report, but circulating this tough-love story is classic Clinton damage control. In preparation for her Senate bid, would Hillary rather have us think that she was hard on with Bill or a total pushover? The former, of course. (Otherwise, forget winning a slugfest against kidney-punching Rudy Giuliani.)

Hillary's response to Monicagate turned feminists into contortionists. For years they had been saying that women don't need men for self-fulfillment. Now they had to explain the First Feminist's own classic clingy-female behavior, adhering to her abuser. Feminists used terms they are comfortable with: This was a woman's right to choose, said NOW President Patricia Ireland on CNN. After months of hibernation during Monicagate, Ireland finally surfaced to rebuke the president, but also to criticize those who were deriding Hillary's new "stand by your man" tack. To question Hillary's choice was to undercut thirty years of efforts to "empower women to make their own decisions [and] have control over their own lives." Ireland suddenly morphed into an opponent of divorce: "Many of us feel strongly that marriage is worth fighting for, and that families are worth preserving." Then the cherry on top—"Marriages are an adventure . . . you have ups, you have downs, you have hard times; if you stick it out you may get closer. . . ." Hillary was enabling Bill and feminists like Ireland were enabling Hillary.

Hillary's loyalty quickly became an excuse for shrugging off Bill's misdeeds. Again and again we heard, "It's between him and his wife, and if she doesn't mind, who are we to say otherwise?" As a New Jersey homemaker put it, "Hillary doesn't seem upset . . . Does it upset me? Nah." As Monica's name was penciled in next to Gennifer, Paula, and Kathleen on the presidential scandal sheet, polls showed the president's "job approval" ratings rise. Hillary helped rally the nation to the view that Bill's libido wasn't the problem, it was Ken Starr and his intrusive band of prosecutors who were the real threat. Jim Carville called Starr sex-obsessed, portraying the independent counsel as a puritanical zealot. The strategy started paying off early on. "Interviews with voters across the nation suggest that most don't much care if the president is a serial philanderer," *The Boston Globe* reported breezily four days after the Lewinsky story broke.

"It's about sex, not perjury," was the one-line battle plan that Clinton defenders used with the media. Affable Democratic consultant Bob

Beckel warned that if the President was impeached over sex, everyone's extramarital adventures would be fair game. (He was shocked when, during our joint appearance on CNN's *Crossfire*, I offered to help him smoke out hypocritical adulterers in Congress.) Later in the year I was amazed when Senator Orrin Hatch, a devout Mormon, announced on NBC's *Meet the Press*, that he thought the American public would forgive the president and let him stay in office if he just owned up. Yet Hatch was actually way behind—the public had already let out a collective yawn about Bill's sex follies. As for me, the more I appeared on television opposite the president's official and unofficial flacks, the more unhip and "out of touch" I began to feel even questioning the president's conduct. That was the whole point of the Clinton counteroffensive during Monicagate—to portray critics as officers in a new sex police, ready to bang down your bedroom door at the slightest hint of impropriety. By October 1998, it was increasingly obvious that the Clintons had succeeded in corrupting the public. I thought, *The guy's going to survive not because he didn't do it—he's going to survive because people knew he did . . . and don't care.*

Most confounding was the ferocity with which the president's female supporters rallied to his cause—from Hillary on down the Democratic food chain. The more details that trickled out about how the president had used his power for sexual gratification, the more unflinching their defense. (Even after they realized that Bill had perpetrated a fraud on the judicial system for months, Senators Barbara Boxer and Feinstein had only tepid words of rebuke.) In the end, pure politics carried the day. Whatever message American youth were taking from all this didn't matter to the administration as much as its own survival.

The Wages of Adultery

In the wake of the disclosures about the big creep and the little intern, oceans of ink and hours of broadcast time were spent reassuring us that illicit dalliances were just a normal part of daily life. A *Newsday* article explained, "Workplaces are sexy places . . . Office affairs are common." Every marriage was susceptible. "No marriage is immune to infidelity, experts say," read a headline in the *Des Moines Register*. The message: Cheating is breaking out all over, so get over it! We were even hearing about all the "positive aspects" of infidelity. Dr. Alfred Kornfeld, chairman of the psychology department at Eastern Connecticut State University, asserted that in some cases adultery "paradoxically strengthens family bonds." *The Detroit News* agreed: "Sometimes, therapists say, the revelation of an affair marks a new beginning, a wake-up call that inspires both partners to reclaim the marriage." The Clinton-Lewinsky tryst, psychologist Miriam Ulrych chirped to a reporter, represents "an incredibly ordinary event . . . It was an older man and a younger woman, an office romance. This is the stuff of many people's lives."

Bill Clinton's adolescent behavior and Hillary's toleration of it surely helped spread this nonchalant attitude. But the moral confusion didn't start with them. Nowadays, distinguishing between "right and wrong" tends to be regarded as a backward, tendentious exercise. In her 1997 book, *After the Affair*, Yale psychologist Janis Abrams Spring explicitly renounced all suggestion of accountability or blame: "I don't categorize partners as 'betrayed' or 'betrayer,' because those words convey a certain moral righteousness or condemnation . . . I don't make blanket judgments about whether affairs are, in themselves, good or bad." Dr. Luann Lindquist's *Secret Lovers: Affairs Happen . . . How to Cope* informs us that "the traditional condemnation of affairs as evil and disruptive is being replaced by a less judgmental view," a development the good doctor heartily applauds. In *Adultery, The Forgivable Sin*, Dr. Bonnie Eaker Weil is keen to dispel "falsehoods about infidelity," chief among them the notion that "adultery is about character."

Some of these modern texts on adultery show more sympathy for the cheater (my word, not theirs) than the cheated on (ditto). An affair, we're told, is really a cry for help. If the errant spouse weren't such a fragile, vulnerable soul, he or she wouldn't be playing around. In *Infidelity: A Survival Guide*, the unfortunately named Don-David Lusterman informs us that "sexual addicts" are usually plagued by that dread modern affliction "poor self-esteem." Bonnie Eaker Weil agrees: "Remember, people who are not in some kind of pain do not commit adultery. Hoping to ease the ache of his emotional emptiness, the adulterer reaches out to new partners just as others reach for food, alcohol, or drugs." Instead of casting blame, we should feel his pain. Could be Hillary's bedside reading.

Lusterman and Weil, at least, recognize infidelity as a problem. Others go further and actually cheer it on. Extracurricular adventures, they assert, can help people grow, find self-actualization, and even juice up their marriages—among other things, by teaching them bedroom skills they can share with their spouses. ("Here, honey, let me show you this great technique I learned from our new intern at the office. . . .") "The affair can let you try out being a totally different person," coos Dr. Patricia Klund. "You can explore new ways of behaving, feeling, and thinking—and learn so much about yourself." In *Secret Lovers*, Luann Lindquist treats forbidden sex as a delicious indulgence, sort of like chocolate cake. "Affairs are brief, like brightly burning Roman candles," she rhapsodizes. "Passion explodes in a fleeting encounter, such as a one-night stand on a business trip." The purported gains for cheaters include "increased feelings of self-esteem, less pressure on their marriages, an opportunity for personal growth, and a validation of their sexual selves.' "

What that exploding passion does to the other spouse is conveniently left out of the discussion. I'm not married, so I can only imagine the hurt a woman or man must feel after discovering a betrayal, and how difficult it is to rebuild trust that has been shattered. It was bad enough for me when I learned that a few boyfriends had been seeing other women behind my back. The combination of hurt and rage overwhelmed my good sense. I became someone I didn't know—depressed and self-destructive. After talking with girlfriends who had been through the same thing, I realized I wasn't alone.

The advocates of "enlightened" attitudes also forget what casual adultery does to children. A child's sense of hurt upon learning that a parent has been stepping out is just as real and just as painful as it is for the wronged spouse. In order to cultivate a healthy ability to trust others, children need examples of trustworthy behavior.

After a few late-night gab sessions in my freshman year at Dartmouth, I discovered that many of my friends—whether their parents were still together or not—suspected or knew that their fathers had cheated on their mothers. All reacted with a mix of disgust, betrayal, and resentment. One night in our dormitory common room, a student who was one of the toughest women on the lacrosse field told a few of us how her little brother found their father in bed with a family "friend," whom he later married. Her parents had been married for more than twenty years. "I have never hugged him the same way since," she said in a deadened monotone.

Then there is my friend whom I'll call Anita, who has, on the face of it, a perfect life: a loving husband, an adorable daughter, a beautiful farm. The idyll bears an underside of pain. Anita told me about it on an early-morning walk on the beach in Delaware one summer. Her parents divorced when she was very young, after her mother took up with a drama teacher. "She put her own happiness before ours," Anita recalled sadly and bitterly. Her stepfather turned out to be a manipulator, and Anita was traumatized by having to leave her father behind in New Jersey. To this day, her relationship with her mother is strained, and she has been in therapy for years.

Infidelity as a tool for female empowerment? Personal growth? An adrenaline shot for a flagging marriage? I'm skeptical, and the damage isn't limited to the accepting spouse. Talk to anyone whose parent has cheated and you will realize that adultery is not just a private matter between husband and wife.

From "Thou Shalt Not" to "Everybody Does It"

Of course Hillary's generation didn't invent adultery. Married men and women have been parallel parking with people other than their spouses throughout the ages. Two thousand years ago, the Roman satirist Juvenal called it "an ancient and long-established custom." But it was always roundly condemned and severely punished as a threat to the foundation of society, the integrity of marriage. In eighteenth-century France, adulterers were excommunicated and publicly beaten; in Reformation-era England, they had to appear barefoot and bareheaded in church and ask forgiveness of the congregation. In *The Divine Comedy*, Dante placed adulterous men and women in one of the circles of hell—including Cleopatra, Helen, and many other famous lovers of history. In *Utopia*, his political romance about an imaginary island, Sir Thomas More had his ideal civilization "punish adulterers with the strictest form of slavery," with a repeat offense "punishable by death." I doubt that Sir Thomas would make an exception for oral sex.

One problem with historical sanctions against adultery was that they applied mainly to unfaithful wives. A man could be punished for seducing another man's wife, but not for cheating on his own. In many societies, men could legally have many wives and concubines but a woman who strayed paid for it with her life. One great achievement of Judeo-Christian civilization was an ideal of monogamy and fidelity for both sexes. In practice, alas, this ideal had lots of loopholes for men: Their extramarital shenanigans were often dismissed with a wink and a nudge, while female adultery was treated as a far more egregious offense. A wife's infidelity, which could cast doubt on the children's paternity, was viewed as uniquely damaging to family honor, presumably much more than a husband's fathering children on the side.

Fortunately, such degrading attitudes have never held much sway in

America. With the rise of feminism, it seemed that they were dead and buried—until, with Hillary Clinton's blessing, self-proclaimed feminists began to dust them off. "A man is a man is a man," pronounced one of the president's defenders during Monicagate. No, not fellow adulterer Dick Morris, but Geraldine Ferraro, former Democratic congresswoman, trying to talk Republican congresswoman Tillie Fowler out of voting for impeachment. Yes, the same Geraldine Ferraro whose vice-presidential candidacy in 1984 was hailed as such a great victory for women.

Maybe we're supposed to take comfort in the fact that adultery isn't just a male privilege anymore. These days, while guys are still more likely to play around, the gals are catching up. A 1994 survey found that only twelve percent of women aged fifty-four to sixty-three had ever been unfaithful, compared to thirty-seven percent of their male peers. However, the infidelity gap was considerably smaller for people in their late forties and early fifties: thirty percent of men and twenty percent of women had strayed. And among those under thirty-four, women were actually more adultery prone: Twelve percent had cheated on a spouse, compared to just seven percent of men. In part, that's probably because men marry later. Still, those numbers can't be shrugged off. Now that women have more freedom, they're using it in bad ways as well as good.

In 1998, I happened to catch a report on CBS *This Morning* on "a growing trend of women committing adultery." While the story was part of a series bluntly titled "Lie, Cheat and Steal," it was careful not to use morally charged language in describing the growing trend of infidelity. "Equal opportunity is making inroads on infidelity," enthused host Jane Robelot. "The women's movement brought change and power to millions of American females . . . Entering the work force meant the old ways that women met men were ancient history. And a new breed of superwoman said, 'I can have it all.'" Including, apparently, a boy toy on the side—or maybe someone else's husband. The "report" featured the usual bunk about how couples might find that infidelity can be just the tonic a troubled union needs, an event that "recharges their marriage."

All this cheerleading for equal-opportunity debauchery would have appalled our feminist pioneers. One of the resolutions passed at the historic women's rights convention in Seneca Falls in 1848 was, "That the same amount of virtue . . . that is required of woman in the social state, should also be required of man, and the same transgressions should be visited with equal severity on both man and woman." They spoke of equal virtue, not vice.

Yet, a hundred and fifty years later, the notion of infidelity as a victory for women's liberation is quite popular with feminists. Dalma Heyn's 1992 book *The Erotic Silence of the American Wife*, featuring interviews with unrepentant wives who had supposedly found empowerment and sexual fulfillment through affairs, declared that "adultery is, in fact, a revolutionary way for women to rise above the conventional." (Heyn also explained that she was "certainly not" advocating affairs. Well, I'm glad we straightened that out!) "Dalma Heyn shows us a new reality and a tantalizing hint of the future—and neither women nor marriage will ever be the same," panted Gloria Steinem in a dust-jacket blurb. "It's about time women gave voice to all their dimensions, including the erotic, without shrinking in guilt," chimed in Gail Sheehy.

Our mothers and grandmothers lived by a very different ethic. If a spouse cheated or a woman dared trespass on another woman's marriage, the social ostracism was swift and severe. In her instructive book *Dumped! A Survival Guide for the Woman Who's Been Left by the Man She Loved*, author Sally Warren recalls coming home from school one day to find her mom sitting in the living room talking about how "that sweet Debbie Reynolds" had been dumped by Eddie Fisher, who had run off with Elizabeth Taylor. "They all agreed it was just terrible," Warren writes. "How could Eddie have done this to that nice girl and those dear little children? . . . It was clear then who was the wronged party, and the conclusion was that Eddie had done something that should make him feel very, very guilty." (If only the soccer moms who form Bill's most loyal constituency were prepared to be so censorious today!)

An example of how the old nosy-neighbor patrol kept infidelity in check comes from my friend Lee Habeeb's mother, Carol, who has been married for forty-two years. "There was this understanding among us that we had to look out for each other—and that included our marriages," Carol told me. In her New Jersey neighborhood, no one could run around without everyone else finding out. So powerful was the fear of social opprobrium that married men would hesitate to take a single woman to dinner in a restaurant. Women themselves, Carol says, deterred cheating and divorce: "Being known as a homewrecker was a social kiss of death." That, ladies, was sisterhood in action. Hillary could have used some of this kind of sisterly advice from her pals.

There was a time when art and literature also reinforced social norms. Some of the greatest nineteenth-century novels—*Madame Bovary, Anna Karenina*—had a clear message: Illicit sex leads to moral degradation, spiritual ruin, and even physical destruction. Far from being refreshed or empowered by her affair with Count Vronsky, Anna Karenina is overcome by shame and torment and driven to suicide. Emma Bovary, the young country doctor's wife who tries to escape her boring marriage through a series of affairs that eventually grow equally boring, ends up swallowing rat poison and dying a grisly death—which novelist Gustave Flaubert, a former medical student, painted in pitiless detail.

These days, the literary treatment of adultery is considerably more upbeat. We have peppy anthologies like *High Infidelity! 24 Great Short Stories about Adultery by Some of Our Best Contemporary Authors*. The foreword sets the tone: "As one of America's favorite clandestine sports, adultery continues to be a topic of fascination," winks editor John McNally, concluding his prologue with a kind of "Adulterers of America, Unite": "If what people are writing about is any indication of what people are doing, everyone is either cheating on someone or being cheated on . . . The way I see it, they should have a good book on their bedside table."

Movies like *The Piano* and *The Bridges of Madison County* portray adultery as enchanting romance. In *Bridges*, the unfaithful farm wife Francesca, played by Meryl Streep, floats through the film in a nimbus of golden light as we watch her fall for roving photographer Robert Kincaid, played by

Clint Eastwood, on a weekend when her husband and children happen to be away. When Robert and Francesca make love, tiny motes of sunlight bounce off their glistening flanks as a throaty female vocalist croons in the background. At the end of the film, most of the audience—yes, myself included—was wishing she had ditched husband and kids for the brooding shutterbug. Critics swooned, too: "A rapturous love story of life and renewal" . . . "Clint Eastwood's gift to women."

A gift? I hope there's a return policy.

When it comes to glorifying adultery, the worst offenders are, without a doubt, popular women's magazines. As Katie Roiphe acerbically put it in an essay in the *New York Times Magazine*, they "practically recommend it to their readers as a fun and healthy activity, like buying a new shade of lipstick or vacationing in the Caribbean." Women who cheat and don't feel guilty are treated as heroines in *Glamour, Elle, Mirabella, Harper's Bazaar*, and especially *Cosmopolitan*, which seems truly obsessed with the topic. (Some magazines then pull off the unwitting self-parody by running features on "how to keep your man faithful" or "how to find out if he's cheating.") In a *Cosmo* article, Dr. Susan Crain Bakos describes the typical adulteress in glowing terms, as having "a high sex drive, an independent spirit, and . . . the ability to keep her own sexual counsel." Another author reports that playgirl wives "tend to view their infidelities as a mark of maturity" and would be enjoying perfect extramarital bliss if the "preachy" disapproval of some unenlightened folks didn't occasionally spoil the fun.

One might ask what all this has to do with Hillary. After all, she never wrote an article for *Cosmo* titled "My Husband Fools Around and That's Okay." However, in her role as the First Enabler, she not only became the symbol of a culture in which adultery is no big deal but helped make such attitudes more respectable. (As people remarked during Monicagate, if Hillary doesn't mind, who are we to say otherwise?) So, when we talk about a social climate in which "judgmental" views of adultery are seldom publicly expressed, we are indeed talking about a part of the Hillary

Trap—a trap that Hillary may not have created, but one that she has rein-forced.

And that is the kind of climate we have today. Where once adulterous lovers felt sufficient social stigma to keep their affairs secret, today many almost flaunt them. The liaison between Sherrie Rollins, ABC News exec-utive vice president and wife of GOP political consultant Ed Rollins, and her married boss, ABC News president David Westin, was splashed all over the papers and magazines in 1997. Not long after the scandal, Sherrie threw a lavish birthday party for David at the Nirvana restaurant, attended by such high-society guests as Diane Sawyer, film director Mike Nichols, and the British ambassador to the United States. Neither Westin nor Rollins suffered professionally—or socially. The ink still fresh on their divorce papers, they wed in October 1998. "I wish them every happiness," gushed gossip columnist Liz Smith. Forget what their pursuit of happiness had done to their ex-spouses, or to the children (three of his, one of hers) from the marriages they had discarded.

Bomber pilot Kelly Flinn, who was booted from the Air Force for hav-ing an affair with an enlisted woman's husband, then lying to her superiors to conceal it and disobeying orders to stop seeing him, was elevated to martyrdom as a victim of military sexism and outmoded prudery. *Newsweek* and *60 Minutes* portrayed her as a talented woman undone by love. The women in Congress rallied to her defense; even Republican Sen-ate Majority Leader Trent Lott joined the chorus, advising the Air Force to "get real." (This must be what they mean by being so open-minded that your brain falls out.) Hardly anyone gave any thought to the real victim— the betrayed wife, Gayla Zigo, who told her side in a poignant letter to Air Force Secretary Sheila Widnall: "Lieutenant Flinn did not care about my feelings . . . She told me once that she wanted to settle down with some-one; I didn't know that somebody was my husband."

A year after the death of beloved television essayist Charles Kuralt, I was stunned by the revelation that the legendary journeyman, the one per-son at CBS I had most wanted to meet while working for the Weekend

Evening News, had led a double life: Married for thirty-five years, he also had a "longtime companion" with whom he shared a secret cabin in Montana. A May 1998 *Charlotte Observer* article about the thirty-year affair sympathetically quoted the "other woman," Pat Shannon: "Mr. Kuralt and I lived a life, and perhaps it was not a life you approve of . . . But it was a life together." Actually, any hint of disapproval was absent from the forty-five-hundred-word story, which was picked up by a wire service and ran in several major newspapers, including the *Chicago Tribune* and the *Fort Worth Star-Telegram*. Author Paige Williams lauded the newsman's "generous devotion" to Shannon and to her three children, "who came to think of him as a father," and noted that "Kuralt took great care never to cross that life with his other, or to 'mix the families.'" (What a prince of a guy.) Recalling his television career, she wrote, "Kuralt had fans everywhere, and he did not let them down." But I, for one, felt badly let down. After this, Kuralt's heartwarming, award-winning stories about the quiet greatness of small-town America suddenly seemed like a giant fraud.

Other examples abound. When writer Lillian Ross detailed her forty-year affair with revered *New Yorker* editor William Shawn in her 1998 autobiography *Here But Not Here*, most critics—except for *The New York Times'* Michiko Kakutani, who had the guts to slam the opus as "unseemly"—bought her premise that their adulterous liaison was as beautiful as any marriage. Kevin Costner's wholesome, rugged all-American image hardly suffered at all when his wife and the mother of his three children, restaurant owner Cindy Silva, got tired of dancing with a wolf and sent him packing in 1995. (Costner heatedly denied romancing some of the women to whom he was linked by tabloids, but, curiously, he has never denied cheating on Cindy.) About a year after the divorce, Costner had an out-of-wedlock child. Yet in 1999, *Redbook*, a family-oriented women's magazine, ran a fawning interview in which the actor talked movingly about coping with single fatherhood and about his love for his children. There was only one oblique reference to "mistakes" he had made.

Of course, the rich and famous have always had their share of sexual adventures and scandals. But never have so many of them so brazenly sneered at fidelity and monogamy. The Hollywood celebrities and media bigwigs who have no problem summoning the requisite righteous indignation for their pet "social problems" (AIDS research, domestic abuse, or children's health care), wouldn't think of speaking out against the epidemic of cheating that wrecks marriages and damages children within their industry. Infidelity can be "very healthy," croons country singer and actress Dolly Parton: "I believe in whatever is right for an individual at the time, as long as you're not hurting other people and you're enhancing your own life." In a 1999 speech, Ted Turner, cable TV mogul and (soon to be former) husband of Jane Fonda, opined that the Ten Commandments, particularly the one about adultery, were "a little out of date."

Married men or women who are caught *in flagrante* don't pay much of a social or professional price anymore. In many states, a company that fires adulterers or forbids married employees to "date" coworkers can actually be hauled into court for violating their civil rights. Ironically, at the same time, in response to aggressive sexual harassment laws, more and more employers are requiring all coworkers who become romantically involved to report the relationship to a supervisor and sign a contract attesting that neither of them is being coerced or harassed. A September 1998 *Los Angeles Times* article about the "new rules of office romance" opened with an anecdote intended to illustrate evolving attitudes:

> *After discovering this spring that two of his executives were involved in an adulterous sexual relationship, the owner of a Los Angeles manufacturing company acted swiftly.*
>
> *But he didn't take the time-honored tack of transferring, rebuking, or firing one or both of the lovers. Instead, he asked them to sign a two-page contract—an "informed consent" agreement intended to crimp their ability to sue the company if the relationship ever turns ugly.*

Monica Ballard, a consultant who was hired to help resolve the situation, gave a glowing assessment of the new, progressive approach to sex at the office. "In the fifties, people sneaked around and had affairs," she crowed. "Now they have the CEO and strangers they've never met coming in to chat in a very adult way about their sex life."

All this opens the door for politicians who promise to lead us to national renewal while practicing serial self-indulgence. Capitol Hill staffers whisper off the record about that pretty young staffer who's working too many late nights behind closed doors with Joe Red-White-and-Blue, junior senator from Blankety-Blank. The 1990s carryings-on of Senators Chris Dodd and Ted Kennedy are now part of congressional folklore.

But family-values conservatives aren't blameless either. And sometimes the right, too, has been willing to look the other way—which may seem politically expedient for a while but usually ends up backfiring. Take the man who was the architect of the Republican revolution of 1994, former House Speaker Newt Gingrich. A brilliant strategist who campaigned on a high-morals, low-taxes message, he was also a man with a cheating heart. In 1980, two years after he was first elected to the House, Newt walked out on his wife of nineteen years and two children, while his wife was suffering from cancer.

Most conservatives were willing to forgive and forget. And how did Newt repay them? By getting embroiled in a scandal that handed a convenient weapon to liberals who want to dismiss all conservative talk about traditional moral values as nothing but hypocrisy. After his abrupt retirement from Congress in 1998, the ex–House Speaker evidently decided it was time for another personnel change in the Gingrich household. He told his second wife, Marianne, that he was leaving her for another woman. What Marianne didn't know was that the young lady about to become Newt's newest mate had already been his playmate for six years. The man who once scribbled a memo to himself modestly describing his mission as "teacher of the rules of civilization," had been merrily breaking the rules with Calista Bisek, a House Committee staffer twenty-three years his junior. This is what it had come to: *The Washington Post* gossip column was smirking that the conservative champion was spotted drinking a $500 bottle of wine in a hideaway restaurant with his new honey.

Needless to say, Gingrich's disgrace caused quite a bit of glee in the pro-Clinton camp. "While Clinton's marriage to Hillary Rodham Clinton is operatic for its baroque mix of passion, ambition, and betrayal, she at least has stood by him, and he has never walked out on her. That's a lot more than can be said for Gingrich," chuckled a columnist in the *San Francisco Examiner*. But the preservation of a marriage based on lies hardly qualifies as a positive message.

A sad moment for me was the day in late 1998 when I watched from the House gallery as Newt's intended replacement as Speaker, Representative Bob Livingston of Louisiana, choked back tears as he said he was withdrawing his name from the speaker's race and leaving Congress. The reason, we found out later that day, was that Livingston had been carrying on an affair with a lobbyist. It turned out his behavior was open knowledge in the House—but not to his constituents or the country. The gallery was stunned and silent as Livingston walked off the floor. I began to think: *Who's next?* You had to wonder how many other dozens of self-righteous congressmen were hiding secret lives.

In a way, the Clinton-Lewinsky scandal was the logical culmination of a long downward slide. The tolerance for Clinton's misconduct reflects not only a diminished respect for the presidency but a diminished respect for marriage, for the principles of fidelity and honor. All of us, and particularly women, have refused to see Bill and Hillary for what they are. He is not an idealistic New Democrat building a bridge to the future, not the first egalitarian husband in the White House, but a relic from an exploitative past. She is not a model of liberated womanhood but an emblem of the worst of both worlds: The old-fashioned view that a husband is entitled to a little fun on the side (while the wise wife will be patient and blame the other woman) and the modern view that moral values are relative, sexual misconduct is trivial, and being "judgmental" is the worst sin of all.

Making Vows Matter

Happily, the good news is that everybody doesn't do it. Despite the any-thing-goes cultural climate and our unzipped president, we really are not the nation of cheaters that self-promoting "sex experts" and *Cosmopolitan* would have us believe. According to a 1996 study, twenty-two percent of husbands and fourteen percent of wives have been unfaithful at least once. Too many, perhaps, but that still means the vast majority take their marriage vows seriously. Fidelity may be a quaint relic in the West Wing of the White House or on Washington talk shows. But in the real world of real people, it's the norm, not the exception.

But that doesn't mean all is well. It is hard to tell whether there is actu-ally more cheating today than there was thirty or fifty years ago: The sex studies done in those years were notoriously unreliable. But if people are led to believe that "everyone is doing it" and that anyone who talks about morality is just a fussy puritan, that attitude certainly normalizes bad behavior. The example set by public figures does mean something. When the Monica circus was in town, conservatives endured a lot of ridicule for warning that kids could use the president's conduct as an excuse for engaging in similar antics. Less than a year later, *The Washington Post* reported that a group of about fifteen students, thirteen and fourteen years old, at Williamsburg Middle School in Arlington, Virginia, had been get-ting together for oral sex parties. When parents confronted the miscreants, one girl shrugged. "What's the big deal? President Clinton did it."

It is fashionable nowadays to deride the 1950s as a pallid and oppres-sive era that enforced conformity at the expense of individuality—the way it's portrayed in the movie *Pleasantville*. But "old-fashioned" isn't always bad. And "individuality" isn't always good—not if it breaks up families and causes suffering. For the last thirty years, our culture has been trumpeting the message that nearly everything about male-female relations pre-1960s was wrong. Plenty was, of course: the sexual double standard, for example, or scant protections for married women in abusive relationships. But the sexual revolution also shattered essential social norms, such as honesty and fidelity.

Americans are beginning to recognize this. Growing numbers say that marital fidelity is an ideal worth fighting for. In 1974, when the sexual revolution was in full swing, fewer than sixty percent of people eighteen to twenty-nine agreed that extramarital sex is always wrong. Twenty years later, seventy-four percent of people in this cohort—now in their late thirties and forties—condemned adultery. Defectors from the war against monogamy include veterans like Erica Jong, whose 1973 novel *Fear of Flying* was among the first to celebrate extramarital adventures by wives. Now in her fifties, Jong has said that abolishing monogamy was her generation's "great experiment," which failed miserably: "We renounced the idea of sexual freedom because it doesn't work," she said recently to *Newsweek*. Young people now in their twenties are even more conservative; they overwhelmingly say that adultery is always wrong. Maybe that's because they've had a chance to see firsthand, as children, what happens when husbands and wives don't take their marital vows too seriously.

Does all this good news mean that young women have successfully avoided the Hillary Trap? Unfortunately, no. The bad news is that a lot of Americans who frown on adultery in theory don't seem to have the guts to condemn immoral behavior by a specific person. Erica Jong's newfound wisdom about the folly of sexual "liberation" didn't keep her from jumping on the Clinton bandwagon during the Monica scandals and deriding the "puritans" who thought the president's outrageous behavior should have some consequences. In a 1996 *Newsweek* poll, only thirty-five percent said they would reject a candidate whom they knew to be an adulterer. Cheating on taxes was seen as a more serious reason for voting against somebody than cheating on a spouse.

Shunning, Amish-style, is obviously not a practical way to discourage adultery. But most of us wouldn't dream of practicing far less extreme forms of ostracism—for instance, saying no to a golf game with the married guy whose late-night work sessions with his secretary are conducted at Motel Sex or refusing a lunch invitation from the suburban housewife whose fitness trainer is giving her more than aerobics lessons. Of course, there are times when we don't know what our friends and neighbors are up to, but there are also occasions when everybody does know—the Sherrie Rollins–David Westin scandal, for example—and the offenders' social lives still emerge unscathed, and are even enhanced.

You can tell a hundred pollsters that you detest adultery and are very concerned about the decline of the family. It doesn't mean a thing if you don't take some action that lets offenders know of your disapproval that then causes them some discomfort. The community—or village, in Hillary's world—must be able to enforce its values or the values amount to no more than empty talk. It takes a village to keep a man faithful.

Some contend that promiscuity and infidelity are in our genes. According to this view, men especially are programmed by evolution to seek sexual variety: Rampant procreation may have helped our hunter-gatherer ancestors to survive as a species, with the prehistoric Bill Clintons more likely to perpetuate their randy genes. Others argue that women too have a lechery gene—female chimps put the *Cosmo* girl to shame—and have historically misbehaved less only because they have faced harsher penalties.

The study of adultery is hardly an exact science, but a few things ought to be clear. Marital infidelity and desertion are unlikely ever to go away. We are all imperfect, and we'll always need to forgive human weakness. However, there's a big difference between forgiving someone who has failed to live up to a moral ideal and giving a nod of approval to someone who doesn't even try. Indeed, if primitive hormonal drives do impel us toward promiscuity, all the greater the need to restrain those urges, whether with religious beliefs, social stigma, or the fear of losing one's marriage and children. A culture that features vast opportunities for straying, no social sanctions, and few personal consequences doesn't provide social incentives for good behavior. Instead, it gives serial adulterers carte blanche.

We have indeed become a society of enablers. Some of the cultural trends that have brought us to this point were around long before anyone had heard of Hillary Rodham Clinton. However, Hillary not only epitomizes these pernicious trends but helps legitimize them. Whatever "bargain" she may have made, the way she has chosen to deal with her husband's philandering has now become a trap for her. Leaving him now, or after he leaves office, would validate what critics have said all along—that she was in it for the power. But the price of staying with him—in loss of self-worth and dignity— is even higher. Every time she looks at him, she must think, *How long will it be before the next Monica snaps a thong and he comes panting?* The message she has sent to an entire nation—Don't sweat adultery; it's not worth ending a marriage over—sets a trap that women who care about preserving their own independence and dignity should avoid at all costs.

Today women are lucky. They no longer are forced to stay with men who mistreat them through chronic cheating. Our hard-won equal opportunity in education and the workplace have given us the means to make it on our own. Hillary thinks she has power because she has used her husband's political office as her own status-builder—by amassing political and media connections, policy influence, and a reputation as a sympathetic figure who persevered through the dark days of Monica. But eventually, she will confront the painful reality that the compromises she has made are irreversible. Each time Bill unzipped himself for another woman and Hillary looked the other way, she chipped off another little piece of her independence. Every time she did the calculation—*Should I kick the bum out?*—she concluded that she needed him too much to let his adultery get in the way. Dishonesty became a way of life between Hillary and Bill, and between Hillary and the American public. But today we should be smarter than that and make better choices. Even as we stumble through life, we know we can make it on our own; we don't have to tolerate behavior we wouldn't have wanted our mothers to tolerate. That is how we exercise true power—with honesty and resolve.

But enabling adultery is not the only Hillary Trap that undermines women's power and autonomy in their family lives. If Hillary's personal example of standing by her cheating husband reduces women to a humiliating dependency on men, the ideology she espouses and the public policies she champions relegate us to an equally degrading dependency on a "village" that, in reality, turns out to be little more than a meddlesome federal bureaucracy. By turning the family into a political football, Hillary sets another trap for American women, as we will see in the next chapter. In this politicized world, inevitably, bureaucrats gain power at the expense of parents.

6.

The
Family Trap

When Hillary Clinton needs a political boost, she often plays the "family" card. That was certainly what happened in late November 1999, when her Senate campaign was in trouble. She had just returned from a disastrous Mideast trip, and amid the uproar, some political veterans in New York were beginning to wonder aloud whether Hillary was up for the job. Political talk shows, including my own, were having a field day with the film clip of Hillary warmly embracing Yasser Arafat's wife, Suha, after she accused Israel of poisoning Palestinian children. Hillary's aides were telling her she had to get back to New York if she was serious about a political future of her own.

Her campaign over before it began? Not a chance. So on November 23, 1999, Hillary flew to New York, abruptly leaving her husband's side during an official European trip. She was going back to tell New York, and the world, that she was going to run—not for herself but for *families*, of course, and for *children*.

"I just became more and more convinced that this is a campaign that needs to be made, that the issues at stake are important ones, and that I have a lot to say about them," she said at a news conference after her address to the United Federation of Teachers, when she first let the word "slip" that she was running. "I believe that if we work together, we really can make a difference for the children and families in New York."

Two weeks earlier, a thirty-second television ad had begun airing on TV stations in upstate New York showcasing Hillary Clinton as the family-friendly candidate. The voice-over urged, "Call Hillary. Tell her to keep fighting for children, for families, for our future."

The "children and families" theme was nothing new for Hillary; for years, it had been a constant refrain when she talked about her role in public life. "I'm a family feminist," she had told an admiring audience at a $1,000-a-plate Democratic fundraiser held by the Women's Leadership Council in New York in December 1997.

A family feminist. It's a friendly, soothing term, conveying a felicitous balance of old-fashioned and progressive values. Hillary says she got it from the late Irish peace activist Joyce McCartan, her host on a 1995 trip to Northern Ireland, who told her that "saving families was at the root of all her efforts." According to Hillary, "This is a brilliant term . . . it captures the very important idea that when women are empowered to make the most of their own potential, then their families will thrive, and when families thrive, communities and nations thrive as well."

But what exactly does "family feminism" mean for American families? That question is rather hard to answer. Hillary rarely comes clean on policy specifics and often cloaks her real positions in misleading traditionalist rhetoric. The fact is, many of Hillary's supposedly pro-family policies would undermine the family, by substituting collective authority—from day-care director to government regulator—in place of Mom and Dad.

It's another Hillary Trap. Without help from the government and guidance from experts, Hillary is basically telling us, women cannot possibly balance career and family—and can scarcely be trusted to do a decent job of raising their own children. She's skeptical of women's competence even in this area in which we have always exercised the most authority, without government programs to empower us. For Hillary, an army of specialists—social workers, psychologists and judges—have to be involved.

If there's one phrase associated with Hillary's crusade for families, it's the African proverb, "It takes a village to raise a child," which inspired the title of her 1996 bestselling book. After she was criticized for seeming to suggest that Mom and Dad can't raise the kids themselves, Hillary protested that emphasizing "the village" didn't mean downgrading families or parents. The book's first chapter does give lip service to the idea that "parents bear the first and primary responsibility for their sons and daughters." Yet that statement rings hollow to me.

The problem is that while the village of the African proverb is a tightly knit community of relatives and neighbors, Hillary's village is made up not of villagers, but of bureaucrats. Her real argument is that only the government, with its armies of social workers and regulators, can secure the welfare of our children. But in fact, far from helping parents make their hectic lives work, these solutions just add another meddlesome layer between parent and child.

I don't have kids of my own, but I know what it was like to be raised by a working mother. From the time I was six, my mom waitressed at various restaurants around our home town of Glastonbury, Connecticut, and tried to tailor her schedule to be home when the school bus dropped me off in the afternoon. It wasn't always possible. On Wednesdays, we were dismissed at noon and I came home to an empty house. Mom arranged for the next-door neighbors, the Cloughs, to take care of me. I played with their daughters, ate snacks with them, and waited until my mother got home at four o'clock. That was my village—neighbors helping neighbors.

My mother could have worked longer hours at a career that consumed more of her time and paid more. But she made a choice to balance a part-time work life with the needs of her kids. Frankly, I don't think my mother or her neighbors would have wanted help in the form of subsidized day care. She regarded raising a family as her business—not the government's.

Today, "the family" has become a political slogan invoked by both left and right. At every opportunity, liberals cry about "the children." Conservatives retort that families are helped most by "tax cuts," which doesn't exactly have the same ring. Democrats say that Republicans don't really care about children and want to dump them in orphanages and Dickensian poorhouses. Let the Democrats run the government, they enthuse, and there will be laws mandating generous family leave and plenty of federal money to subsidize day care, family planning, and social services for everybody. These programs may sound good to harried parents, but they combine to produce Hillary's Family Trap.

Uncle Sam, Baby-sitter

On April 17, 1997, Hillary Rodham Clinton opened with great fanfare the White House Conference on Early Childhood Development. Attended by scientists, public officials, pediatricians, educators, and activists, the symposium was beamed by satellite to nearly a hundred universities, schools, and hospitals in thirty-seven states. Her mission, Hillary declared, was "to give the leading experts in the field of early childhood development . . . the opportunity to explain their discoveries" and put their knowledge at the service of American parents, child-care workers, doctors, policy makers, and just plain old concerned citizens. The gist of the conference was that the neurocircuitry of a baby's brain isn't fully formed until the age of three, making the first three years vitally important. Miss out on proper nurturing and mental stimulation early, and you'll go through the rest of your life with a poorly wired brain.

A couple of years later, this theory took quite a pummeling in a well-regarded book entitled *The Myth of the First Three Years*. Author John Bruer didn't argue that baby care didn't matter but that the brain's capacity to learn and improve doesn't stop at three and that the growth of the little gray cells won't be stunted except in cases of severe deprivation. So Hillary may have been using questionable science. What's more interesting, though, is that she was using it to advance one of her pet projects: day care.

Let's examine this issue a bit more closely. Suppose for a moment that the vital importance of the first three years is a fact. What conclusion would you draw? You might think that it would be all the more important for Mom and Dad to spend more time with the children, maybe even for one parent to stay home during that crucial period when the baby's brain is being wired. Only if you were an unenlightened, old-fashioned sort, clinging to the hoary myth of the family as a self-sufficient unit, that is. In Hillary's world, there's only one answer—ever more government funding for child-care programs for working parents. Not tax cuts returning money to single- and dual-income families alike. Not elimination of the marriage penalty. Predictably, close on the heels of "Hillary's brain conference" (as it was dubbed by West Wing staffers), in October 1997 came another event, the White House Conference on Child Care, to present Hillary's standard canned solutions for the issue she had trumped up earlier.

"Child care" as understood by the White House means work by paid caregivers. As columnist Lori Borgman observed:

> *There was little recognition of stay-at-home moms and the parents who design tag-team work schedules to care for their children. There was no mention of grandparents and relatives who offer working solutions to day-care dilemmas. There was a brief mention of neighborhood women who provide child care, primarily that parents never know when one of them can turn out to be a wacko, hence the need to have them all federally trained and certified.*

The work that millions of moms (as well as dads, grandmas, and grandpas) do at home every day is occasionally given lip service by the Clinton Administration, in rhetorical response to conservative critiques. But at the Conference on Child Care the only player consistently mentioned in solving the child-care dilemma was the federal government—Big Nanny.

The policy proposals Bill Clinton presented at the conference were actually pretty modest: $300 million in scholarships over a five-year period to train child-care workers, legislation making it easier for parents to do background checks on care providers, the use of AmeriCorps national service volunteers in after-school programs for latchkey children. His hands were, after all, tied by the Republican-inspired spending caps, which made it tougher to fund government programs than in the past. The Clintons had learned a big political lesson from the health care debacle: Trying to address a social problem by foisting a national, centralized, one-size-fits-all bureaucratic plan on a large sector of the economy is not a good way to win friends among American voters.

Yet Hillary's vision for child care remains extremely ambitious and expensive. In *It Takes a Village*, she heaps praise on the French state-subsidized day-care system, the "maternal schools" attended by over ninety percent of preschoolers in France. These strictly regulated centers have "sparkling classrooms," well-stocked with educational toys; the teachers and directors are required to have extensive training in childhood development and education. "It may sound too good to be true, but it's not," gushes Hillary. "When I went to France . . . as part of a group studying the French child-care system, I saw what happens when a country makes caring for children a top priority."

On the next page, Hillary adds a little disclaimer. She doesn't mean we love our kids any less than the French or that "their system can or should be duplicated wholesale here." Still, unlike the French, it appears, we don't make our children a "top priority." She goes on to tell us reproachfully that when she asked French politicians how they could achieve a consensus on government subsidized day care, they replied in shock, "How can you not invest in children and expect to have a healthy country?"

A quick reality check might be in order. French government-run day care may not be as much of a fiasco as British government-run health care, but it's no utopia, either. It's extremely expensive and its costs keep rising. Financing the French welfare state has added to its fiscal woes and its twelve percent unemployment rate. The quality of the day care all those taxes buy isn't all it's cracked up to be either. Those allegedly fabulous preschools have a ratio of one teacher per twenty-eight children, while day nurseries have one caretaker per twenty-two infants (with occasional help from aides). That means French day-care centers would get an F from the

American Academy of Pediatrics, which recommends a child-to-staff ratio of three to one. Nor does Hillary mention that despite the French government's generous spending on day care, parents often have to wait up to a year for a vacancy. You won't find those details in *It Takes a Village*.

There are other problems, too. According to *The New York Times*, French psychologists worry that day care as a sacred entitlement in France is beginning to undermine many mothers' and fathers' trust in their own parental competence: They just don't think they can "civilize" their children any more without institutional care. Even stay-at-home mothers in France pack *les enfants* off to the "maternal schools." Maybe Hillary should stop and think before she engineers a new dependency culture in America, at vast expense for dubious benefit.

More recently, Hillary has praised a model child-care system closer to home: that of the U.S. military. Leave it to the author of *It Takes a Village* to find what may be the only big federal day-care program in the United States to hold up as a "bright spot" and a "shining example." At the White House Conference on Child Care, the First Lady boasted that "our Defense Department runs the largest child-care system in the world." She proudly announced that her husband had directed the Defense Department "to work with the private sector to take the experience they've gained, their guidelines . . . and bring those to the table to discuss with more child-care centers and family day-care providers what can be done to use [federal money] to make models that can be replicated."

Well, at least this Vietnam War protester has gotten over her distrust of the military. Our cold-blooded generals might not be worthy of our trust when it comes to the battlefield, but when it comes to day care I guess they're four-star Benjamin Spocks.

Of course, one might ask if the experience of the military, which has a rather unique relationship to its clientele and its employees, can really be replicated in civilian life. But is child care in the United States really in such a state of emergency that we need a civil defense plan to step in? If kids are getting too little care, discipline, and attention these days, where does the fault lie—with parents or the government? A "crisis" exists only if you believe, as Hillary apparently does, that parents are chumps when it comes to child care in comparison with accredited day-care providers and teams of federal experts.

The same day that Hillary was calling for "national discussion and action" on the child-care crisis at her White House Conference on Child Care, the Cato Institute, a libertarian, free-market think tank in Washington, D.C., released an exhaustively researched paper by policy analyst Darcy Olsen debunking Hillary's "crisis."

Based on careful examination of the government's own data, the 1991 National Child Care Survey conducted by the Urban Institute (a traditional liberal policy group) and co-sponsored by the Head Start Bureau of the Administration for Children and Families in the Department of Health and Human Services found that more than ninety-five percent of working parents at all income levels were satisfied with both the cost and the quality of their child-care arrangements. Fewer than a quarter said that if they could have any type of child care they would choose some other option.

The same survey found that, far from stumbling helplessly in the dark, "many parents are fairly well-informed consumers of child care"—not only about the care their own children are getting but about the costs and the quality of various alternatives. The fact is, different parents have different needs and priorities when it comes to child care. Many emphasize educational activities above all else, just as Hillary would have them do. Others think it's important for the caregiver to be someone the child and the parents know personally. Some prefer a structured school-like environment, others an informal and spontaneous homelike atmosphere. An overwhelming majority want child care that reinforces the religious and cultural values they are trying to impart to their children.

You'd think that a "dizzying" variety of child-care arrangements in America would be a good thing, right? Not to Hillary. Our system, she laments in It Takes a Village, "looks more like a patchwork quilt than a security blanket"—neighbors and relatives helping each other out, nannies, neighborhood family-care homes, day-care centers, and church-affiliated preschools. In Hillary's world, diversity is good if it refers to skin color quotas, but not when applied to diverse individuals' ideas about child care.

Is it really true that, as Hillary keeps telling us, the quality of this "patchwork" of child care is so "abysmal" as to endanger our kids? It's the kids warehoused in federally regulated day-care centers we ought to worry about. Children these days often don't get enough warmth, emotional nurturing, and one-on-one attention—the kind of things that are hard to measure in studies, and the kinds of things institutional day care isn't very likely to give, no matter how many educational toys the classrooms are packed with. This is not to say that there are no good, warmhearted, nurturing caretakers in day-care centers. But I would rather rely for loving care on the blue-haired lady next door, whose only expertise in child development is her experience raising five kids of her own.

In fact, according to the Census Bureau, fewer than thirty percent of working parents send their children to organized day-care facilities. The percentage of preschoolers with working moms who are cared for by their dads (nineteen percent), grandparents (fifteen percent), other relatives (nine percent), moms at work (five percent), or nannies at home (five percent) adds up to more than half of the total. About fifteen percent are in family day-care homes—many of which are unregulated. Is that a problem? A study conducted for the Department of Health and Human Services, Family Day Care in the United States, has found that most family day care, regulated or not, "provide[s] a stable, warm, and stimulating day-care environment that caters successfully to the developmentally appropriate needs of the children" and that "parents who use family day care report it satisfactorily meets their child-care needs."

Hillary and her fellow child-care crusaders keep pointing to a couple of studies that are said to show that most nonregulated child care for infants and toddlers is of poor quality. But the definition of "quality" can be distinctly subjective. The National Research Council, for example, advises that child-care centers and family day-care homes should have separate areas reserved for specific activities, such as "an art table, a dramatic play corner, a building-block corner, a reading corner." By such standards, even most suburban middle-class homes would flunk the quality-control test. The studies that paint a dismal picture of child care in America—which are then used to call for more federal funds—look disproportionately at home-based care and care by relatives in low-income groups. (In one study, by the Families and Work Institute, nearly forty percent of relatives and unregulated providers who were caring for children had not graduated from high school and nearly sixty percent had a family income below $20,000.) Their ways of caring for children are especially likely to be disparaged by the experts.

The National Institute of Child Health and Human Development released a study to media acclaim in the spring of 1997 that gave working mothers a thumbs-up. It concluded that kids with working moms are doing just fine. Contradicting Hillary's view that there is a child-care crisis, it found that seventy to eighty percent of young children with working mothers are getting good or excellent care—the best of which is provided by unlicensed, untrained, and unregulated fathers and grandparents. Family day-care homes got somewhat lower grades. Hillary's day-care centers came in dead last. What's more, the researchers concluded that a child's healthy development is far less affected by the quality of day care than by the quality of his or her home environment and relationship with Mom. That's the good news for working mothers. The bad news is that when babies and toddlers are trundled off to day care for more than thirty hours a week, the quality of that all-important relationship with Mom can deteriorate, as mothers become less attuned to their children's needs and children become less responsive to their mothers.

This might go under the heading Yet Another Amazing Discovery We Really Didn't Need Federal Money to Prove. But it shows how misguided Hillary's vintage 1970s' policy obsessions are. The truth is, Hillary hasn't bothered to re-examine the basis of her deeply held beliefs on issues like day care and abortion since they became activist "causes" for her generation twenty-five years ago. She hasn't had much incentive to. Those causes have generated lobbying groups and organizations, and yes, big government bureaucracies, with plenty of good intentions, but also a vested interest in their own survival. They're Hillary's friends and campaign supporters and they make up her liberal political power base. They don't want to hear that their approach might be misguided or irrelevant. Then who would pay their salaries?

It turns out that if we really want to "invest in our children," what we should do is help mothers (and fathers) spend more time with their kids. That, as it happens, is exactly what most parents actually want. Overwrought conservatives might occasionally go overboard insisting that women dream of nothing but becoming Donna Reed again. But in fact, in a 1997 Pew Research Center poll, forty-three percent of mothers who were employed full-time did say that they'd rather work part-time if they could, and nearly one in four would have preferred to stay home. Other surveys find that both mothers and fathers would prefer to work shorter hours.

Maybe if the government let parents keep more of their earnings, more families would be able to fulfill that wish. Tax cuts—yes, boring old tax cuts—just might be more beneficial than government-funded research on the neurocircuitry of a child's brain.

Uncle Sam's Surrogates

American parents are failures by other measures, too, in Hillary's world, and their deficiencies beg for the intervention of the regulatory apparatus. Indeed, while insisting so fervently on "privacy" for adulterers, Hillary evidently doesn't believe that parents should be left alone to decide for themselves when to have children and how to raise them. That's the message that pervades *It Takes a Village*.

Hillary has lamented, for example, that many Americans are more thoughtful about planning their weekend entertainment than about planning their families; she has even called it a "national shame." Let's suppose for a moment that this is true. Maybe that's because Americans regard children as a miraculous gift to be cherished whenever it arrives, not as an item to be scheduled into their Palm Pilot. Why is it Hillary Clinton's business, or anybody else's for that matter? There's no evidence that unplanned children turn out worse than those who were planned or that they're any less precious to their parents. If you don't happen to accept the Planned Parenthood gospel, do you need to be scolded from a bully pulpit?

Hillary also frets that many parents, especially in working-class and poor families, don't spend enough time talking to their small children, give them too little praise, and make too many "statements of disapproval, such as 'That's bad,' 'You're wrong,' 'Stop.'" Obviously, people should treat their children with kindness, but some children these days are excessively coddled and overpraised. Maybe school discipline wouldn't be such a disaster if some kids heard more "statements of disapproval" at home when they misbehave. In a biting review of *It Takes a Village*, political philosopher Jean Bethke Elshtain points out that while the book is full of rhetoric about "diversity" in the usual sense of race, ethnicity, sexual orientation, and the like, little tolerance is shown for diversity of child-rearing methods. Elshtain also wonders if, in Hillary Clinton's vision, "government, or some agency somewhere, [must] step in" and do something about parents who talk to their kids too little, or too strictly. Hillary concludes that less affluent, less educated moms and dads need "coaching" to help them become better parents, presumably by government-certified child development experts.

As an example of what "the village" can accomplish, she cites the Abecedarian Project, launched in North Carolina in 1972, in which over a hundred babies whose parents had little education and low IQs were "gathered" at four months of age and "placed in a preschool with a very high ratio of adult staff to children" and a high-quality educational environment. Several years later these children scored considerably higher on academic and intellectual tests than kids from a similar background who had not been in the program.

Many other researchers caution that such findings are far from conclusive. Of the four successive groups of infants in the Abecedarian Project, only two showed an improvement. One did worse than a comparison group that hadn't been given any help. Even if the Abecedarian Project itself was a spectacular success, holding it up as a model has disquieting implications. The babies "gathered" into the program were from families deemed to be at high risk. They were placed in eight-hours-a-day, five-days-a-week, year-round day care. Their parents received special assistance from social services. For all intents and purposes, the day-care center became these children's second home. Such intensive institutional care for newborns may be appropriate in cases of seriously dysfunctional families. But as a national policy it resembles the communist fantasies of universal nurseries more than anything that Mr. and Mrs. America would want for their kids. And extended to a broad population the cost of what amounts to round-the-clock institutionalization (sounds like orphanages to me!) would be prohibitive.

What, then, is the "village" that Hillary has in mind? Even the most dyed-in-the-wool individualist would agree that, to quote a chapter title from It Takes a Village, "no family is an island." Many people helped shape our world when we were growing up: neighbors, relatives and family friends, priests, ministers and rabbis, teachers, librarians, and police officers. (And let's not forget the ice-cream truck driver!) In her book, Hillary, too, talks about this informal network of caring adults when she movingly retells her own childhood experiences from a simpler and more innocent small-town America. But that village, which provides so many anecdotes and so much charming local color, vanishes once you get to the meat of the book and its policy recommendations. "This is real, America," a beleaguered working mom is quoted as saying. "We ask you, the government, and you, the employer, to help us, the working people, to make child-rearing work."

In the words of Vassar psychologist Gwen Broude, who reviewed It Takes a Village in Reason magazine, "[T]he kinds of villages to which the [title] proverb refers are small, homogeneous, and kin-based. They are little platoons. People know each other, interact with each other on a day-to-day basis, and form voluntary associations in which I watch your child and you watch mine. By contrast . . . the village Hillary Clinton has in mind is Uncle Sam." Hillary takes a proverb about the importance of communities and transforms it into a plea for a bigger government.

Deploring "antigovernment rhetoric," Hillary rejects any suggestion that the state can sometimes hinder rather than help parents who are trying to raise good children. Ironically enough, she bemoans the difficulty of teaching character and virtue in today's world, the "spiritual emptiness" and the temptations of drugs and sex. But wasn't it the government that set out to purge every mention of God from our public schools? Overzealous enforcement of federal civil rights laws and bureaucratic micromanagement are what brought us, for instance, a high school valedictorian being barred from saying a prayer at graduation, and ubiquitous federally subsidized sex education classes in which twelve-year-olds master the fine art of slipping a condom on a banana. Hillary's friends at the National Education Association are the same experts who replaced the teaching of old-fashioned virtues with "values clarification" exercises, where kids are expected to figure out for themselves whether it's moral to cheat and steal without the "oppression" of clearly stated rules about right and wrong.

Many mothers and fathers—not just the religious extremists constantly conjured up by the liberal imagination—today see the schools as actively hostile to the values they are trying to impart to their children. They agree with the social critic Thomas Sowell who writes that our schools "have set sail on an uncharted sea of social experimentation"—an effort to "re-shape values, attitudes, and beliefs to fit a very different vision of the world from what children have received from their parents." Today's widely used sex education textbooks decry the "traditional ideas" held by parents and religious leaders. One popular text, *Changing Bodies, Changing Lives*, describes parents as typically "hung up" and burdened with "old-fashioned stereotypes" and "negative attitudes toward bodies and sex." The tax-subsidized education "experts" whom Hillary is so eager to empower are much more interested in personal turf-building and grand schemes to "revolutionize" education according to their latest (often crackpot) theories than they are in cultivating boring, old- fashioned common sense solutions.

It's not just a matter of sex. More and more, the educrats are prying into family life and undermining parental authority under the guise of "life skills" and "health" courses. Imagine your son or daughter having to fill out class worksheets asking what presidential candidates you voted for, whether any close relatives have ever suffered from alcoholism or mental illness, and whether your family income is a private issue or can be discussed in the classroom. A paranoid Big Brother fantasy? No, actual assignments in a required ninth-grade Human Interaction, or HI!, course in Petaluma, California, as reported by columnist Debra Saunders in the *San Francisco Chronicle*. Other class materials include a "Family Systems" handout extolling "open" families that function on a model of " 'pure' democracy," in contrast to "hierarchical" and "closed" families. Parents who wanted to pull their kids from the course were told that they would have to sign a waiver not only explaining their reasons for doing so but promising to provide "alternative educational experiences" on HI! topics at home—"under penalty of perjury." It took the threat of a lawsuit from the Rutherford Institute, a religious freedom advocacy group, to make the school district back down from that bizarre requirement.

An aberration? I wish. In her extensively researched book *The Assault on Parenthood*, scholar Dana Mack documents plenty of such follies—courses that not only substitute Therapy 101 for learning, but seek to remedy what the "experts" obviously regard as inadequate parenting. In one widely used "values clarification" curriculum, students are quizzed on such academically challenging topics as "What disturbs you about your parents?" A popular health education course suggests that substance abuse is learned in "chemically dependent homes," from parents who enjoy an occasional beer or a glass of wine. Many child abuse prevention programs encourage tykes as young as six to be wary of "wet kisses" and "tight hugs," even from parents or close relatives, and to regard all corporal punishment as abuse.

The schools are not just trying to re-educate children about values and attitudes. They're trying to use the children as agents of re-education for parents on matters from recycling to alcohol consumption to methods of discipline. One mom told Mack "with a bemused chuckle" that she used to think she was doing a good job raising her kids until she sent them to school: "I found out differently from my son!" But to most parents, the contempt that Hillary and her friends the professional educators show for their supposedly outdated methods of child-rearing is no laughing matter.

The Cops on the Beat

Public schools aren't the only place where Hillary favors surrogate parenting. Across the country, family courts and departments of social services employ armies of bureaucrats who are convinced that they know what's best for your kids. In *It Takes a Village*, Hillary agrees.

Intervention by government is sometimes needed, of course, as in such taxpayer-funded positions as Public Guardian. Neglect and abuse of children, the elderly, and the disabled must be met with public action. Hillary has said that physical and sexual abuse of children calls for "strong, unambivalent prosecution of perpetrators" and the removal of children from a dangerous situation—and no one would disagree with that. The problem is, when Hillary calls for rapid and vigorous intervention by an army of police officers, child protective workers, social workers, judges, and other "qualified citizens" representing "the village," she seems unaware of the perils of overzealousness. She never mentions highly publicized prosecutions of parents, day-care workers, and preschool teachers falsely accused of child sexual abuse, which have sometimes resembled the Salem witch trials. In case after case, "expert" abuse therapists and investigators have been shown to have manipulated children into making false charges of molestation by implanting them with abuse scenarios suggested by the experts themselves. Yes, real child abuse can shatter lives, but political demagoging of "the children" can also breed hysteria, with the so-called experts interested in nothing but feeding the flames.

Richard and Renee Althaus, a middle-class couple in Mt. Lebanon, Pennsylvania, suffered a Kafkaesque ordeal at the hands of liberal crisis-mongering about child abuse. In 1991, their fifteen-year-old daughter

Nicole, depressed over family problems including her mother's illness, was befriended by a teacher, Priscilla Zappa. Zappa told students that she had been a victim of child sexual abuse. She encouraged her class to share such experiences and somehow became convinced that Nicole was being molested. Despite the girl's denials, Zappa kept prodding her and gave her literature on child abuse, telling her it sounded "very similar" to her family. Finally, Nicole began to think that maybe something really had happened to her. One day, Zappa marched her to the principal's office and announced that the girl had been abused by her parents.

That was enough for child welfare officials to remove Nicole from her home and send her to live with Zappa. Soon, the girl was claiming that her father and mother had subjected her and other children to unspeakable perversions, tortured her, and made her have two abortions. No physical or medical evidence was ever found to support these wild tales, but that didn't deter the social workers, the therapists, the police, or the district attorney's office. Richard Althaus was arrested three times. Renee was arrested twice and was suspended from her teaching job. The nightmare went on for more than a year until the presiding judge began to feel that the case was getting too weird and ordered an independent psychiatric evaluation. It concluded that there had been no abuse. Shortly thereafter, Nicole recanted her charges, the case was dismissed, and the family reunited. With a veritable village of the high-minded having ganged up on them, the Althauses were out $150,000 in legal fees and lost wages, not to mention the emotional devastation. Meanwhile, Priscilla Zappa continues to teach and was never even reprimanded.

What happened to the Althaus family was admittedly extreme. But there's no shortage of head-turning stories about government and child welfare expert intervention so intent on protecting children from their parents that they literally invent cases against them. We would wait in vain for Hillary to acknowledge this reality, or to consider the possibility that government intervention—which she espouses—has contributed to the problem.

In 1995 in New York, fourteen-year-old Jazmine Rivera was taken into the custody of the Children's Services Administration after she told a school counselor she had been beaten by her mother, Lisette Samuel. Soon, according to an account in the New York *Daily News*, Jazmine admitted that she made it all up to get back at Mom for being too strict and not letting her stay out late. The police concluded that there was no evidence of child abuse. But the Children's Services bureaucrats still thought they knew better. They continued to treat Lisette as a criminal, while Jazmine, who was begging to go back to Mom, kept getting bounced from one foster home to another. At one point, she tried to kill herself. Finally, after several months, the girl was able to persuade a Family Court judge to send her home. Lisette Samuel's joy was tempered by bitterness toward the system: "My integrity as a mother was taken away from me," she told the New York *Daily News*. "They destroyed my family." Where was she supposed to turn to regain her dignity and good name?

It's a question that might well be asked by Bobbie Sweitzer, an anesthesiologist at Massachusetts General Hospital, who was startled to find a message from the police on her answering machine about an "incident" outside a store. She thought she was being accused of hitting another car. She never dreamed that her crime was stepping inside the store to drop off a roll of film while her one- and four-year-old children slept in the backseat of her car. She was gone for less than two minutes, but that was enough time for some anonymous do-gooder to write down her license plate number and call the police. Dr. Sweitzer explained that her car alarm was on and she could see the car through the store's glass entry. That wasn't good enough for the Department of Social Services, which informed her that there was "reasonable cause to support the allegations" of neglect.

It took Dr. Sweitzer eight months and $15,000 to clear her name and get the state agency to reverse its finding. "If you don't have the ability to spend thousands of dollars to fight, you end up getting lost in the system," warned her attorney, Robert Sherman.

Need more? The Reverend Frank Fowler, a father of three and a minister in Plattsburgh, New York, slapped his son's face when the eleven-year-old was having a violent tantrum, swinging and kicking at his parents.

Word of the incident got out at school, a teacher made a report, and the wheels of the child protective system were set in motion. Reverend Fowler was charged with assault; he went to trial, acting as his own attorney, and won an acquittal. But there was some part of "not guilty" the authorities didn't understand. Reverend Fowler was still listed in the statewide registry of child abusers and the caseworkers quickly cooked up new charges: They alleged he had mistreated his son by calling him as a witness at the trial and questioning him on the stand. The relentless harassment forced the Fowlers to move to another town. Finally, the embattled dad sued his tormentors for false arrest and malicious prosecution and won.

Dana Mack interviewed hundreds of parents and attended focus groups while researching her book. "I have been shocked at how commonly parents report that they or close relatives have been visited by child protection authorities—and for acts no more sinister than disciplining a wayward child or seeking medical help for a playground injury," writes Mack. As many as one out of five parents she met had such tales to tell—"frightening tales of long-term investigations, irresponsible therapeutic interventions, even child removals." One man found himself battling social workers after he grounded his out-of-control teenage stepson (the boy had assaulted his mother, a cancer patient). The wicked stepfather and his wife were forced into counseling, where they were told, among other things, that they shouldn't make the poor lad sit at the dinner table with the rest of the family: If he wanted to eat in the living room in front of the TV, that should be just fine.

Are there cases in which horrendous incidents of real abuse fall through the cracks and children are allowed to remain in life-threatening situations? Sure, but the more the system is bogged down in investigating every call from every busybody who overheard a next-door neighbor threatening to spank Junior, the less time and attention it has for children who are starved, tortured, and subjected to truly unspeakable things. Well-meaning laws requiring health professionals, teachers, and child-care workers to report any suspicion of child abuse may have helped some victims but they have also opened the floodgates for trivial or unfounded complaints. Of course, nobody wants serious cases of child abuse to be missed, but some discretion should be exercised as well.

Take the case of Margaret "Kelly" Michaels, a New Jersey nursery-school teacher who became the victim of one of the most egregious cases of sex abuse hysteria. Her ordeal began when a little boy who was having his temperature taken rectally by a nurse at the pediatrician's office remarked that his teacher did this at school. When the nurse asked what he meant, the boy replied, "She takes my temperature." There was nothing sinister about this; at the nursery school, the staff routinely took the children's temperature, not rectally but with a strip applied to the forehead. Nonetheless, the nurse decided that the boy's words just *might* mean that he had been rectally penetrated. She reported the incident. Before long, an investigation was launched, all the parents were told their children might have been sexually molested, and after extensive and relentless grilling many of the children agreed that they had indeed been abused. Michaels was convicted and sentenced to forty-seven years, and later released after she won an appeal.

No wonder the child welfare system is, as Hillary Clinton laments in her book, "overwhelmed." Some of those wounds are self-inflicted.

The standard social welfare response of erring on the side of caution often results in errors, humiliation and invasion of privacy of the people involved. Adults wrongly accused of heinous crimes aren't the only victims. What happens to many children at the hands of their would-be saviors can only be described as brutal psychological abuse or worse. According to one report, children in foster or group care are ten times more likely to be maltreated while in the custody of the state than in their own homes. Hillary is always quick to call for professional counseling in every catastrophe—except when government meddling is the cause.

In the world according to Hillary, government blunders are easily overshadowed by all the exciting possibilities of what it can do to improve the lives of families and children. In the real world, that's not the way it looks to many exasperated parents who are starting to feel that their children aren't theirs any more but belong to the state. In most parents' eyes, the one best thing the government could do would be to adopt the time-honored principle of the Hippocratic oath, which doctors have taken since the days of Ancient Greece: "First, do no harm."

Doing Some Good

Is there anything the government can do to help families, besides give them a break come April 15 (which wouldn't be a bad start)?

Hillary lobbied hard for the Family and Medical Leave Act, which her husband signed in 1993. It allows employees up to twelve weeks a year of unpaid leave to care for children or sick family members. Throughout the 1996 presidential campaign and after, Clinton hailed the millions who had allegedly benefited from this new law—exaggerating every bit as much as when he bragged of bringing "one hundred thousand new police" to America's streets when the true number was just a fraction of that. Republicans, for their part, were so terrified of appearing to be anti-children, they crowed to the press about their own support of the bill.

But in fact, it's a bad law that can burden employers without doing much at all for employees. While the Clinton Administration touts a survey in which ninety percent of business owners said that FMLA compliance imposed little or no extra costs on them, a December 1999 article in the Raleigh, North Carolina, News & Observer paints a much more complicated picture. Most employers interviewed by the newspaper supported allowing workers to take time off for family and personal emergencies, but they complained that the law created tons of paperwork—when employees go on leave, records must be kept, supervisors formally notified, and sometimes certification from doctors obtained as well—and often resulted in absences that were difficult to handle. Since the twelve weeks of unpaid leave can be stretched out over a year, a worker could just put in a few hours a week and keep his or her job. As we already know (see The Work Trap), the overburdened business owners are often women. "The FMLA causes a hardship to the company because of the added administrative work and the time away from work," Becky Bullard, head of an 850-employee footwear company, told the *News & Observer*. "You can see the enormous headache it can require. It's an added expense to the company." Sometimes, she said, she had to ask another worker to volunteer for overtime to cover for the absent employee.

Meanwhile, many parents either can't afford to take the time off or wouldn't dare to ask, knowing how difficult it would be to accommodate the request. Nearly sixty percent of working mothers aren't covered by the act anyway, because they either work part-time or for small companies that are exempt from the FMLA. Besides, do employers really need Uncle Sam breathing down their necks on behalf of their workers' families? To ignore your workers' needs isn't good business and employers know that far better than Uncle Sam—despite tales of the occasional Scrooge who gives a despondent mom the boot for taking a few hours off to visit her ailing child in the hospital. A year before the FMLA became the law of the land, ninety-three percent of mothers and eighty-four percent of fathers reported that their employers already had parental leave benefits, and about ninety percent said that they could always make special arrangements for time off to care for a sick child or family member, according to research studies from the Families and Work Institute.

The government could do a lot more good if it corrected some bad laws that make it more difficult for parents to balance work and family. For instance, our legislators could revise badly drafted existing regulations that actually make child care less available, such as city zoning codes that prohibit homemakers or retired schoolteachers from providing child-care services at home under the guise of keeping "businesses" out of residential neighborhoods. Or they could encourage flextime, not by strongarming businesses, but by allowing them to do so.

Suppose Mom wants to take a day off when Johnny has the flu or Mary has a soccer game, and then make up for it by working an extra eight hours the next week. Under current law, it's not allowed unless the employer pays overtime for the makeup hours. For several years, Republican Senator John Ashcroft of Missouri has been pushing for a law, the Family Friendly

Workplace Act, which would let employees trade overtime pay for extra time off. More than two-thirds of working women surveyed in 1997 liked this option. It's endorsed not only by social conservatives like the Family Research Council but by *Working Mother* magazine. But don't expect support from the Democrats who love to profess their devotion to working parents. Or from the National Organization for Women. Or from Hillary Clinton. Senator Ashcroft's bill, after all, is ferociously opposed by the Clintons' most powerful constituency—the labor unions, with their time-warp mentality in which workers are so oppressed and bamboozled by evil capitalists, they can't possibly be allowed the choice to bargain away their overtime pay.

By and large, families, businesses, and communities have adapted to the past thirty years' changes in women's roles with dynamic, quintessentially American resourcefulness—mitigating the hardships sometimes created by the influx of mothers into the marketplace and accentuating the positives. Businesses are voluntarily introducing flextime and giving employees opportunities to work from home, as well as providing on-site day-care programs. Parents are working out ways to share child-care duties, with other family members and relatives pitching in, too. Churches and community groups have stepped up to the plate.

Instead of celebrating all these options, Hillary bemoans the notion that "parents alone can always determine and then provide—personally or through the marketplace—what's best for their children" and calls for "a nationwide consensus on how to best nurture our children." Set by her, no doubt. But deciding how best to bring up children really isn't a matter of national consensus—it's something only mothers and fathers can decide.

Will the Real Children's Advocate Please Stand Up?

Those who haven't blocked out all memory of the 1992 presidential campaign may recall the controversy over Hillary's articles on children's rights from the 1970s. Her critics charged that they revealed a radical antifamily agenda to strip parents of their authority and enable children to sue over having to take out the garbage. Her defenders angrily countered that they were misinterpreted and that she was only talking about giving underage children some say in major decisions affecting their lives. I looked at those articles. While the critics might have gotten a wee bit hot under the collar, they had a point.

Basically, Hillary maintained that our "child citizens" ought to have the same civil rights as adults and should be presumed to be legally competent to make their own decisions unless proven otherwise. (She also warbled about empowering a child to file lawsuits against "future technological changes that may damage him or her.") If enacted into law, this concept would have been an unmitigated disaster, instigating an avalanche of litigation. In an insightful analysis of Hillary's views on children's rights in *Harper's* magazine, even the late, left-leaning social critic Christopher Lasch noted that "her position amounts to a defense of bureaucracy disguised as a defense for individual autonomy." She opposes the control of children by families but "has no objection to bureaucratic control of children as long as it preserves the fiction of treating them as if they were adults." In a 1977 article in *Yale Law Journal*, Hillary also openly deplored the "cautious attitude about government involvement in child rearing," mocked "politicians [who don't want] to appear as advocates of interference with the family," and urged American policy makers to "overcome the noninterventionist impulse." As Lasch observed, Hillary's defense of children's legal competence is really an argument that parents are incompetent to raise their children.

Examine her more recent pronouncements and writings and it's clear that Hillary's views have, shall we say, evolved. She no longer thinks that children are just smaller versions of adults and that they should be able to make their own decisions about everything from schooling to cosmetic surgery. She proclaims herself a believer in benign but firm parental authority, strong discipline at home and in school, and school uniforms. She has even come out against divorce, single motherhood, and teenage sex, much to the dismay of some feminists like writers Katha Pollitt and Ellen Willis who still think that promiscuity and family breakup equal women's liberation.

But Katha and Ellen needn't fret. Hillary's conservative morality is about as deep and genuine as Bill's devotion to personal responsibility. She may lament "the confusion and turmoil that divorce and out-of-wedlock births cause in children's lives," but when it comes to actual policy recommendations, she suddenly becomes uncharacteristically shy. The most she can muster is that she's "ambivalent about no-fault divorce with no waiting period when children are involved." It's telling that Hillary has not uttered one word in support of actual legislative efforts to roll back no-fault divorce or of the "covenant marriage" movement that has been gathering steam in recent years. Covenant marriage laws, passed in Louisiana and Arizona, allow couples tying the knot to choose a form of marriage that will be more difficult to dissolve, except in cases of the three As: abuse, abandonment, or adultery. This modest measure has liberals up in arms about the religious right trying to "impose" its rigid moralism on people. But, after all, the laws leave the choice to the couples involved. The National Organization for Women and other feminists have joined in the attacks on covenant marriage, with a lot of hand-wringing about how these laws hurt women. Meanwhile, when Hillary criticizes casual attitudes toward divorce, who does she single out? She pillories unnamed right-wingers who "protest loudly against welfare, gay rights, and other perceived threats to 'family values' " but are "silent about divorce." But it looks like it's really Hillary who's silent about divorce. She's adept at trying to have it both ways.

In Hillary's political universe, Marilyn Quayle was treated as a national laughingstock when she talked about "family values"—but a few years later, when Marilyn's "controversial" views became conventional wisdom, "family" was the tag line of choice for Hillary herself in her Senate campaign. (Remember that "Call Hillary. Tell her to keep fighting for children, for families" ad?) And yet, only two years after Hillary deplored absent fathers in *It Takes a Village*, she attended a book party for *On Our Own: Unmarried Motherhood in America* by her friend and fellow Wellesley alumna Melissa Ludtke. *On Our Own* featured sympathetic portraits of educated women who became single mothers by choice and felt that marriage would get in the way of their self-fulfillment. The book bemoaned societal prejudice in favor of "the two-parent heterosexual family." For Hillary to come out too decisively in defense of marriage would alienate too many of her supporters. For her, family values is just a slogan, and raising a child doesn't *really* require Mom and Dad.

If you read *It Takes a Village* carefully, it's packed with traditionalist messages that Hillary didn't intend. Take her story used to illustrate the plight of parents forced to fend for themselves without an organized childcare system. One morning when attorney Hillary was due in court, two-year-old Chelsea had a fever and was throwing up. Her nanny called in sick with the same symptoms. This happened during the Clintons' two-year absence from the governor's mansion so no state police or Secret Service were available to come to the rescue. Bill was out of town and the neighbors weren't home. What's a working mom to do? The solution, it turns out, was only a phone call away:

> Frantic, I called a trusted friend who came to my rescue. Still, I felt terrible that I had to leave my sick child at all. I called at every break and rushed home as soon as court adjourned. When I opened the door and saw my friend reading to Chelsea, who was clearly feeling better, my head and stomach stopped aching for the first time that day.

This episode is actually an example of "the village" at work—not Hillary's theoretical village of bureaucrats, experts and top-down managers, which she advocates as public policy, but the flesh-and-blood village of friends, neighbors, and community members who assist and support each other in "uncoordinated" ways.

Or take her affectionate stories about her own parents and relatives. Her mother, born Dorothy Howell, had a tough childhood—practically abandoned by her parents at the age of eight, raised by grandparents who provided for her material needs but weren't very affectionate. Yet she found support, love, and encouragement from a kindly great-aunt and then from a couple for whom she worked as a housekeeper at the tender age of fourteen. Better by far than being snatched by a social welfare agency and carted off to foster care, don't you think? Her father, Hugh Rodham, was nearly left crippled for life when his lower legs and feet were mangled in a traffic accident and the doctors at the hospital wanted to amputate both feet. By Hillary's account, "His mother, a formidable woman, barricaded herself in his room, refusing to let anyone in until her brother-in-law, a country doctor, arrived. Then she ordered him to 'save my sonny's legs.' "

The moral of this story, according to Hillary, is that "sometimes Mother knows best too"—that is, mothers are as capable as fathers of acting in strong, authoritative ways to protect their families. But, of course, we already know that. The other lesson, that a parent can know best, stand up for herself, and do a better job than a state surrogate, is simply lost on Hillary.

In Hillary's memories of her own childhood, not a government worker is in sight. There is the father who supports his family as a hardworking small businessman but is also there to provide his children with guidance and is present "at dinner, on weekends, during holidays, [and] as part of our daily lives." There is the mother who "organized our daily lives and fed us with her devotion, imagination, and great spirit," who taught Sunday school and helped out at her children's public school, and who is no less of a person in her own right for not having a job outside the home. There are "grandparents, aunts, uncles, and cousins" who pitch in when the family goes through hard times. There are other grownups in the community who look out for the children and know that they need to present a "united front" of adult authority.

That was Hillary's village then. And sometimes, the adults in it behaved in ways that wouldn't meet with the approval of what she regards as her village now. "When I brought home straight As from junior high," recalls Hillary, "my father's only comment was, 'Well, Hillary, that must be an easy school you go to.' By raising the bar, he encouraged me to study even harder, and in fact, comments like that spurred me on." While Hillary describes her mother as the more nurturing parent, her account leaves no doubt that Dorothy Rodham could be pretty tough-minded herself. After the family moved to a new town, four-year-old Hillary was teased and bullied by the neighborhood kids until she ran back home in tears. This went on for several weeks, until one day, her mother stepped in: "She took me by the shoulders, told me there was no room for cowards in our house, and sent me back outside . . . I stood up for myself and finally won some friends."

I wonder what today's parenting experts would say. Would Hugh and Dorothy Rodham be faulted for undermining their daughter's self-esteem? Would young Hillary be quizzed by a school counselor about her relationship with her parents? Might the Rodhams be accused of "emotional abuse" and have to spend huge sums of hard-earned money on defense lawyers?

Yet after sharing her memories of a childhood in a strong family and a tightly knit community, Hillary rebuffs any suggestion that we might want this kind of environment for our own children. That, she says dismissively, is for "nostalgia merchants." In "today's busier, more impersonal and complicated world," the "network of relationships" that sustains our children has to expand to include "the whole nation." So, bring in the counselors, the cops, the therapists, and the judges. Jean Bethke Elshtain said it best: "The big, shapeless, amorphous, infinitely extended 'village' of her book is no village at all."

When Hillary Rodham was growing up, America was indeed a very different place, where stay-at-home motherhood was the norm. That's no longer true. We have more freedom to pursue our goals and ambitions outside the home—and less freedom to be "just" wives and mothers. While most feminists regard this social shift as only glorious progress, most Americans recognize that it involved a few drawbacks as well, especially for our children. The social bonds essential for their healthy growth have worn dangerously thin.

Can we go back to exactly the way things were? Of course not. But that doesn't mean we can't strengthen our families and communities without the state holding our hand every step of the way. In the two decades since Hillary Rodham published her over-the-top articles about enacting new civil rights laws for children, a lot of politicians have successfully "overcome the noninterventionist impulse" toward the family, just as Hillary urged. We've all seen the results of the swelling welfare state. Millions of parents around the country feel that their authority has been usurped by government agencies, while others are trapped in a dependency culture. Having lost confidence in the ability to raise their own children, they now look to the government for family entitlements.

Instead of falling for the promise of new laws mandating goodies from employers or new social services from the state, women should worry about the state's encroachment on family life. The family is the domain where women have always wielded the most power and enjoyed the most respect. Today, we can exercise our talents and our energies in many fields, but family remains central to most women's happiness. Surrendering our parental authority and autonomy to the experts and the bureaucrats of Hillary's "village" does not liberate us, it disempowers us. If we can learn any lessons from Hillary when it comes to family, it's from her own life experience as a daughter and a mother, not her work as a "child advocate."

As Hillary herself said in a 1995 speech to the Child Welfare League: "No government can love a child, and no policy can substitute for a family's care." In that one sentence she tells us how to avoid the Family Trap. Too bad that for her, they were just words.

7.

The
New Age
Trap

It is my very firm conviction that there is a growing awareness of the need for a spiritual renewal in our country and a willingness on the part of many to act and work in good faith together to fill that sense of emptiness with the Word and with an outreach that is grounded in real Christian values.

So spoke Hillary Rodham Clinton at the National Prayer Luncheon in 1994—undoubtedly causing many of her usual admirers and allies to reach for the Maalox.

The modern feminist movement, after all, is not exactly known for its friendliness toward traditional religion. In the 1992 book *Revolution from Within*, Gloria Steinem bewails the lot of religious women who have supposedly traded "self-respect and freedom" for "safety." When a 1999 poll showed that three out of four women considered religion a very important part of their lives and saw religious organizations as a positive force in society, many feminists deplored these findings as "very disturbing." Such irreligious attitudes certainly were not shared by the Founding Mothers of

American feminism, the suffragettes. They might have assailed sexist clergymen who misused the Bible to justify the subjugation of women, but never religion itself. Many of these women were devout Christians who saw their quest for justice as grounded in religious principle. Suffragist leader Elizabeth Cady Stanton spoke of the Christian idea of "the individuality of the human soul" as the foundation of feminism.

Today's feminists, however, are allied with a secularized elite that views religious devotion as something to be ridiculed or at best treated with benign neglect. Often, too, they espouse such pseudo-alternatives to religion as New Age and feminist "spirituality." These fads, with their psychobabble about "the inner child," their crystals, and their talk of witches and goddesses, may look like harmless silliness. But they replace established forms of religion that are rooted in time-tested authority, firm standards of right and wrong, and belief in a higher power; in place of these absolutes, they substitute amorphous beliefs based on warm and fuzzy feelings and worship of the self.

Of course, if you agree with pro wrestler-turned-Minnesota governor Jesse Ventura that all religion is "a crutch for the weak-minded," then it hardly matters which crutch you pick. But if you believe that the soul needs nourishment just as the body does, then nutritional content is important. New Age spirituality offers Twinkies for the soul: sweet and seemingly filling, but lacking in any real substance or value. Worse yet so-called feminist spirituality actually perpetuates the most sexist of stereotypes, extolling women's intuition and women's reproductive functions over reason and critical thinking.

Hillary Clinton has always seemed to differ from her feminist counterparts in this regard. Profiles of the First Lady typically mention that she is a devout, old-fashioned Methodist, which is often cited as evidence that "right-wing" critics have unfairly caricatured Hillary as an elitist cultural radical. Indeed, Hillary has more than once talked about her faith as a source of strength and inspiration. She wrote about religion and children's religious training in *It Takes a Village*. She has even chided those who would banish God and spirituality from the public arena and criticized the press for its inability "to talk about religion except in stereotypes."

Yet, without pretending to judge whether Hillary is in her heart a good Christian—which is between her and her God—I believe that in subtle but important ways she has contributed to a cultural environment that undermines respect for religion and allows flaky alternative pseudo-religions to flourish. (As the British writer G. K. Chesterton observed nearly a century ago, people who stop believing in God don't believe in nothing, they believe in everything.) Losing our religious moorings should be a concern for all of us, but especially for women, who have always been drawn to a spiritual life more than men and who, for reasons I'll tackle later, are even more susceptible to spiritual fakery. The erosion of faith threatens to deprive us of vital sustenance.

Throughout this book, I have talked about the importance of self-reliance and independence, which are feminism's true gifts to women. But I also know that the self is not enough. None of us can ever have perfect wisdom or knowledge, and our ability to take charge of our lives will always be limited by events beyond our control, from tragic accidents to devastating illness. Reliance on God's love does not diminish our independence; on the contrary, it gives us the strength not to have to rely on less exalted sources of support, whether they're men or government. We may try to believe that we're able to cope completely on our own, but sooner or later we'll find out that it's only an illusion.

That's something I know all too well.

I have had an on-again, off-again relationship with the Episcopal and Catholic churches over the years. My reluctance to seek regular guidance and inspiration from the church, to submit myself completely to Christian teachings, is something I think a lot of people of my generation have experienced. I was living the yuppie life and church was just something that I couldn't seem to fit into my schedule. Sunday mornings were inconvenient. They were for leisurely reading the entire *New York Times*, maybe going outside to exercise, and *sleeping*. Plus, reading the Scriptures forced me to rethink my whole way of life, which I was usually too tired or too stubborn to do. I began to think of church as a weekly recrimination that I didn't need. Besides insisting that I love and serve the Lord more than *anything* or anyone, the Bible would tell me to slow down, appreciate the goodness around me, help my fellow man. I was too busy to slow down and think such big thoughts! Even as I knew deep down that chasing "success" wasn't the path to glory and that I was always happiest when I was giving to someone else, somehow I just couldn't be bothered to work on my faith.

Then I got the call. I remember the day, where I was, what I was doing, everything. My father and mother had just returned from her pulmonary specialist.

She had been having pain in her upper right chest for several weeks and a persistent cough for years. At one point the doctors had told her she was just getting old and she might have chronic bronchitis. But when the new pain developed, they did an MRI, which showed a seven centimeter lump on the upper right lung. The lump was biopsied. I told my mom I was sure it was just a benign cyst, some harmless polyp that could be zapped with a laser or something like that.

I was wrong. It was Stage 3 lung cancer—which meant my mother would likely be dead within six months.

I dropped the phone.

Throughout the next several months, my mother went through hell: chemotherapy, radiation, hideous drug cocktails that were supposed to bring back her appetite but which only seemed to make her sicker. She lost her hair and was weaker and more frail every time I saw her. None of the grueling treatments worked and so her oncologists told me it was time to move into a "pain management" phase of treatment. That was a nice way of telling me that my mother would die soon. We decided not to tell her, but she knew. She could feel the cancer move up her legs, see the tumor on the back of her head growing larger.

I spent as much time with her as I could—I lived in Washington, was hosting a daily television show, and would fly up on the weekends to be with her. When my mother started to eat again, she'd say, "Get me out of this house! Let's go to Harry's," the hot dog stand that served her favorite 'kraut dog with onion rings. When she couldn't walk anymore, I'd push her in her wheelchair around the neighborhood so she could see the new flowers popping out and the robins. She loved birds. It was springtime and my mother smelled and saw everything, and cherished simple things like a warm bowl of soup at the local bookstore or a drive through Connecticut. Something was happening to me, too. I realized that I was praying several times a day—at work, in the car, when I woke up, and when I fell asleep.

My mother wasn't the church-going type. It had been more than twenty years since she had attended church regularly, at Pilgrim Baptist Church in Glastonbury. I don't know why my mother stopped going to church. She never talked about it. But maybe it was because my father wasn't interested and she had grown tired and embarrassed of taking the kids by herself.

But church or not, my mother was always praying—mostly for the health and happiness of my three brothers and me. In my twenties, when I would call her to tell her about a guy problem or a work problem, she'd always tell me she was praying for me.

We started praying together during her illness. I hadn't done that since saying my bedtime prayers when I was six. Now it was different, because, invariably, one of us would start crying. But it brought us together.

Two weeks after Mother's Day, the hospice nurse called me and said, "It's her time now, and she wants her children here." I rushed to the airport, flew to Hartford, and raced home. My mother was sitting up in her wheelchair when I walked in; she was waiting for me. Tears welled up in her eyes. "I don't want to leave my children," she sobbed, her tiny hands gripping a ball of tissue. "But I am at peace." Self-help books couldn't help her now. Her faith in God was what kept her going during her final week. My mother held my head in her lap—*she* was comforting *me!*—telling me not to be sad for too long, to believe that we would all be together again and that she was going to a place that was pain-free. She said she felt closer to Jesus because she was suffering just as he suffered on the Cross for us. I couldn't believe how brave she was.

A few hours after my mother died, my brother's family and I went to church and prayed with a deacon who had visited my mother only a few times, but who had been taken by her grit and determination, by her humor and serenity. He was one of a small squadron of hospice workers, nurses and volunteers who had cared for my mother in her final months. They bathed her, fed her, brushed her teeth, took her to the bathroom, read to her, held her hand, rubbed lotion on her skin so she wouldn't get bed sores—everything she could no longer do for herself. My mother called them "angels." Among her favorite angels was an African-American nurse. I was stunned; I had always thought my mother was hopelessly prejudiced. But the two of them had bonded. The nurse was a devout Christian and read the Bible aloud to my mother in the darkest days. "I love her so much," she cried at my mother's deathbed, "I don't know what I'm going to do without her." My mom had touched so many people during her illness and I suddenly had no doubt that God was taking care of her. My mother, befriending a black woman from the inner city? There *had* to be a God.

Hillary Clinton could probably relate to my experience. She has talked about the role of prayer in her daily life and about how, when her father Hugh Rodham lay dying, it made her realize that success and worldly possessions were empty without spiritual values. On *Live with Regis and Kathie Lee* in 1996, discussing the need to fight feelings of "hopelessness and helplessness," she said, "I'm blessed with the kind of religious upbringing that has given me a lot that I can fall back on."

But where is Hillary when it's time to stand up and be counted in defense of the importance of religion? In spring 1998, in the early months of Monicagate, one smear tactic the Clinton camp tried against the special prosecutor's office was to suggest that it was run by a bunch of Bible-thumping extremists whose piety had driven them to become obsessed with the president's sexual sins. Their definition of an extremist was a pretty broad one. Independent Counsel Ken Starr, for example, was ridiculed by Clinton adviser James Carville for his practice of praying and singing hymns aloud while jogging by a creek near his house: "He goes down by the Potomac and listens to hymns, as the cleansing water of the Potomac goes by, and we're going to wash all Sodomites and fornicators out of town." Meanwhile, White House aide and a well-known FOH (Friend of Hillary) Sidney Blumenthal blasted Starr as a "zealot on a mission divined from a higher authority" and Starr's chief deputy in Little Rock, W. Hickman Ewing, as a "religious fanatic." The basis for this slur? According to the *New Yorker*, Ewing is a born-again Christian who prays daily, regularly attends a small evangelical church he helped found, and credits his faith and prayer with helping him overcome a drinking problem.

Blumenthal eventually apologized, after fifty-three congressmen wrote a letter to Clinton demanding that the White House repudiate his offensive remarks. But one voice that was not heard in this chorus of outrage was that of Hillary Clinton. Just as Hillary the feminist stood by silently while the Clinton attack machine trashed women who accused the president of sexual impropriety, Hillary the Christian stood by silently while her associates trashed Clinton's critics for their faith.

Obviously, when it came to sliming Ken Starr, the end justified any means in the Clintons' eyes. But Hillary Clinton's failure to speak up against antireligious bigotry also seems to reflect a reluctance to alienate the secularist cultural elites that are the Clintons' most devoted constituency.

Consider what happened in the fall of 1999 when New York mayor Rudolph Giuliani threatened to cut off city government subsidies to the Brooklyn Museum of Art unless it canceled an exhibition called "Sensation," filled with works that turned Christian symbols into a target of vulgar jokes—such as a painting of the Virgin Mary decorated with elephant dung and porno magazine cutouts of buttocks and genitalia. At a news conference in New York, Hillary not only lambasted the mayor but tiptoed gingerly around criticizing the show: "I share the feeling that I know many New Yorkers have that there are parts of this exhibition that would be deeply offensive." (She couldn't even muster an unequivocal statement that they *are*—not "would be"—offensive.) Even many of Hillary's fellow Democrats who also decried Giuliani's actions, such as former mayor Ed Koch, were far more vigorous in denouncing "Sensation" as deliberate Christian-baiting of the kind that, alas, has become all too common in the art world.

Surely, if the offensive works had treated rape as a joke or lampooned the suffering of Jews in concentration camps, Hillary would have been among the first to denounce the museum. She might even have been able to make the distinction between free expression and forcing taxpayers to pick up the tab for "expression" that insults their dearly held values. Mind you, I'm not expecting the First Lady to become a crusader against heresy. I just wish she could summon the same outrage when artists or filmmakers bash religion—when, for example, movies like *Dogma* or *Stigmata* depict the Catholic Church as an evil empire—that she does when movies like *My Best Friend's Wedding* seem to glamorize smoking.

Maybe the fear of offending her habitual allies, the cultural elites—who regard religious devotion as virtually unmentionable in polite society—accounts for another curious fact. Except when she talks specifically about matters of faith (and often in a religious context, such as the National Prayer Luncheon or an interview with a magazine's religion correspondent), Hillary Clinton rarely mentions religion. References to faith are largely absent from her speeches about social issues, even when it would seem to be highly relevant—when the subject is youth violence, for example.

I don't expect Hillary to wear her faith on her sleeve. But it's odd when the First Lady gives speech after eloquent speech on the importance of nongovernmental organizations, or NGOs—voluntary associations that bring citizens together and form the backbone of democracy—and barely ever mentions religious groups. I was truly taken aback when I read a speech Hillary gave on October 5, 1999, in Warsaw, Poland, at a conference called "Partners in Transition: Lessons for the Next Decade." She talked movingly about the rebirth of Eastern and Central Europe after the long winter of communism, about "choosing the path of democracy, free markets, and freedom," and about the role of NGOs in making this transition.

Yet I looked in vain for a single reference to one NGO that by all accounts had played the decisive role in the resistance to communism in Poland: the Catholic Church. What's more, when praising the revival of the civil society in the ex-Soviet bloc, Hillary mentioned newspapers, activist and charitable organizations, health clinics, even small businesses—but did not utter a word about churches or other religious organizations as "partners in transition." A few days later in Reykjavik, Iceland, at a conference sponsored by the Vital Voices Democracy Initiative, Hillary again spoke at length about NGOs. And again, churches and religious associations were the "vital voices" missing from her talk. In a total of nearly twenty speeches in which she has lauded NGOs, churches and synagogues rated a mere three or four references—compared to dozens for women's groups.

Hillary's refusal to discuss the public role of religion is consistent with the desire of many liberals to eliminate any reference to religion in American public life. While Hillary has asserted that "freedom of religion does not mean, and should not mean, freedom from religion" and that expressions of faith should not be banished from the public sphere, she has not spoken out against policies that suppress religious speech under the guise of "separation of church and state." In *It Takes a Village*, she praises Department of Education guidelines that allow students to "participate in individual or group prayer during the school day . . . when they are not engaged in school activities or instruction." But these guidelines would never have been needed if liberal judges and administrators had not adopted extreme positions in an apparent effort to ban religion from any public places.

Take, for example, the battle fought by Carol Hood, an artist and mom in Medford, New Jersey, for the civil rights of her young son Zachary.

When Zachary was in kindergarten, the kids were given a Thanksgiving assignment: Each had to make a picture of something for which he or she was thankful. The pictures were put up on the wall. Then, a teacher's aide took down Zachary's picture. You see, he had chosen to draw Jesus. Unacceptable.

Carol and her husband called up school officials and complained. The picture went back up—but in an inconspicuous spot a safe distance away from the drawings of his classmates.

The following year, when Zachary was in first grade, each child in the class was supposed to select a story and read it aloud in class. He picked a story from *The Beginner's Bible: Timeless Children's Stories.* The story was about Jacob and Esau, two brothers who were estranged from each other but later became reconciled. It did not mention God or miracles. Carol reviewed it and decided that there couldn't possibly be any problem with its content.

But she was wrong. Zachary's teacher, Grace Oliva, told the little boy that the story was a "prayer" and therefore could not be read aloud in a public school classroom. The school principal sided with the teacher, explaining to Carol that Zachary's reading selection could have offended Jewish or Moslem students—which is rather ironic, considering that the story of Jacob comes from the Hebrew Old Testament, which Moslems also consider to be a part of their tradition.

Outraged, Zachary's parents filed a lawsuit. Even Nat Hentoff, a left-wing civil libertarian who believes that the First Amendment prohibits the use of publicly funded vouchers in religious schools, wrote in *The Washington Post* that the boy's constitutional rights had been blatantly violated. Yet, amazingly, federal courts have sided with the school: To let Zachary read the story in class, they declared, would have been tantamount to the school "endorsing" the Bible.

It's not just first-graders who are muzzled when they want to express their religious beliefs in a school setting. On many occasions, schools have not only banned voluntary student-initiated prayers at high school graduation ceremonies, but forbidden valedictorians to mention Jesus or to talk about the importance of God in their lives in their commencement speeches.

Obviously, the bureaucrats who make these rules haven't noticed that the First Amendment, which says that "Congress shall make no law respecting an establishment of religion," goes on to add ". . . or prohibiting the free exercise thereof." Policies of this type go well beyond separation of church and state and actively discriminate against religiously based viewpoints. (Imagine the howls of indignation if a valedictorian was stopped from mentioning feminism or gay rights in a graduation speech!)

Now this hostility to religious speech cannot be regarded as simply the overreaction of a few isolated radicals. Since the Warren Court began issuing its decisions on the Establishment Clause in the 1950s and 1960s, American liberals have consistently demonstrated their commitment to eradicating religion from its traditional role in American public life. Traditional Christmas displays have been prohibited in numerous cities. The Ten Commandments have been torn from schoolrooms. Prayers at countless events—from graduations to football games—have come under attack. School voucher programs that would allow poor children access to better schools have been struck down because some of those children might go to religious schools. A federal court recently issued a permanent injunction prohibiting the town of Republic, Missouri, from including a fish—which supposedly represents Christianity—on its city seal. The ACLU even brought suit to prevent Ohio from displaying the words "With God All Things Are Possible"—which just happens to be the state motto—on the Capitol Square Plaza in Columbus.

No one can seriously believe that having a fish on a city seal endangers the freedom of non-Christians. But the determination with which liberals pursue such trivial issues underlines their real goal: The government—which teaches our children, taxes our incomes, regulates our businesses, and orders our soldiers into battle—can *never* take even the slightest step that could be construed by the fertile imagination of an ACLU lawyer as support of religion. These liberals envision a government that can constantly make moral judgments—on issues ranging from abortion to war—but that can never mention God. Religion in such a society can never be more than a mere hobby—like coin collecting—and could never serve the unifying role it has traditionally played in American life.

Hillary must bear some responsibility for this effort to purge religion from American life. As the best-known liberal in the country, Hillary could have urged her fellow liberals to cease this crusade. She could have reminded them of how Abraham Lincoln and Martin Luther King invoked the Bible in the name of freedom. Instead, she has treated religion as something to be discussed only in the privacy of one's home, with all the windows closed and the blinds drawn. Her silence on these issues suggests that her defense of spirituality in the public sphere amounts to little more than lip service.

When Hillary *does* talk about religion as a basis for social action, it's nearly always in the context of support for progressive causes—the one exception that secular liberals make to their general distaste for the intrusion of religion into the public sphere. "My church took seriously its responsibility to build a connection between religious faith and the greater good of a society full of all kinds of people," she writes in *It Takes a Village*, recalling her childhood religious experiences. She recounts how the youth minister at the First United Methodist Church in Park Ridge, Illinois, the Reverend Donald Jones, arranged for her youth group to share worship with black and Hispanic teens in Chicago and had the group discuss civil rights, war, and other controversial issues of the day. And there is nothing wrong with that. Indeed, clergy and activists motivated by religious faith have played a key role in the movements that have helped realize the American promise of liberty and justice for all, from abolitionism and women's rights in the nineteenth century to the civil rights movement in the 1960s.

But there is danger in reducing religion solely to a "social gospel." For one thing, commitment to progressive causes can overshadow faith and personal conduct based on biblical morality. At some gatherings of the "religious left," such as an ecumenical conference of Christian feminists held in St. Paul, Minnesota, in April 1998 called "Re-Imagining Revival," the only sins you'll ever hear mentioned are racism, sexism, homophobia, Western imperialism, and exploitation of the environment. On a more popular level, the same attitude surfaces in *Touched by an Angel*, the series many conservatives have lauded for introducing unabashedly religious themes to prime-time TV. The show's sinners are usually guilty of crimes like racial insensitivity or working for a gun manufacturer or a tobacco company.

What's more, some believers who try to translate their religious principles into social action start looking to the state, rather than individual men and women, families, and communities, to build a moral society. The most common error is to confuse true Christian charity with the "compassion" that politicians practice with other people's money. This blurring of the lines between God and Caesar has led to some pretty strange twists of faith. After the Russian revolution, there were "social gospel" Methodists who hailed Soviet Communism as an embodiment of Christian brotherhood—a "Red Star of Hope" in the East. In the 1960s, they were succeeded by activist clergymen such as the Reverend William Sloane Coffin, who, as the chaplain at Yale during Hillary's Yale Law School years, proclaimed that "white oppressors" had no right to judge terrorist acts committed by black revolutionaries and that the prosecution of several Black Panthers on charges of murdering a New Haven police officer "might be legally right but morally wrong." In the 1980s, members of the "religious left" worshiped at the altar of the Sandinistas and were far more passionate about nuclear disarmament than they were about the persecution of Christians in the Communist bloc.

As a student at Wellesley in the turbulent 1960s, when she abandoned her parents' political conservatism to become a McGovern Democrat, Hillary Rodham, too, was tempted by the interpretation of Christianity as a mandate for the politics of the left. Her favorite reading at the time was *Motive*, a magazine for college-age Methodists funded by the United Methodist Church. "I still have every issue they sent me," she told *Newsweek* in 1994. Hillary recalled being particularly impressed by Carl Oglesby's article "Change or Containment?" questioning the war in Vietnam. Oglesby, however, was no mere Christian pacifist but a leading New Left ideologue, a cofounder of the radical group Students for a Democratic Society (SDS). In the pages of *Motive*, Oglesby inquired, "What would be so wrong about a Vietnam run by Ho Chi Minh, a Cuba by Castro?" and exonerated the violence of foreign terrorism or of inner-city riots in the U.S., which, he asserted, was "reactive and provoked" and therefore "culturally beyond guilt." Extending its "progressive" mindset to religious doctrine, *Motive* wrote favorably about the rites of Wicca, a neo-pagan cult with feminist overtones, associated with witchcraft and goddess worship (to which I'll return later). In 1969, the year that Hillary got her Wellesley diploma, the magazine finally overtaxed the patience of even the liberal Methodist leadership and was stripped of its funding.

The extent to which devotion to a social gospel can devolve into a vaguely spiritual creed cut off from any real religious content is most evident in Hillary's famous (many would say, infamous) call for a "politics of meaning." In a speech in Austin, Texas, in April 1993, the First Lady declared that "a sleeping sickness of the soul is at the root of America's ills" and talked about a nation in a profound "crisis of meaning," gripped by "alienation and despair and hopelessness." At the heart of it all, she asserted, was a

> *sense that somehow economic growth and prosperity, political democracy and freedom are not enough—that we lack at some core level meaning in our individual lives and meaning collectively, that sense that our lives are part of some greater effort, that we are connected to one another, that community means that we have a place where we belong no matter who we are.*

Many conservatives would probably agree with Hillary's grim assessment of the spiritual state of our nation. But they would quarrel with the implication that the answer to it can be found in politics—whatever the "politics of meaning" stands for. Hillary was evasive on the details, both in the Austin speech and in subsequent interviews. The phrase itself was

coined by rabbi and New Age psychotherapist Michael Lerner, founder of
the liberal Jewish magazine *Tikkun*, whose ideas the First Lady found sufficiently appealing to invite him over to the White House for some discussions. Lerner, too, was hazy about the meaning of the "politics of
meaning"—he offered a lot of verbiage about empathy, caring, community,
and the evils of a market economy that rewards selfishness. However, a
few specific proposals outlined in the May/June 1993 issue of *Tikkun* provide evidence that in Lerner's vision, Uncle Sam would be in charge of
America's spiritual regeneration. For example, the Department of Labor
would direct every workplace "to create a mission statement explaining its
function and what conception of the common good it is serving and how it
is doing so"; it would also "train a corps of union personnel, worker representatives and psychotherapists in the relevant skills to assist developing a
new spirit of cooperation, mutual caring, and dedication to work."

When Lerner met with Hillary at the White House, he came up with
another brilliant proposal: As he explained to journalist Michael Kelly, he
suggested that the Clinton Administration formally adopt "a policy where,
for any proposed legislation or new program, there would have to be written first an Ethical and Community Environmental Impact Report, which
would require each agency to report how the proposed legislation or new
program would impact on shaping the ethics and the caring and sharing of
the community covered by that agency." According to Lerner, Hillary liked
this idea a great deal, though she was also "worried about using words like
'caring' and 'sharing' and 'love' in talking about government policies"—
mainly, it seems, because of concerns about being mocked in the press.
Evidently in Hillary's world, it's okay to mix "meaning" and the state—but
not religion.

Spirituality Lite

While Hillary Clinton has usually talked about her Christian faith in fairly
traditional terms, she has also embarked on less orthodox pursuits in the

spiritual realm. Her connection to New Age gurus Jean Houston and Marianne Williamson made headlines and invited plenty of speculation and ridicule, despite Hillary's later attempts to downplay the contacts.

Hillary's flirtation with New Age mumbo-jumbo may have been fairly mild. Just because she has dabbled in Houston's flaky "spiritual growth" techniques and expressed interest in Williamson's rambling sermons doesn't mean that she buys the whole package. Certainly, this experimentation has not steered Hillary away from her traditional faith. But those who have grown up in a more secular society and who, unlike Hillary, have not had the benefits of solid religious training, may find it far more difficult to avoid the trap of fake spirituality.

In discussing New Age beliefs and Goddess worship, I'm not suggesting that Hillary Clinton actually endorses these notions. Rather, I want to show what lies at the end of the slippery slope down which Hillary has taken a cautious first step.

The First Lady's relationship with psychologist Jean Houston was first revealed in 1996 in Bob Woodward's book *The Choice*. Woodward wrote about White House sessions where, under Houston's tutelage, Hillary conversed with imaginary friends Eleanor Roosevelt—her designated "archetypal spiritual partner"—and Mahatma Gandhi. According to Woodward, Hillary was instructed to close her eyes and visualize Eleanor, then talk to her and then talk back for Mrs. Roosevelt, who she had saying things like, "I was misunderstood . . . You have to do what you think is right." Mrs. Roosevelt probably would have demanded better lines.

Stung by the ridicule that followed Woodward's disclosures, both Hillary and Jean Houston insisted that Houston was not a "psychic," a "guru," or a "spiritual adviser"—a term that, Hillary said, she reserved for her pastor—but just a friend. They also explained that the chats with Eleanor were not "séances" or "channeling" but merely "guided visualization," "role-playing" and an "imaginative exercise," a way of establishing a connection with a famous woman from the past who Hillary could regard as a role model. (Though, as one Methodist pastor pointed out in *The Washington Times*, she would have made a better connection with Eleanor

Roosevelt by studying and reflecting on writings than by putting fake words in her mouth.)

But Houston, who runs the Foundation for Mind Research in Pomona, New York, with her husband, Robert E. L. Masters, is more than just a psychologist with a creative streak. As Martin Gardner reported in *The Skeptical Inquirer* in 1997, Houston and Masters have conducted hundreds of sessions in which people in a trance "channeled" the voices of the dead—or in one case, of an ancient Egyptian goddess named Sekhmet. Unlike some even wackier New Agers, Houston does not actually think she was hearing from the dear departed or from Egyptian deities, but she does believe that her "channelers" were tapping into humanity's "collective unconscious"—something like a huge computer storing the psychic and mental energies of the human race from time immemorial—and that their prattle was full of the wisdom of the ages. She has also suggested that the "channeled" entities may represent "disembodied" intelligence "pulsing" through the universe.

The Jean Houston flap could be dismissed as just a mistake: So what if Hillary sought advice and intellectual stimulation from a psychologist who turned out to hail from Cuckooland? But the fact is, it wasn't even Hillary's first "guru-gate." A year earlier, she had to defuse a minor controversy surrounding her relationship with another New Age prophetess, best-selling writer and popular lecturer Marianne Williamson. The winsome Williamson has been dubbed "the Guru to the Stars"; she "officiated" at the last of Elizabeth Taylor's weddings, in 1991—even though she has never been ordained in any faith—and her disciples include Cher, Richard Gere, and Bette Midler. Was she also the Guru to the First Lady? In 1995, *Esquire* reported that Williamson had been lunching with Hillary and had stayed overnight at the White House. Hillary fired back a two-page denial: "I have no 'gurus,' spiritual advisers, or any other New Age alternative to my Methodist faith and traditions." She described Williamson as "a political supporter who has an intriguing view about popular culture" and merely one of many interesting people she had met while at the White House. But the connection may have been a little closer than that. It was

Williamson who the Clintons asked to put together a group of "communi-
cators" for a long weekend at Camp David in late 1994. It was also
Williamson who recruited Jean Houston as one of the "human potential"
mavens for that meeting—and who thus brought Hillary and Jean
together.

Generally, Williamson's wisdom ranges from the banal (we need better
communication in relationships) to the kooky (people stricken with cancer
or AIDS should invent a correspondence between themselves and the
virus or tumor). While her books are sprinkled with Christian terminology,
her message has little to do with Christianity or with any other religion.
For one, while Jesus is mentioned in *A Return to Love* as the Son of God,
it's clearly not in the conventional Christian sense: He is simply one of any
number of "enlightened beings" who fulfilled the potential for perfect
unconditional love within all of us.

Whereas traditional religions teach that we are born with a potential
for evil as well as good, and have the free will to choose either,
Williamson's message is very different: "When we were born, we were programmed perfectly." Then how did things get all messed up? "We were
taught to think unnaturally. We were taught a very bad philosophy"—
everything from competition to limitations to guilt. (Of course, it's not
entirely clear who could have started teaching children all this terrible
stuff if all humans are "programmed perfectly" at birth. Did an e-mail virus
get in the files along the way?) The good news, Williamson tells us, is that
none of the bad stuff is real. There is no sin, only "error in perception." As
Williamson explains:

> A sin would be something so bad that God is angry at us. But since we
> can't do anything that changes our essential nature, God has nothing to
> be angry at. Only love is real. Nothing else exists.

Williamson also tells us that "the traditional notion of forgiveness" is
actually bad because it is "an act of judgment"—that is, it involves the
recognition that the person you forgive is guilty of something.

Obviously, this feel-good faith has no room for anything as stuffy as the Ten Commandments. (If there's one, it's "Thou shalt not be judgmental.") Even Ten Suggestions might be a little too restrictive. Here's Williamson, in her 1993 best-seller, *A Woman's Worth*, on the subject of marital fidelity:

> *While monogamy can be a beautiful, even sacred bond, it might not be the agreement that best suits everyone. Our thinking that monogamy is inherently a nobler arrangement than any other has created a nation of hypocrites—which is what we've become.*

Williamson frets that all the preaching about fidelity makes it "very difficult to be clear about what you want." Just think: wouldn't it be a shame if you were so hemmed in by traditional morality that you didn't even *realize* you wanted to have a fling with that married guy at the office!

It's easy to see why the gospel according to Marianne—no guilt, no sacrifice, the only thing God wants from us is to be happy—would be popular with the Hollywood crowd and with many other people whose approach to religion is akin to that of "eat all you want and lose weight" fad diets. New Age "spirituality," a grab bag of everything from aromatherapy and crystals to ancient pagan myths to witchcraft and magic, has millions of adherents and sells millions of books that usually have all the depth of a coloring book and all the insight of a fortune cookie.

For the men and women of the Me Generation, raised on such principles as "do your own thing" and "if it feels good, do it," an unstructured "religion" that encourages its followers to make up their own morality and replaces the worship of a supreme being with an endless quest for the inner self is a convenient way to fulfill one's spiritual needs without cramping one's lifestyle. New Age is where 1960s counterculture meets 1990s consumerism: You get to question authority and think happy thoughts about peace and harmony, and you get to mix 'n' match whatever bits and pieces you like from different religions, just like at a shopping mall. One 1999 article in the *Fort Lauderdale Sun-Sentinel* described a South Florida

woman with a home altar that sports a Buddha, a crystal heart, angel fig-
urines, and a statuette of the elephant-headed Hindu god Ganesh.

Although the exact numbers would be difficult to pin down, it seems
that New Age fads, whether inside or outside of traditional religious struc-
tures, are most popular among women. Why? For one (WARNING: politically incorrect statement ahead!), we tend to be more susceptible to cheap
emotionalism than men. You may be appalled by this sexist stereotype, but
feminists peddle such stereotypes all the time, just with a positive gloss:
Women and girls, they proclaim, are more in touch with their feelings and
more likely to emphasize caring and relationships over justice and rules. If
anything, many feminists, like Harvard psychologist Carol Gilligan, are
prone to exaggerating these differences.

To a certain extent, these qualities may have served women well in
their maternal and domestic roles. However, I would argue that today, as
we enter most spheres on an equal footing with men, it is especially important to encourage women to be more tough-minded. When we run businesses, work in scientific research, write computer programs, perform
surgery, or practice law, we must rely on our brains, on facts and objective
reality, not on feelings and "love." Unfortunately, even in mainstream
churches, as Douglas and Rebecca Groothuis report in *Christianity Today*,
there is a tendency for men's groups to encourage men to study theological
issues and to have a sense of mission to the world, and for women's groups
to focus on sharing feelings and life stories. It's an approach that, the
Groothuises worry, unnecessarily divides the sexes and limits women to a
narrow, personal perspective. And it is certainly true that in excess, being
more oriented toward relationships and nurturance makes women more
prone to fall for psychobabble and feel-good pseudo-piety.

But there is another reason women make up a majority of the consumers of the new spiritual junk food. New Age spirituality, which
includes goddess worship and witchcraft, is frequently peddled to women
as a feminine alternative to the oppressive, traditional, patriarchal religions. According to many feminists, this is the ultimate step in women's

liberation from male dominance. But is this step only taking us into a new trap?

Witches and Goddesses:
Ancient Tradition or Modern Snake Oil?

In the 1999 book *Rebels in White Gloves*, a group portrait of Hillary Clinton's Wellesley class of '69, reporter Miriam Horn noted that quite a few of the women have embarked on New Age quests for spiritual fulfillment. Horn found that "the goddess movement in particular boasts a surprisingly high number of acolytes in Hillary Clinton's class." Their bookshelves often feature the works of Starhawk, a.k.a. Miriam Simos, a "teacher of witchcraft and licensed minister of the Covenant of the Goddess," and *Women Who Run with the Wolves* by Clarissa Pinkola Estés, who urges her readers to reclaim their inner "wild woman" by drawing on images of mythic heroines. According to Horn, "[A] number of Hillary's classmates actively participate in rituals meant to evoke such matriarchal traditions": lighting candles for the winter solstice, "raising energy" for a troubled part of the world, holding ceremonies to celebrate menstruation and menopause.

Much as some of Hillary's political opponents would be thrilled to discover that she is an honest-to-goodness witch, there is absolutely no evidence that she has ever dabbled in Wicca or Goddess cults. Elements of "feminist spirituality," however, are present in the work of Jean Houston— who, by Bob Woodward's account in *The Choice*, told Hillary that she (the First Lady) was a stand-in for the rise of female power, "carrying the burden of five thousand years of history, when women were subservient." But that's nothing compared to Marianne Williamson, who announces, in *A Woman's Worth*, that "we are now living at the beginning stages of the resurrection of the Goddess."

The source of all our problems, writes Williamson, is that we women have been denied our "mystical powers" because our culture has rejected and devalued the Goddess: "The Goddess has been raped when she should have been honored. She has been abused when she should have been worshiped." As a result, we have forgotten that we are all "priestesses and healers," "glorious queens" and "mystical princesses."

While it's a little bewildering that a Yale Law School graduate like Hillary Rodham Clinton would find this drivel "interesting," Williamson is not necessarily advocating literal goddess-worshiping rituals. (Sometimes, she uses "Goddess" as shorthand for "feminine essence," rather stereotypically defined as "the values of intuition, nurturing, and healing.") On occasion, however, she comes pretty close, urging women to establish a "relationship" with a symbol of female divinity, be it the Virgin Mary, Gaea, Isis, or any Hindu or Chinese goddess.

More and more American women—estimates range from one hundred thousand to an improbable four million—are taking this route. Goddess workshops, seminars, lectures, and retreats can be found everywhere from New York and San Francisco, where you'd expect to find such fare, to the Bible Belt. Stores that deal in goddess books and paraphernalia are multiplying, as are Internet sites and chat rooms. Not only eccentric artsy types but ordinary-looking librarians, teachers, health care workers, and even lawyers gather in "sacred circles," tap drums, dance around fires and chant, invoking deities like Artemis, the ancient Greek goddess of the moon and the hunt. Hollywood stars like Sharon Stone and Cybil Shepherd have talked about turning to the Great Goddess for inspiration.

Goddess worship is closely intertwined with another offshoot of "feminist spirituality": Wicca, a.k.a. witchcraft, now officially recognized as a religion by the National Council of Churches, the Internal Revenue Service, and the federal courts. We even have practicing witches in the U.S. Army—probably flying on Pentagon-issued broomsticks that cost $1,000 each. In 1997, the first official Wiccan group was sanctioned at the largest U.S. military base in Fort Hood, Texas; much to the dismay of some conservatives in Congress, witches in uniform are now holding full-moon rites and chanting around bonfires at bases from Florida to Alaska (though even the newly sensitized Clinton-era Army won't allow them to conduct their ceremonies in the nude, as some covens like to do).

Witchcraft is a growth industry. Minneapolis-based Llewellyn International, which specializes in Wicca, more than tripled its annual sales from $4.5 million to $13.8 million between 1992 and 1996. Altogether, there are said to be anywhere from seventy thousand to a million Wiccans in the United States, probably overlapping with Goddess worshipers. While slightly over a third are male, this movement has a distinctly feminine face. Many covens are all-female and dedicated to Goddess worship (the largest Wiccan organization is called the Covenant of the Goddess); the coed covens usually have all-female holidays and rituals and relegate the male god to a secondary role. Forget about the wizened crone bent over the cauldron mixing up raven's eggs and crocodile's blood: The typical witch of our time is a college-educated woman in her twenties or thirties.

Teenage girls, too, have become a prime target audience for modern witchcraft. (Why aren't all those feminists who worry about girls taking too few science and computer courses railing against the insidious attempt to fill girls' minds with occult nonsense?) They've edged out boomer women as the major buyers of witchcraft books, with *Teen Witch*—a how-to manual for Generation Hex—raking up the biggest sales. Some teen witches have fought in court for the right to wear a pentagram to school, arguing that it's no different from a cross or a Star of David. In 1999, *The Toronto Sun* reported that in a recent survey of adolescent girls, witchcraft came *first* on a list of sixty interests.

Oddball cults and spiritual quackery are nothing new—especially in America, where respect for religious diversity has created a fertile ground for such loony experimentation. But today, with the decline of traditional authority and the rise of secularism, the fringe is taking over the mainstream. And, like New Age fads in general, the wackiest forms of "feminist spirituality" have sometimes found a haven in established and respected religious institutions.

At one 1993 gathering of nearly two thousand women in Minneapolis, Minnesota, the participants sang a liturgy to a female creator: "We are women in your image: With the hot blood of our wombs we give form to new life; with the milk of our breasts we suckle the children; with nectar between our thighs we invite a lover, we birth a child; with our warm body fluids we remind the world of its pleasures and sensations." Just another gathering of Wiccans or Goddess-heads? No, the ecumenical Christian feminist conference called Re-Imagining, funded by the Presbyterian Church, the United Methodist Church, and other mainline Protestant denominations.

When reports about Re-Imagining began to trickle out, even a lot of liberal Christians felt a bit queasy. There were rituals honoring "Sophia," nominally the spirit of divine wisdom but often treated more like a sensual goddess with breasts and a womb. There were slurs against established churches, such as the comment that "Christianity as practiced in today's world demonstrates a nightmare more than a vision." A Lutheran pastor practically bragged that the name of Jesus was never mentioned in the opening-night service; a seminary professor sneered at the belief in Jesus' atonement for the sins of humanity through the crucifixion, saying, "I don't think we need folks hanging on crosses and blood dripping and weird stuff."

After offended congregations voted with their pocketbooks and with-held millions of dollars from their national leadership, mainline Protestant churches pulled back from overt support for Re-Imagining. But Diane Knippers, president of the Washington-based Institute on Religion and Democracy, reports that the Re-Imagining movement is still going strong: it is influential on seminary campuses, in many church agencies, and espe-cially in laywomen's organizations such as the venerable ecumenical Protestant group Church Women United. Nor have the Re-Imaginers calmed down. At their later gatherings, women were invited to honor Eve's eating of the forbidden fruit—"re-imagined" as an embrace of "freedom, choice and knowledge" rather than Original Sin—by biting into an apple.) The 1996 Re-Imagining conference featured a wall decorated with femi-nine images of the sacred: the Virgin Mary side by side with the randy Babylonian love goddess Ishtar; the ferocious Hindu war goddess, Kali;

and Diana of Ephesus, a multi-breasted fertility goddess. There were also instructions on how to pray to these deities or interact with them in dreams.

Many mainstream denominations have been quite hospitable to Christian feminism, which they see as an expression of women's quest for justice and respect. But the truth is, the new feminist spirituality is not simply about a more equal role for women or more gender-inclusive language in religious texts (such as replacing "And I, when I am lifted up from the earth, will draw all men to myself" with "draw all people to myself") or even women's ordination. It's about replacing a God-centered religion with a women-centered one. Even when they don't put up shrines to pagan goddesses, the new "Christian" feminists elevate women's feelings—or, as they put it, "intuition" and "personal experience"—above everything else, including church doctrine and reason. They encourage women to "re-imagine" God in their own personal ways: as a force within themselves, a friend, a nurturer, but certainly not a supreme being who sets down rules or judges our behavior.

Adherents of the goddess claim to be practicing an old-time religion— the oldest of all, suppressed and covered up by the patriarchy for thousands of years. Once upon a time, they say, most of humanity lived in peaceful, nature-loving, harmonious societies that worshiped the Mother Goddess, revered women, and knew nothing of such evils as war or social inequality. Then, around 5000 B.C., the Goddess civilization was overrun and destroyed by male-dominated, violent nomadic tribes who imposed their male gods on the conquered peoples. The Great Goddess was either broken up into a bunch of lesser goddesses who were subordinate to male gods, as in ancient Greece, or rooted out altogether, as among the ancient Hebrews.

This feminist version of Paradise Lost is a basic tenet of goddess literature. It is embraced by feminists like Gloria Steinem, novelist Marilyn French, and numerous women's studies professors. And it may be a nice story—at least if living among noncompetitive tree huggers is your cup of tea—but history it's not.

In his well-documented 1998 book *Goddess Unmasked*, Philip G. Davis, a professor of religious studies at the University of Prince Edward Island in Canada, conclusively shows that it's highly unlikely that any ancient culture worshiped one goddess rather than multiple deities of both sexes or that there ever were any flourishing matriarchies. Many of the cultures that Goddess acolytes claim as their peaceful feminist utopias have left scant archeological evidence, but what evidence there is shows that they had violence, war, human sacrifice, and probably even male dominance. In any case, what makes the Goddess devotees think a female-run society would be peaceful and egalitarian? Obviously, they've never been in a sorority. Numerous studies have found that while men and boys are more likely to engage in physical violence, women and girls in groups are just as likely to bully and abuse, using words as their weapons. Many of us don't need studies to know that. Elizabeth Fox-Genovese put it best in her 1991 book *Feminism Without Illusions*: "Those who have experienced dismissal by the junior high school girls' clique could hardly, with a straight face, claim generosity and nurture as a natural attribute of women." And those who, like Fox-Genovese herself, have experienced ostracism by women's studies professors could also have some things to say on the subject.

Just as actual women are quite different from the beatific feminist ideal, the goddesses who were actually worshiped in antiquity—and are still worshiped in places like India—couldn't be more different from the feminist fantasy of the nice, nurturing Great Mother. The Hindu goddess Kali, depicted as wielding a cleaver and wearing a necklace of human skulls, is tougher than Demi Moore in *G.I. Jane*. In biblical times, the Canaanites described their goddess Anat as wading joyfully in the blood of her slain enemies.

Not only does Goddess worship not ensure peace and social harmony, it doesn't even ensure the high status of actual women. In ancient Greece, Athena was the patron goddess of the city of Athens. But while Athena's priestesses were revered, the average woman in Athens had far fewer rights than they did in medieval Christian Europe.

If witchcraft and the Goddess religion as practiced in the United States today are not time-honored female traditions, what are they? According to Davis, whose work is praised by leading historians like Wellesley professor Mary Lefkowitz, the answer is simple: a fable of modern, and decidedly male, origin. Ancient Goddess-worshiping matriarchies are the brainchild of nineteenth century German historian J. J. Bachofen, who could hold a candle to any women's studies professor when it comes to building big speculative theories out of thin air. Wicca was invented in the 1950s by one Gerald Gardner, a retired British civil servant with an interest in Asian philosophy, magic, and nudism—which may explain why the cult he founded has such an emphasis on rituals conducted in the buff.

In many ways, like much of New Age spirituality in general, Wicca and the Goddess religion are tailor-made for the self-involved. Look closely, and you'll see that Goddess worship is actually female self-worship. A popular bumper sticker says, BACK OFF—I'M A GODDESS! That may be facetious, but Goddess devotees are not trying to be funny when they exchange the blessing, "Thou art Goddess!" in their rituals. Carol Christ, a Goddess guru whose 1978 essay "Why Women Need the Goddess" is a staple of women's studies courses, exults, "I found God in myself and I loved her fiercely." Radical "Christian" feminism isn't very different. Writes Diane Knippers of the Institute on Religion and Democracy, "The object of Re-Imagining worship is ultimately women themselves."

Does traditional, patriarchal religion elevate men in the same way? Mary Daly, the wacky feminist theologian, thinks so: She has written that "[I]f God is male, then the male is God." But this "logic" is far removed from the Judeo-Christian view of the relationship between God and man. Can you imagine a serious Christian or Jew putting a BACK OFF—I'M A GOD! bumper sticker on his car, even as a joke? The Judeo-Christian God is separate from his creation; human beings are made in God's image, but they are certainly not the same as God. Despite non-gender-neutral language like "Father" and "the Lord," which so irks feminists, the Judeo-Christian God—unlike male and female pagan gods—has no sexual characteristics and the Bible clearly says that both men and women are made in God's image and likeness.

On the other hand, a basic tenet of the Goddess religion is that the Goddess is "immanent," that is, inherent within the physical world. "The Goddess is also earth—Mother Earth, who sustains all growing things, who is the body, our bones and cells . . . Thou art Goddess. I am Goddess," bubbles Starhawk, the Wiccan priestess. The Goddess is within all living and even inanimate things, but she is particularly manifest in women: "This is what the Goddess symbolizes—the Divine within women and all that is female within the universe. . . . The responsibility you accept is that you are divine, and that you have power," writes Zsuzsanna Budapest, another self-styled feminist witch. Female physiology, seen as embodying the eternal cycle of life, death, and renewal, becomes a special object of veneration. Hence, the importance of childbirth, menstruation, and menopause in Goddess rites. Carol Christ rapturously describes a ritual in which women "marked each other's faces with rich, dark menstrual blood" and concludes, "From hidden dirty secret to the hidden power of the Goddess, women's blood has come full circle."

Maybe it's feminism that has come full circle with Goddess worship: from challenging a view of women as defined by biology and motherhood to celebrating biology and fertility as the essence of divine womanhood. As Rene Denfeld wrote in the 1995 book *The New Victorians*, "In the end, goddess religion places women's identity right where traditional sexism does: our genitalia." What's more, the view of "the feminine" in Goddess religion is just as much of a throwback to sexism: Women are seen as repositories of intuition, nurturance, and oneness with nature.

But if the obsession with female physiology in Goddess religion is silly and retrograde (not to mention messy), its tendency toward self-deification takes us down a much more dangerous path. Elizabeth Achtemeier, a biblical scholar at the Union Theological Seminary in Richmond, Virginia, who believes that feminists have many valid points about historical sexism in the church, cautions:

The radical feminists, believing themselves to be divine, think that by their own power they can restructure society, restore creation; and overcome suffering. But the tortured history of humanity testifies to what human beings do when they think they are a law unto themselves with no responsibility to God, and those feminists who are claiming that God is in them will equally fall victim to human sin.

Predictably, the fuzzy thinking of "feminist spirituality" leads to fuzzy ethics. There is, after all, no transcendent deity who sets down rules or standards of right and wrong. Rabbi Paula Reimers has pointed out that if the Goddess is one in the universe, "then nature and its cycles are held to be an expression of the divine will. In such a cosmology, good and evil lose all meaning, everything being good in its proper time." The Goddess devotees seem to agree: "The immanent conception of justice is not based on rules or authority, but upon integrity, integrity of self and integrity of relationships," writes Starhawk in her 1982 book *Dreaming the Dark*. The Wiccan ethical code consists of the precept, "If you harm none, do what you will." The catch, of course, is that it's up to each person to define "harm." In a 1999 article on teen witches in the *Bergen* (New Jersey) *Record,* Jaime Anderson, a high school junior who wears black clothes and a pentagram to school, was quoted as saying, "You can really incorporate yourself into the religion. You don't have to follow a lot of rules. You basically do what you feel is right."

To get this sort of message, you don't really need religion. *Playboy* or *Cosmopolitan* will do just fine.

Losing Our Religion

Many women have understandable grievances about the way their religious institutions have stereotyped them and relegated them to second-class roles. But traditional religion was sexist because it existed in sexist societies, not the other way round. The "Christian Women's Declaration," signed in 1997 by an ecumenical group of women supporting equality of the sexes but opposing radical feminism, pointed out that "[T]he Bible is the most effective force in history for lifting women to higher levels of respect, dignity and freedom."

Many young women today have been so indoctrinated in the notion that "male" religions have been a leading cause of misogyny and patriarchal oppression that they may find this statement startling, even laughable. Yet Judith Antonelli, author of the 1995 book *In the Image of God: A Feminist Commentary on the Torah*, points out that "far from oppressing women, [Judaism] began to improve women's status in the ancient world," albeit "in small steps," in such areas as divorce, property ownership, and parental rights. In the Middle Ages, as French historian Georges Duby shows in *History of Private Life* (1988), the Catholic Church played an often overlooked yet crucial role in elevating the position of women. Until the twelfth century, marriage in feudal Europe was treated as a pragmatic matter and was established by physical consummation following mutual promises of marriage. As clerics gained more influence over private life, marriage became a sacrament, resulting in greater protection not only for the dignity but for the economic rights of wives. What's more, it was priests who insisted on verifying that both the groom and the bride had freely consented to the marriage.

Today, there are legitimate disagreements among Christians and Jews about such issues as the ordination of women and the question of whether the biblical model of marriage is based on male leadership or mutual submission. But that has nothing to do with replacing God with the mysteries of the menstrual cycle or nature worship. It also has nothing to do with trading a clear moral code and the virtues of self-discipline and sacrifice for a touchy-feely, therapeutic "morality" that differs little from the hedonism of secular culture.

It might seem at first glance that "feminist spirituality" is genuinely pro-female. Who wouldn't find it enticing to be regarded as divine? But it's a false promise, a trap rather than a path to true happiness. First of all, if spirituality is segregated by gender—and especially if women are "goddesses"!—it bodes ill for women's ability to have loving relationships with their fathers, brothers, husbands, or sons.

However enthusiastically the New Age gurus, the Wiccan high priestesses and the Goddess worshipers try to persuade us that we have supreme powers, anyone who buys that will be disappointed sooner or later. However smart, strong, and fortunate we may be, we will eventually, at one time or another, experience failure, illness, and grief. If spirituality is only about looking within, then we have nowhere to turn for consolation and guidance when we fail, left to our own fallible devices.

Faith can be, in a very literal sense, a healing force in our lives. In his books *Healing Words* and *Reinventing Medicine*, Larry Dossey, M.D., a former agnostic, reviews more than a hundred studies persuasively showing the positive health effects of religious devotion. Going to church has the same benefits for your longevity as not smoking. Not only do patients who pray do better, but patients who have someone else praying for them—whether they know about it or not—generally recover faster, require fewer drugs, show fewer side effects of the drugs they do take, and are at lower risk for heart failure. These findings have been convincing enough for dozens of medical schools to start courses dealing with health and religion. On the other hand, vaunted New Age therapies have flunked the scientific test. "Therapeutic touch," in which a healer supposedly manipulates a patient's energy field without physical contact, was debunked by nine-year-old Emily Rosa, whose fourth-grade science project demonstrated that practitioners could not accurately identify which of their hands, concealed by a screen, was in proximity to Emily's hand. But to turn religion into simply a form of therapy is to trivialize it. Real faith is hard work. It requires things that are unfashionable in our me-first culture: obeying rules and acknowledging an authority higher than our own self.

Hillary Clinton is right about the spiritual hunger and the emptiness so many Americans feel in the midst of our freedom and prosperity. It's too bad that she can't wean herself from dependence on the cultural elites that have done so much to create this emptiness by banishing all talk of God, and of right and wrong, from the public square.

Sadly, our search for something to fill the void has taken many of us, especially women, down the wrong roads. The pop gurus like Marianne Williamson, the Goddess worshipers, and the feminist theologians all hold out the promise of love without judgment and spirituality without authority. But in the end, all they do is put a spiritual veneer on the self-absorption that pervades our culture. No less than the secularists, they deny us the presence of a loving and caring God.

Epilogue: Escaping the Traps

Hillary Clinton finally did it in 2000: She moved out of the White House to her new home in Chappaqua, New York, and formally kicked off her Senate campaign. In one telling respect, the scene at Hillary's "formal" announcement was very different from that of her unofficial kickoff/birthday gala five months earlier: Bill was not at the microphone. Instead, he sat behind the First Lady, barely in camera view, with Chelsea. The large banner that hung behind the podium read simply "Hillary for Senate." The message she wanted all of us to take away was clear—she had finally come into her own as a woman and a political force. No longer would she be mopping up after Bill's messy sexual escapades. At last she'd use that Wellesley brainpower and a lifetime of experience to make sense of the country's political problems. She'd be Hillary Unplugged, without the trappings of the White House and her position as First Lady.

But how real is this transformation? Has Hillary really escaped the traps that ensnared her at each passage of her life? Has she broken the cycle of dependence—personal and political—that kept her from becoming a star in her own right? Is she finally on her way to becoming a true role model for women? It won't surprise readers that my answer is *no*. It takes more than changing residence and purging her husband's last name from her campaign paraphernalia to strike out on her own. In fact, a Hillary fundraising letter, mailed earlier this year, echoed the same old "I'm-a-victim" theme: "They can launch anti-Hillary websites. They can use their limitless war chest to run negative television ads. They can publish mean-spirited books and press releases. But they can never stop me from standing up for what I believe in."

Who am I to judge Hillary? It's a fair question. She has lived longer than I have, seen more of the world, and experienced life as a wife and mother. I can't see into her heart and I know that in many ways she must be a good person. To her, what I've written will probably seem like just another personal attack by a Clinton hater. But Hillary's inner self—her sense of humanity—isn't what this book has tried to untangle. I'm no psychologist. Instead, I've tried to look at her political beliefs and how those beliefs have intertwined with her life and marriage. That's an area where we *need* to make frank judgments.

What would I tell Hillary if I could have a few minutes alone with her? (Okay, not likely, but humor me.) I'd tell her to start being honest, personally and politically. None of us like to admit it when something we've believed in hasn't worked. But we all know that without frank self-examination, we can never learn from our mistakes. We remain caught in the same cycles of self-destruction and hypocrisy—the same traps—that have us staying in bad marriages or clinging to bad ideas. Yes, it's more comfortable to keep lying to yourself and those around you. But the price is intellectual and emotional paralysis.

I'd tell Hillary to stop running away from the truth. Her private life stopped being private when she married a man with presidential ambitions. Her travails are a matter of public record. The only things that're still hidden—perhaps even from herself—are her true feelings. Hillary tells friends she hates to be seen as the victim. Well then, she should stop acting like one. Even her Senate campaign is said to have its roots in the

Monica Lewinsky scandal. It was a kind of payback, as if she were saying: My husband humiliated me all these years, but now it's his turn to be the dutiful spouse.

I'd tell Hillary to be honest about her politics, too. Listening to her, you sometimes wonder if she's ever modified her views on anything. Has she taken a hard look at what her brand of liberalism created? "Question authority!" was the loudest rallying cry of her 1960s generation and the denunciation quickly extended beyond the Vietnam War establishment to every major American institution—our universities, churches, and government. Traditional values were suddenly under attack. Ethics were now "situational." No belief was necessarily more moral than any other—it was all relative. Truth was "multicultural" and up for grabs. *No more absolutes!* was the motto of Hillary's generation.

Take a look around and you'll see what Hillary's political ideology created: public schools that don't teach our children core subjects or reinforce values parents try to teach at home; a workplace constricted by government edicts that are meant to help "protected classes," yet end up hurting women and minorities most; a permissive sexual culture that tolerates rampant infidelity and divorce. We've become a nation prey to mindless television programs, ultra-violent movies, Internet pornography, and school massacres conducted by children. In these prosperous times, we may be rich in material things, but we have become impoverished in the values that hold society together.

Hillary, you got what you asked for. There are few absolutes anymore. The country is drifting into the future, looking for answers that liberalism can't provide. The liberal campaign to purge all mention of God and faith from our schools has left children adrift in a valueless sea, where teachers who try to teach students what's right and wrong risk being called intolerant zealots. Before the shootings at Columbine High School, murderers Eric Harris and Dylan Klebold were giving each other the Nazi salute in the hallways. What would have happened if a teacher had stood up to these young thugs and demanded that they stop—and when they refused, suspended them? The ACLU might have denounced this violation of the students' freedom of expression and school administrators would have been scurrying to apologize. That's where we are now as a country, Hillary, and your value system helped create this mess. So isn't it time to take a fresh look at thirty years of mistaken social engineering and begin to set a new course based on common sense?

And despite all the wrong turns she has taken, I'd tell Hillary it's not too late to be a role model. Millions of Americans admire her and look to her to embody what's right. She can start by speaking out, from the heart. Instead of meaningless chitchat with Rosie O'Donnell, she should finally tell the truth about her husband's behavior. We'd cheer for a woman who said: *I won't tolerate my husband's lying and cheating another day. From now on, I'm going to act like the free and independent woman I am, and I won't ride on my husband's political coattails anymore.* I'd love to hear Hillary speak those words. Finally, rather than excuses and recrimination, she'd be sending a real message of liberation and self-reliance. But I won't hold my breath. Given Hillary's past, even the subject of divorce would be test-marketed with a focus group.

There's a sense that Hillary Clinton is Everywoman. Her life symbolizes the tug-of-war going on within all our minds, between our desire to seize new opportunities and our old habits of dependence on men and ideas that limit us. Hillary's problem isn't that she's made mistakes—we all do that—it's that instead of recognizing them for what they are, she's turned them into a life philosophy and a political platform.

But as I've tried to show, Hillary's answers are really a series of traps. The returns are in: Over the last thirty years, Hillary's ideas about marriage, education, the workplace, and family politics have set women back rather than forward. Her liberal feminism has created a culture that rewards dependency, encourages fragmentation, undermines families, and celebrates victimhood.

In this sense, Hillary is a figure of the past. Her way of thinking about politics and personal life is foreign to many younger women, who are strong and confident enough to live their lives on their own terms. They might empathize with Hillary. But they wouldn't dream of putting up with a perpetually cheating husband, or demanding special gender privileges to get ahead, or letting the government intrude into their family lives. Indeed, polls in early 2000 showed women voters beginning to reject Hillary's message.

The future belongs to the new feminist pioneers, not to Hillary and her tired ideas. These women are starting their own companies, battling bureaucrats to regain control of their schools, taking responsibility for their own safety, and making tough choices about careers and families without looking to the government for help. It's hard work avoiding the Hillary Traps, but it's the only way to a truly independent, fulfilling, and honest life. By taking responsibility for ourselves, we start to look for power in all the right places.